NOSTRADAMUS
& OTHER PROPHETS AND SEERS

Fig. I.

Saturnus
Iupiter
Mars
Sol
Venus
Mercurius
Luna

Cauda
Leonis

Orbita Saturni

Spica
Virginis

Virgo

30

Libra

Fig. VI.

NOSTRADAMUS
& OTHER PROPHETS AND SEERS

JO DURDEN SMITH

Capella

This edition published in 2008 by Arcturus Publishing Limited
26/27 Bickels Yard, 151–153 Bermondsey Street,
London SE1 3HA

ISBN: 978-1-84837-021-0

Printed in China

Cover design by Paul Oakley and Beatriz Waller
Book design by Alex Ingr

CONTENTS

Introduction

W E NO LONGER LIVE in an age of prophecy or of inexplicable phenomena – miracles – which have somehow to be accommodated into an explicative world view. Or rather we do – except that the miracles of today are scientific ones, and the things we don't understand are presumed to be ultimately explainable by the scientific enterprise – once, that is, the scientists have got round to them.

Prophecy, too, has given way to prediction, the pillar of the scientific method and the formal rationale of all experimentation: "Is this prediction correct or foolish? Let's see." And so we are inflicted with the figure of the scientist-as-final-arbiter who decides what is real and testable and what lies beyond the pale. Somewhat like an art expert, he or she announces what is 'right' (an echt, authentic picture or area of experience) and what is wrong (a fake or a delusion). When predictions of the future are called for (by and for the contemporary right-minded), it is scientists who arrive at the television studio or the book, bringing with them, if not a shining certainty, at least the apparently reasonable conviction that the future will be like the present, only more so.

The problem with this, of course, is that science deals almost entirely with the physical world, the seizable, the 'real': with the electrical charges across neural synapses in the human brain, for example; with the movement of massive objects in space and particles so tiny that their presence (or absence) is almost undetectable. Those sciences which deal with the emotions and aspirations and perceptions of 'real' people are called – by common consent – inexact. At the same time, all kinds of prodigies and mysteries are ignored, the sort of prodigies and mysteries collected by the reclusive American Charles Hoy Fort in the early part of the 20th century – and characterized by Louis Pauwels and Jacques Bergier in their book *The Morning of the Magicians* as:

> *Red rain over Blankenbergue on 2nd November, 1819; a rain of mud in Tasmania on 14th November, 1902. Snowflakes as big as saucers at Nashville on 24th January, 1891; a rain of frogs in Birmingham on 30th June, 1892. Meteorites. Balls of fire. Footprints of a fabulous animal in Devonshire. Flying disks. Marks of cupping-glasses on mountains. Engines in the sky. Erratic comets. Strange disappearances. Inexplicable catastrophes. Inscriptions on meteorites. Black snow. Blue moons. Green suns. Showers of blood.*

Fort doggedly collected accounts of twenty-five thousand of these strange phenomena, not because he necessarily gave credit to each one of them, but because he didn't believe that they should all be totally dismissed *a priori*. He saw science, in fact, as a motor-car pursuing a narrow and self-elected path along a highway, but wilfully ignoring all the wild country that lies on either side, away from all the neon lights and the asphalt.

In all this, of course, we – the thralls of science – still long for some way of foretelling the

future, of harnessing the supernatural. Slightly shame-facedly, we devour horoscopes in newspapers and magazines, aware that it is almost certainly all tosh, but unaware of the uncomfortable fact that certain professions seem to be inexplicably clustered under particular birth-signs. We have been successfully persuaded that oracles, too, are flim-flam, superseded ju-ju, but we don't know that the Dalai Lama, a universally respected figure, still keeps an oracle – and regularly consults it – in his hill-station in India. We no longer believe that visionaries and seers are either crucial to the community or extremely dangerous to it. Instead we tend to dismiss them as poor unfortunates, mad people, who suffer an imbalance in the brain of serotonin or acetylcholine or some other substance that regulates the proper firing of brain-cells. We don't attend to them or burn them. We cosh them into conformity with drugs.

We still have forecasts, of course, but they are weather and economic forecasts, predictions of future consumption and climate based upon past experience. But – however much we flock to charismatic churches and to classes in the Kabbala – our capacity to believe in spiritual forecasts or presagings of the future has largely gone. And yet the world is a very strange place indeed; and the things that happen in it cannot all be dismissed as untestable, unreliably observed or delusory. What are we to make of Jacques Cazotte, for example, who at a dinner party correctly predicted the Reign of Terror after the French Revolution and the individual fate of his fellow-guests? Or of the writers who predicted the Final Solution and the sinking of a great liner called *Titan*? Or the palmist and

clairvoyant Cheiro who warned the editor of *The Times* of London not to travel by sea during the period of the *Titanic's* sinking? (He went down with the ship.) Or of Jeanne Dixon, the so-called 'White House seer', who predicted through visions, among many other things, the death of President Kennedy? Or of 'the Sleeping Prophet', Edgar Cayce, who in a trance could diagnose a patient's illness and prescribe unorthodox medicines to cure it?

Yes, there are objections and explanations, of course, to cover all these cases. Cazotte's prediction was only written about in detail long after the event. The forecasts of the Final Solution and the sinking of the *Titanic* were written by a) an unusually deep political thinker, and b) one of the early writers of the sci-fi school who saw that one day such a disaster would inevitably happen – as it did. As for Dixon and Cayce, Dixon's predictive success-rate was way below the almost a hundred per cent claimed by her biographer; and Cayce – as a prophet – made many foolish claims about Atlantis and the Pyramids and many predictions (as Dixon did) that were just plain wrong.

And yet... is it possible that contemporary Western society, with its scientific view of the universe, is barking up the wrong tree? Is it possible that, like the early Christian Church – if for different reasons – science is proceeding on its way to final authority by suppressing awkward facts and unassimilable human abilities like clairvoyance and second sight? Or that, like the medieval Church, it demonizes the heterodox and the visionary? The answer, of course, to these questions is that it is entirely possible. But they will have to wait for another book.

I

THE ROOTS OF PROPHECY

There is not to be found anywhere a race of men, no matter how highly civilized and cultured, or, for that matter, how utterly savage and brutish, which is not firmly convinced that there are portents which point to coming events, and that certain persons are able to recognize these portents and to predict from them what the future holds in store.

CICERO: CONCERNING DIVINATION

IN CHINUA ACHEBE'S NOVEL *Arrow of God*, set in a Nigerian village in early colonial times, one of the Chief Priest Ezeulu's tasks is to identify the new moon. This is not easy during the rainy season, but it is vital, since the new moon kicks off the pumpkin festival, during which Ezeulu has to perform a ritual dance to absolve the community of its sins. It is also his responsibility to respond to the voice of the god Ulu and announce the time of the yam harvest, the equivalent of the New Year. The trouble is that the old ways are dying in the village; Ezeulu's authority is under attack and he fails to hear the voice of Ulu. So the yam harvest is put off; food stocks run low; and the village, "locked in the old year", as Achebe puts it, goes through a period of profound stress.

What Achebe is describing is the passing of a way of life in which time and the supernatural were inextricably linked. The arrival of the new moon and of the 'right' time for festival and harvest were not predictable events, measured by clockwork or by written calendar: they required the intervention of a priest. Indeed, in virtually all early (or so-called 'primitive') societies we know of, priests were – to use Damian Thompson's expression in his book *The End of Time* – "the first specialists in timing". As a privileged caste, sustained by the community and delivered from the need to labour for their own food, they were free to watch the skies for the signs of the passing of the seasons and to select the 'right' moment, not only for sowing and harvesting, but also for the ceremonies which marked and celebrated the passage of the agricultural year.

These ceremonies were not by any means mere feasts and frolics. They were acts of propitiation, expiation and worship, designed to take care of the community's spiritual well-being. It is notable, for example, that a special period was almost universally set aside for the expulsion of demons, diseases and sins by a variety of means, from fasting to fire rituals; and that this commonly coincided with the celebration of the New Year. Thus the renewal of life beneath the earth and the beginning of a new cycle went hand in hand in prehistoric societies with the regeneration of the human psyche.

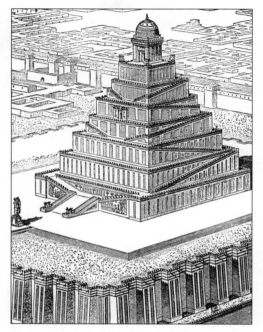

Ziggurats were used, particularly by the Chaldaeans, to observe heavenly activity

THE MARKING OF TIME

This primordial connection between the marking of time and spiritual health is echoed down through the ages. Even after the development of the calendar as an instrument for the ordering of more complex societies, it remained in the hands of priests, since it codified and enshrined a powerful magic with profound effects on the life of the community. When Julius Caesar, for example, wished to change the calendar, he had first to consult the Pontifex Maximus, the high priest or 'Chief Bridge-Builder' between the gods and men; even today in the Catholic Church, as Thompson observes, "the dates of the moveable feasts for the coming year are proclaimed from the pulpit, in a special chant on the feast of the Epiphany".

It is no great step from the marking of present time – the duty, for example, of Mesopotamian astronomer-priests who were required to pass the news of each new moon to the royal palace – to the prediction of events in the future. Indeed, the presumption that future cycles would repeat past ones was precisely what gave birth to the first calendars, the result of reiterated readings and interpretations of the mechanical clock-face of the skies.

The clock-face was seen as the manifestation of divine will for the ordering of man's life on earth, his destiny – and this idea naturally gave rise, in Mesopotamia in the first instance, it seems, to its corollary: that the fate of a society or empire, personified by its king, could be also read in it, *if only sufficient skills could be developed*. It fell to the Mesopotamian priesthood, in other words, to look deeper into celestial phenomena than mere yearly recurrence, and through what they learned to advise the royal household of impending disaster or success.

Though lunar eclipses had, it seems, been regarded in an earlier period as foreboding disaster – and though a sect called the Chaldaeans had much earlier built stepped pyramids (or ziggurats) to observe the heavens and their connection to the ups and downs of human life – it was during the so-called first dynasty of Babylon (c. 1800-1600 BC) that cuneiform texts devoted to celestial omens began for the first time to be collected, emerging in modern times inscribed on some of the 20,000 or so tablets and fragments dug up from the library of the 7th-century BC King Ashurbanipal in Nineveh.

READING THE OMENS

The omens found in these texts can be divided into four categories, named for the four gods under whose jurisdiction they fell. Thus Sin (the Moon) covered eclipses, first crescents and conjunctions with fixed stars; Shamash (the Sun), observations of two suns, solar haloes and perihelia; Ishtar (Venus), stations, risings and first and last visibilities; and Adad (the weather god), a variety of meteorological phenomena, such as thunder and lightning, earthquakes and cloud formations.

All of these were duly reported back to Nineveh by a network of observers throughout the Assyrian empire, and were interpreted there by a court prognosticator called the *baru*, who applied them mostly, it seems, to the military prospects of the imperial armies and to the personal lives of the royal family. As the article 'Divination: astrology' (under the general heading of Occultism) in *The Encyclopaedia Britannica* comments:

> *Since the celestial omina were regarded not as deterministic but rather as indicative – as a kind of symbolic language in which the gods communicated with men about the future and as only a part of a vast array of ominous events – it was believed that their unpleasant forebodings might be mitigated or nullified by ritual means or by contrary omens… [The] omens provided a basis for intelligent action rather than an indication of an inexorable fate.*

The reading of these celestial omens fell out of favour in Mesopotamia, it seems, after the fall of Nineveh to the Persians in 612 BC. By the time it was revived again as a priestly art two and a half centuries later, it had already spread to Egypt, Greece and India. There is evidence, for example, of Mesopotamian lunar omens in an Egyptian papyrus of about 500 BC, and of a wider knowledge of Mesopotamian omen literature in a book written in Greek in the second century BC, a book which was probably one of the main sources of later accounts that emerged in Greece and Constantinople.

As for India, the traditions contained in the Nineveh tablets (known collectively as *Enuma Anu Enlil*) appear to have arrived there during the so-called Achaemenid period (named for the Persian dynasty which ruled a vast eastward-stretching empire from the fifth century BC onwards) and to have been quickly incorporated into Buddhist texts that were subsequently carried by Buddhist missionaries to Tibet, China and east Asia. They also became part of a separate Hindu cosmology – in which the planets are revered as gods whose decrees can be altered by supplication and ritual – which appeared for the first time in the oldest recorded manuscript in Sanskrit, dating from the first century AD.

It is clear from all this that the desire to foretell – and to forestall, if possible – future events was more or less universal, especially in settled agricultural communities whose economies allowed for the upkeep of an independent priesthood. The priesthood's responsibility was to announce the most favourable times for the annual rituals of sowing and harvest, to placate the gods and to predict the collective future, so that steps could be taken either to guarantee or to avert it. But what of each individual's future? It was upon the base of the priests' slowly-gathered knowledge of the skies that what we today call astrology – though in its origins no different at all from astronomy – was built.

THE FOUNDATIONS OF ASTROLOGY

The listing of constellations and prominent stars was already in hand in Babylonia in the second millennium BC; and with it the project that we now know as astrology. It was clear to early observers of the heavens that, though the background pattern of the skies remained more or less unchanged, there were a number of bodies which moved through it, constantly changing their relations both to it and to the watcher below.

Not only were there the sun and the moon – which was early seen to influence tides and to chime with the menstrual cycles of women – there were five others visible to the unaided eye, which we now know as solar planets. Each of these was identified with a divine being and each was seen as passing by night through sections of the sky that were ultimately defined as the twelve constellations. These were named after animals – and later became the signs of the Zodiac.

In the sixth century BC or thereabouts, the Chaldaeans – spurred on, no doubt, by the curious multifariousness of human beings – began to speculate that the sky-pattern present at the time of an individual's birth might well explain why humans were so temperamentally different from one another (compared to, say, domesticated animals). Advances in astronomy, particularly in Egypt and Greece, gave further shape to these speculations; and eventually a recognizable cosmological (and human) order emerged.

Earth and its human inhabitants were at the centre of the universe, with transparent spheres rotating around them, each carrying one of the seven heaven-wandering bodies. The Moon's sphere was nearest; and concentrically around it were six other moving spheres carrying Mercury, Venus, the Sun, Mars, Jupiter and Saturn. Beyond Saturn's was a further sphere, which bore the stars in their constellations; and beyond that yet another, which imparted motion inward to all the others.

It was the planet-passengers of the inner concentric spheres, however, that came to be regarded as the ultimate directors of human destiny. The Sun's was the most important (and visible) of these; and its ecliptic (its apparent orbital circle round the heavens each year) was divided into twelve equal parts of thirty degrees, each corresponding to one of the constellations. Thus the Sun was said to be 'in' Aries (the Ram) during the part of the year we now assign to late-March and early-April; 'in' Taurus (the Bull) during the rest of April and part of May; and so on. The date of an individ-

ual's birth was all-important because it was this that determined his or her so-called Sun-sign or birth-sign – said to have a critical influence on his or her personality.

As for the other moving bodies, they too had an important part to play in an individual's make-up, as is still clear from the names given them by classical astronomers. 'Mars', 'Venus' and the rest, in fact, as they come down to us from the Romans, represent the personality-traits thought to be engendered by each of the planets' influences, which were then assigned in a kind of theocosmical shorthand to the god who represented them most aptly. The fifth planet's influence, for instance, was thought to

Ancient civilizations were the first to make a connection between the positioning of the planets and human behaviour

produce varying degrees of strength of character, assertiveness and short temper – so it was taken to be the planet of the god of war, Mars.

Each of the planets, furthermore, was seen as being naturally domiciled (or housed) in the various signs of the Zodiac – and when subdivisions were introduced into these, representing 10 degrees (or a third of each constellation's domain), these too were regarded as being dominated by one or other of the planets.

Thus Libra, like Taurus, is the house of Venus, but its thirds – or decans – are ruled by the Moon, Saturn and Jupiter, while those of Taurus are ruled by Mercury, the Moon and Saturn. Equally, Gemini, like Virgo, is the house of Mercury, but their decans are governed by different planets: Jupiter, Mars and the Sun in the case of Gemini, and in Virgo's the Sun, Venus and Mercury.

Also thrown into this dizzying mix as astrology developed were further subdivisions of each Zodiacal sign (each of them also ruled by one or other of the planets), and such elements as the degree of exaltation (high influence) or dejection (low influence) arrived at by each planet at various points during the ecliptic. The signs of the Zodiac, too, came to be associated over time with a multitude of different things – with parts of the body, for example, and with the four elements and their different qualities. The article in *The Encyclopaedia Britannica* (by D.E.P and R.A.Gi), gives some idea of the diverse characteristics accorded to them:

> *Numerous pairs of opposites (male-female, diurnal-nocturnal, hot-cold, and others) based on the speculations of Pythagoras... are connected with consecutive pairs of signs... [and a] wide variety of substances in the elemental world and attributes of human character are more or less arbitrarily associated with [individual ones]... These lists of interrelationships provide the rationale for many of the astrologer's predictions... Furthermore... the modes of the planetary motions [have to be] carefully considered, since their strengths are partially determined by their phases with respect to the Sun. Also, they exert a mutual influence both by occupying each other's houses and by means of conjunction and aspects.*

Who exactly developed this complex system of correspondences and connections – and in effect mathematicised the relationship between the macrosm (of the universe) and the microcosm (of the human being) – is not known. It seems to have taken more or less complete shape during the time of the Ptolemies, a Greek dynasty which ruled Egypt during the last three

centuries BC; and it was a further Ptolemy, a mathematician and astronomer of the second century AD, who laid the ground base for what was to become the Western tradition of astrology with the writing of the *Tetrabiblios* (or 'Four Books'), which is still in use today.

THE COMING OF THE PROPHET

The reading of time and the interpretation of celestial omens – the core around which classical astrology grew – were not the only ways in which ancient Middle Eastern priests seem to have mediated between past, present and future, and between the community and what they saw as the working-out of divine will. The priests, in fact, appear to have played multiple roles – roles which academics today tend to separate out into those of the shaman, the diviner, the mystic and the prophet.

Texts found in northwestern Mesopotamia, for example, dating back to the 18th century BC, refer to two types of prophets, both speaking the words of the god Dagon (just as the Israelite prophets were later to speak the words of Yahweh). One type is characterized by a word meaning 'an ecstatic' or 'frenzied one'; the second is described as 'the one who responds' – and they operated rather differently.

The 'ecstatic' type received revelations directly from the god (perhaps via trance), while 'the one who responds' was more institutionalized, operating formally within some sort of group or guild. However, their recorded pronouncements cover the same sorts of ground: exhortations about the king's duties to his subjects, warnings, threats, admonitions, accusations and predictions of good and bad outcomes.

In these early texts we may be seeing the shamanic tradition of older, nomadic societies sitting side by side with the development of a more settled priesthood, dedicated to communal forms of worship. The shaman was (and is) an individual healer endowed with psychic powers who communicates with the spirit (or divine) world through ecstatic states, but can seldom remember the messages transmitted through him when possessed.

It may be, by contrast, that the 'responder' prophets were conscious of what they had 'heard', and had begun the process of re-transmitting it in the form of homiletic ritual. They were, if this is the case, the forebears of contemporary Christian priests who preface scriptural readings with the words 'Thus saith the Lord,' while the 'ecstatics' formed part of a line of descent that led to Christian mystics such as St. Teresa of Avila, say, and Muslim Sufis.

How far these two prophet-types overlapped in an individual in ancient times is again unknown. Both, however, spoke directly, one way or another, to the divine – and were themselves imbued with it. They were at the same time representatives of the god and the god himself: they spoke with his voice.

The likelihood that emerges from the early texts, though, is that while 'responders' were the members of an organized body of prophet-priests, the 'frenzied ones' could be either priests or lay people, seized by the spirit of a deity as a result of secret trance-inducing practices, or suddenly, unexpectedly, in the manner of the Russian 'holy fool'. In an Egyptian text of the eleventh century BC, for instance, there is an example of the latter occurring in what is now Byblos in Iraq. An Egyptian temple priest named Wen-Amon had been sent there to procure timber; and while his request was being considered, a young nobleman was suddenly seized by his god to deliver a message to the city's king that it should be granted – as it indeed was.

The tradition of 'frenzied ones' operating within the priesthood, for all this, remained strong – and may well have been the origin of a new religion that was founded perhaps as early as the fourteenth century BC. This was Zoroastrianism, which became the official religion of the Persian empire and spread rapidly from the Middle East to northwest India, Afghanistan and China.

ZOROASTRIANISM

Zoroastrianism was founded by the prophet Zoroaster (the Greek form of the Persian name Zarathustra), who has often been dismissed as a mythological figure. However, he may well have been a *zaotar*, or ecstatic priest-singer – in other words, a 'frenzied one' who used special techniques to induce trance-states and (in Zoroaster's case) attacked the institutionalized priesthood for having lost touch with the divine. He preached, instead, the coming of the kingdom of the god Ahura Mazda after a period of crisis and judgment, when there would be a transformation known as 'the making wonderful' and the dead would be resurrected. According to Damian Thompson in *The End of Time*:

> This would be followed by a great assembly, in which all people would be judged. The wicked would be destroyed, while the righteous would become immortal. In the new world, young people are forever fifteen years old, and the mature remain at the age of forty. But this is not a reversion to the original paradise; nothing in the past approaches its perfection. It is the End of Time.

Zoroastrianism – as recorded in its sacred writings, the *Avesta*, revealed to Zoroaster by Ahura Mazda himself – was in other words the world's first eschatological and apocalyptic faith. It was to have many descendants, as we shall later see. In one section of the *Avesta*, Zoroaster refers to himself as a *Soashyans*, a sav-

Zarathustra, also known as Zoroaster, founder of Zoroastrianism, the official religion of the Persian empire

iour; and Messianic prophecies of the end of the world are common. Norman Cohn in his *Cosmos, Chaos and the World to Come* believes that the emergence of Zoroastrianism was to do with conflict, perhaps between 'ecstatic' and more institutionalized forms of worship and the different societies which gave them shape:

> [Zoroaster] *is the earliest known example of a particular type of prophet – the kind commonly called millennarian –. and the experiences that determined the content of his teaching seem also to have been typical. Prophets who promise a total transformation of existence, a total perfecting of the world, often draw their original inspiration from the spectacle not simply of suffering, but of one particular type of suffering: that engendered by the destruction of an ancient way of life, with its familiar certainties and safeguards.*

DIVINATION

We have already seen how, in Mesopotamia, astronomer-priests, in addition to their duties as observers of celestial omens, also made a close record of the weather, and of other phenomena like earthquakes and lightning which came under the aegis of the weather-god, Adad. (The reading of lightning-patterns later became a particular speciality of the Etruscans.) Obviously, this was of eminently practical concern, since the weather was crucial to the successful negotiation of the agricultural cycle; the coming of rain, drought or natural disaster was something it was vital both to predict (if possible) and take precautions against.

What the priests were involved in, though, was not merely a primitive form of speculative meteorology: they were attempting to read the divine will – and the divine will was expressed everywhere: not only in dramatic but also in seemingly small phenomena, such as the flight-

patterns of birds, cloud-formations, or the shapes taken on by smoke and fire. They were also involved in processes by which the divine will could be placated – and the main one of these was sacrifice.

THE IMPORTANCE OF SACRIFICE TO ANCIENT CIVILIZATIONS

Sacrifice, from the texts we have available, seems both to have played a major role in the religious practices of the Sumerians and the Babylonians who followed them, and to have been closely connected to augury, the reading of animate nature to reveal the gods' will. Why this should be so, we do not fully understand. But since the practice of sacrifice to the gods arose very early in human history, it seems reasonable to believe that the place where it took place became over time in settled communities the central theatre of worship. The sacrificial altar, in other words, came to be seen as a focus of the gods' presence and an accumulator of the cosmic energies which dictated the life of the community. It therefore took on the role of the vantage-point from which all the signs we know about were read: the rising of smoke from the sacrificial fire, for instance, the movement of birds in the vicinity, and above all – and most curiously, perhaps, to modern minds – the state of the entrails of the central player in the drama: the sacrificial victim.

Perhaps the most famous example in history of this 'reading of the entrails' is that of the soothsayer in Shakespeare's *Julius Caesar* with his "Beware the Ides of March!" He was, in fact, as we know from the orator and statesman Cicero, a senior priest called Vestricius Spurinna, who had found the liver of a sacrificed goat to be missing a major lobe. The liver was of particular importance, since it (rather than the heart) was regarded as the centre of the vital force, the seat of the emotions, and the 'mirror of the soul'. It was also a mirror in

Julius Caesar made a costly mistake when he chose to ignore the advice of a soothsayer

another sense, since, when it is removed from the body, the liver has a sheeny surface in which the sacrificing priest could see not only his own reflection, but also the reflection of the heavens above him.

It was probably from this that there had early sprung a further association – as in Vestricius Spurinna's case – between the state of the liver and predictions involving astrology. Each section of the liver had come by this time to be linked to a particular division of the skies, and therefore carried within itself (depending on its condition) a favourable or unfavourable astro-

logical meaning. It was also linked among the Etruscans – from whom the Romans seem to have inherited the practice – to an individual deity, as we know from an inscribed fourth-century bronze model of a sheep's liver now in a museum in Piacenza.

The Etruscans – who were "stark-mad on the subject of entrails", according to Cicero – almost certainly passed on to the Romans, too, the identification of the large intestine, with its complex doubling-back on itself, with the planet (and god) Mercury, which seems to follow the same sort of pathway in the sky. But

from where did the Etruscans themselves, a mysterious people who colonized west-central Italy in the 8th century BC, inherit their own predilection for entrail-reading? The most likely answer is, from the Greeks. The Greek philosopher Plato, in his *Timaeus*, for example, takes it as read that the state of the liver is a sure predictor of future events:

God... placed the liver in the house of lower nature, contriving that it should be solid and smooth, and bright and sweet... in order that the power of thought, which proceeds from the mind, might be reflected as if in a mirror... Such is the nature of the liver, which is placed as we have described in order that it may give prophetic intimations.

Paying attention to the entrails – and waiting – proved beneficial to Xenophon and his men

tory – he recounts how at almost every major turning-point his priests were required to read the entrails of sacrificial victims before a decision was finally made.

Even before setting out, with the whole army of 10,000 men starving and under attack, he refused to allow his men to move for three days until the entrail-omens had improved. Finally, on the fourth day, an ox delivered the goods, and almost immediately a Greek ship, carrying food, unexpectedly arrived – a ship his men would have missed had they moved on earlier. Once they had eaten, Xenophon gave the order to attack the enemy (as quoted in Damon Wilson's *The Mammoth Book of Prophecies*):

> *It is better for us to fight now, when we have dined, than tomorrow, when we may be without dinner. The sacrifices, soldiers, are favourable, the omens encouraging, the victims most auspicious. Let us march against the foe.*

Xenophon finally got back to Greece with the remnants of his force; and an avid reader of how he did so was Alexander the Great, who led an army eastward, back across the Hellespont, using his *Anabasis* as a guide-book along the way.

Alexander too relied upon the interpretation of victims' entrails for advice about the future. He often made sacrifices himself – along with his own readings – as he gradually expanded his empire, first across Mesopotamia and Persia, then to north-west India and what is now Afghanistan.

Finally, returning westward after eight long years, he and his by-now exhausted army headed for Babylon, but he was forestalled by a message from its Chaldaean astrologer-priests saying that a bitter fate would await him if he

Plato's rough contemporary, the Greek general Xenophon, also talks a great deal about the importance of entrail-reading in general. In his book the *Anabasis* – the account of a Greek expedition to Asia Minor which became embroiled in a Persian civil war and was forced to beat a long and harried retreat back towards the Hellespont over 1500 miles of hostile terri-

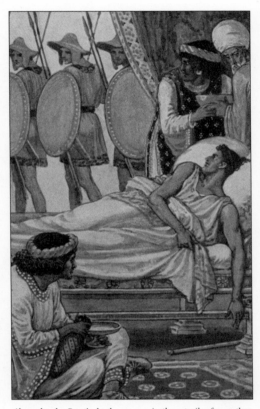

Alexander the Great's death was seen in the entrails of more than one sacrificial victim

Soon after this, still camped before the gate, Alexander fell ill with a fever or was poisoned. He was taken into the city for treatment, and there died.

The art, then, of entrail-augury – like that of astrology, to which it is strongly linked – has a relatively clear line of descent: from the Mespotamians to the Greeks, and from the Greeks to the Etruscans and Romans. But these were by no means the only peoples to practise it. Julius Caesar, for example, in his accounts of his conquest of France and southern Britain in the first century BC, attacked the cruelty of the Celtic Druid priests, who not only read the entrails of animals, but also those of human sacrificial victims.

The Toltecs, too, who dominated central America between about 700 and 1200 AD, may also have read the livers of their human offerings. For, as Robert Temple in his *Conversations with Eternity* points out, the god in whose name these human victims were slaughtered was called Tezcatlipoca, which means 'Smoking Mirror'. The 'Mirror', he suggests, may once again refer to the reflective sheen of the newly extracted liver, while 'Smoking' might be a description of the steam given off a freshly killed and opened body – as anyone who has ever slaughtered an animal will know.

entered the city. For a while he ignored the warning, but as he neared the city he received word that his own appointee as city-governor had made a sacrifice and had also found extremely disturbing omens in the entrails. He decided to camp outside Babylon's huge walls, and he immediately, according to the historian Plutarch, sent for the priest who had performed the sacrifice and questioned him:

> *The soothsayer answered that the victim's liver had lacked one lobe. "Really!" exclaimed Alexander, "that is indeed a terrible omen!" He did the soothsayer no harm, but regretted that he had not listened to the warning* [of the Chaldaeans].

ORACLES

Another Mesoamerican people, the Maya – who developed from about 1000 BC and eventually absorbed the Toltec culture – used a different form of sacrifice to read and determine god's will. Young girls were thrown into a sacred cenote or deep well and then, after a few hours, brought up again. Those who were fortunate enough to survive and were still alive were then required to recite the messages they had received from the gods during their trip to the underworld below.

Socrates, who believed himself inspired by spiritual guides, meets his death by poisoning

QUESTIONING THE ORACLES

This practice had a counterpart in ancient Greece, in the so-called Oracle of Trophonius, a shrine over a deep cave on the Hereynos river in Boeotia. Suppliants who required the answer to a question from the god – in this case Apollo – were first locked in the nearby Temple of Fortuna for three days and three nights with no food nor drink. They were then taken out and led to the shrine, where they were given two cups of water, one from a spring called Lethe (or 'Forgetfulness') and the other from a spring called Mnemosyne (or 'Memory'), so that all thoughts of their past lives would disappear and their minds would be open to nothing

but the visions to be vouchsafed by the god.

At this point they were told to descend by ladder, in total darkness, to the cave below and then writhe down a long narrow tunnel to where a trolley was waiting. Here they were handed two sacred cakes and sent hurtling away into the darkness of the cave complex, clinging on for dear life not only to the trolley but to the cakes – since the penalty for dropping them during the journey was death on arrival at their final destination. This sequence of events – isolation, starvation, dehydration, intimidation and sense-deprivation, perhaps enhanced by drugs in the cups of water and/or the cakes – eerily resembles modern brain-washing techniques.

For some suppliants, it was an altogether

overwhelming experience. A pupil of Socrates called Timarchus, for example, visited the Oracle shortly after his master's execution by poisoning in 399 BC to ask its opinion of the spiritual guide, or *daimon*, by whom Socrates had believed himself inspired. In the silence and darkness that awaited him at the end of the pell-mell trolley-ride, he eventually had a vision of a lake of fire, dotted with islands, and heard a voice addressing him by name, telling him that Socrates was one of those pure souls who had crossed the fiery lake to one of the radiant islands. But "you cannot yet understand this mystery"; the voice said, "[only] in three months will it be revealed to you".

Timarchus, like a number of others who had gone through the experience, never, according to the Roman historian Plutarch, recovered; three months later he died, "babbling about luminous islands, lakes of fire and holding out his hands to the picture of Socrates, who, he said, was coming closer to him". Whether the psychological manipulation apparently practised at Trophonius' Oracle was a late addition or not to priestly oracular techniques, we simply do not know. But we do know that prediction of the future by oracles goes back a very long way.

The oracles of the Chaldaeans, for example, probably established in the second millennium BC, remained famous throughout classical antiquity, and their reputation lasted well into the Christian era (though we know very little of how they worked or what they said). There is a direct reference to 'an oracle of God', too, in the *Second Book of Samuel* in the Old Testament in which 'to enquire of God' or of 'the Lord' seems routinely to have meant 'asking questions of an oracle'. There is a further record of oracular consultation in Homer's *Iliad* – though this seems to have consisted of a divine revelation by dream while sleeping in a temple precinct after conducting certain rites, a practice that was also common from surviving records in Egypt.

It is not altogether surprising, then – given these interconnections – that the oldest oracles we know of in the western world were founded in Greece and in north Africa apparently by Egyptians at least a thousand years before Christ. Two black doves sacred to the goddess Isis, the story went, were released from Thebes in Egypt and flew to two places later favoured by the gods, one at Dodona in Epirus (southern Macedonia) in Greece, and the other at Siwah, an oasis in the Libyan desert. An ancient grove of oak-trees at Dodona was subsequently dedicated to the Greek god Zeus, and a temple built to house the oracle at Siwah, to the horned and goat-headed Egyptian god of wisdom, Ammon – whom Greek suppliants thereafter, maintaining the connection, referred to as Zeus-Ammon.

THE ORACLE AT DODONA

A related story, recorded in Egypt, suggests that the sacred doves of the legend may actually have been Egyptian priestesses, not in their first prime, who set out on long journeys and finally came to rest on what was then declared consecrated ground. Interestingly the word for 'dove' in the ancient Epiriot language is the same as that for 'old woman'; and there are suggestions in classical literature that the priestesses at Dodona, at any rate, may well have been foreign.

Though the main method used there to interpret the god's will seems to have been attending closely to the rustling of leaves in a particular 'voiceful' oak tree, much attention was also again paid to the mourning of the doves in its branches – which the historian Herodotus took to be a metaphor for the language the priestesses spoke:

> The story which the people of Dodona tell about the doves came, I should say, from the fact that the women were foreigners, whose language sounded to them like the twittering of birds.

'To speak like a bird' was in fact a common Greek expression for 'talking unintelligibly', like a foreigner. When the Trojan princess Cassandra is accused in Aeschylus's play *Agamemnon* of twittering 'like a swallow', what is meant is the impenetrability, to Greek ears, of her native tongue.

How exactly the priestesses at Dodona, foreign or not, though, went about answering questions put to Zeus, we really don't know – except that it involved interpreting the whole world of sound presented in the grove, not only by the birds and the trees, but also by bronze vessels hung from the branches, rather similar to wind-chimes today, and even perhaps by a fountain described in the literature as 'murmurous'. A brook that ran through the grove was one of the wonders of the place – it stopped flowing each day from midday to midnight; and one can only assume that it was daily dammed up so that these complex aural readings could be made without interference from its babbling.

The priestesses, presumably – most of them elderly, it seems – must have gone through a long period of training on-site and consultation with the records before being called on to exercise their skills. It is possible that these skills of theirs, passed down from priestess to priestess, were gradually eroded over the years – either that, or a cheaper method of questioning the god came later to be offered at Dodona.

Hundreds of lead slips have been found in modern times at the site, with the name of the questioner on one side and the question itself on the other. Most of these questions are both simple and banal. Cleotas, for example, asks whether he should take up sheep-farming; Leontios wants to know whether his son will recover from an illness and Gerotion wonders if he ought to marry. Questions like these, of course, require no more than a 'yes' or 'no' answer, and this suggests that the priestesses used a method known from elsewhere, either throwing the slips into a jar full of, say, black and white beans and seeing which colour, signifying 'yes' or 'no', attached to them, or else serially taking a slip from one jar and an answering bean from another.

Some of the questions discovered at Dodona, however, did require a fuller and more complex answer: 'By what prayer or form of worship may we enjoy greatest good fortune?', for example. So it is possible, at least, that a two-tier system of interpreting Zeus's will evolved there, with simple enquiries dealt with in short order at special prices, and complex enquiries from both important individuals and embassies from city-states addressed at higher rates in the ancient way.

The answers in these cases – though again we know little of them – were apparently complex and often extremely baffling. There is an account, for example, of a legation from Boeotia arriving to ask a question of great importance, to be duly informed by the priestess Myrtile after her matching of the grove's susurrations to keys contained in the scrolls that 'it would be best for you to do the most impious thing possible'. Bemused, the members of the legation consulted with one another and then threw Myrtile into a cauldron of hot water, this being the most impious thing they could think of at the time.

THE ORACLE AT SIWAH

As to Dodona's sister-oracle at Siwah, we again know very little; what little we know comes mainly from a single visit, that of Alexander the Great after his conquest of Egypt in 313 BC. It is recorded that Alexander crossed 200 miles of desert with a small entourage to get to it and was only saved from death by thirst along the way by a sudden rainstorm sent by Zeus-Ammon.

Alexander was hailed by the shrine's priests when he finally arrived there as the god's son and the ritual of the oracle was explained to him. "When an oracle is wanted," he was told, "the priests carry forth the jewelled symbol of the god in a gilded boat, from whose sides dangle cups of silver. Virgins and ladies follow the boat, singing the traditional hymn in honour of the deity."

At this point, the pilgrim would ordinarily have to proclaim his question to the god, who would then give his answer in one of three ways. If he pushed the boat forwards, the answer was 'yes'; if backwards, 'no'; and if the boat merely rocked from side to side, then it meant that the god thought the question stupid and not worth answering. Fortunately, though, Alexander did not have to go through this semi-public rigmarole.

As a newly crowned pharaoh, he had the right, he was told, to a personal interview with the god in a private chamber. He accepted this option, though all he would say afterwards was merely that he had received the answer he was looking for. What his question had been, he never said, though it's generally believed that it was whether his planned invasion of the Persian empire would be successful – either that, or whether his mother was right in claiming that he'd been fathered by a god. Certainly from then on he expanded his empire with the implacable confidence of a man utterly convinced of eventual victory – or of an immortal; and he later had his coinage stamped with his head topped by a fillet sporting two small goat-horns, perhaps to record his close relationship-ship to the goat-god Ammon.

THE ORACLE AT DELPHI

Although not as old as the oracles at either Dodona or Siwah or as long-lasting as the oracles of the Chaldaeans, the oracle of Delphi at Phocis in central Greece was the most famous of the ancient world. Probably founded in the middle of the second millennium BC, it was originally dedicated to an earth-goddess, Gaea,

but was then taken over by the familiar classical Greek god Apollo.

Gaea, so the story went, gave birth to a monstrous snake called Pytho, which lived in a deep ground-crevice at Delphi. But the snake was challenged and killed by Apollo, who then took over his lair. Diodorus Siculus, the Greek historian of the 1st century BC, takes up the story:

At the spot where the adytum [the inner sanctum] of the present temple is, there was once a chasm in the ground where the goats used to graze [and Pytho ruled]. Whenever one of them approached this opening and looked down, it would begin skipping about in a startling fashion and bleating in a quite different voice to its normal one. Then, when the goatherds went to investigate this bizarre phenomenon, they too were similarly affected but, in their temporary possession by the god, would prophesy the future. As news of what was happening at the chasm spread across the countryside, many peasants flocked to test its strange power. As each approached the cleft, and breathed the vapour that emerged from the recesses, they would also fall into a sacred trance, through which Apollo would voice the coming of things yet to pass.

In the aftermath of this discovery, locals used the site as a place where they could simply prophesy to one another, without the intervention of any priest or priestess. But so many of them became giddy and fell into the chasm that it was decided to channel the god's words through a single individual, a priestess called the pythia – perhaps in honour of the earlier snake cult – though the name only appears for the first time much later, in the writings of the 5th-century BC historian, Herodotus.

The procedures for consulting her – and through her the god Apollo – are swathed in mystery, since "the practice of consulting the oracle was so completely established in classical

Anxious enquirers await the utterances of an entranced pythia

Greece that no author thought it necessary to give a plain straightforward account of what happened", as the classical scholar H.W. Parke puts it. It does, however, seem to have been more of less standardized.

The enquirer – an individual, a city or a state – first put his question to the Delphic priests, who after the appropriate rituals and sacrifices, then placed it before the pythia. At this point she entered the inner sanctum, took up her position over the fissure, went into a trance and began speaking in the voice of the god. How intelligible this voice was we simply don't know. Did the pythia understand what came out of her mouth? Did the priests have later to interpret and make sense of them?

Again classical writers are mostly silent. Sometimes, though, the message seems to have been utterly direct. When asked, for example, whether there was any man wiser than Socrates, the pythia simply said 'No.' When the people of Cnidus, stricken by all kinds of diseases and misfortunes while digging a canal, asked what they should do, the response was quite plain: 'Do not dig'. And when Alexander the Great

visited Delphi – apparently outside the oracle-season, for the priests refused to prepare the pythia – he simply rushed into her private apartments and began to drag her towards the inner sanctum. Unable to resist him, the pythia cried out 'This young man is unstoppable' (in another version: 'You can do what you like') which was quite enough oracle for the would-be invader of Persia. He let her go and, as Damon Wilson points out, "he never lost a battle in his life".

Another later enquirer, though, the Pythagorean philosopher Apollonius of Tyana, describes a rather more complex procedure (in the first century AD). Questioners, he says, were first ritually purified and then encouraged to sacrifice a goat to Apollo. They were then conducted to the sanctuary, but were kept from going too near the fissure to prevent them from either breathing in the fumes or disturbing the pythia.

He describes the air in the inner sanctum as having 'a wonderfully sweet perfume', though he acknowledges that this smell may have come from incense. The pythia then went into a trance. Her chest heaved, her face changed colour and her arms and legs convulsed. She foamed at the mouth and her hair stood on end. Finally she gabbled out a few unintelligible phrases, took off the sacred woollen fillet from her head and threw it to the ground – at which point Apollonius was rushed out by the priests, who had been taking down her words on his behalf.

The question Apollonius has asked was whether his name would live on after his death – and eventually the answer came via the priests: 'You shall be spoken of in centuries to come, but only for insults to be levelled against your name'. Apollonius records that he tore up this prediction and stormed away in a rage, like many another unsatisfied customer. But the pythia's words – if such they were – in the end came true, for Apollonius's Pythagorean beliefs were singled out by the early Fathers of the Christian Church and subjected to intense ridicule.

Another first-century AD account is that of the Latin poet Lucan, who describes the visit to the shrine of a man called Appius, who is anxious about his survival in a coming civil war. He takes his anxiety to the pythia, at that time a woman called Phemonoe. Michael Wood, in his *The Road to Delphi*, recounts what follows:

> She struggles against her approaching posses-
> sion by the god, and says that "all time is
> gathered up together", that the centuries
> crowd her breast and torture it. She also
> says… that she knows the number of the sands
> on the seashore. But now she is speaking as
> the god, not as herself, and she gives Appius
> his apparently consoling prophecy. He will
> "escape the awful threats of war" and "stay at
> peace" in Euboea. As indeed he does. He dies
> there before the civil war has really got
> started…

The fume-filled fissure at Delphi, if it ever existed, has long since disappeared, the victim of successive earthquakes – and scholars have tended to dismiss it as a myth, suggesting instead that the pythia was given some sort of hallucinogenic drug. However, in 2002 a group of geologists announced that it had discovered two underground faults in the region's oil-bearing limestone which crossed directly beneath the site of the temple.

It was entirely possible, the geologists announced – even probable – that petrochemical fumes would have arrived at the surface at the precise point where the pythia sat. One element in these fumes would have been ethylene, which is both sweet-smelling (as in Apollonius' account) and was once employed as an anaesthetic. In small doses it produces what the team head described as "aloof euphoria", which is a good description of the state of the peasants who first discovered the cleft, according to Herodotus, and of the pythia's mixture of trance and frenzy.

THE ACCURACY OF THE DELPHIC ORACLE

Whether the pythia was under the effect of ethylene or not, the process of consultation with her seems to have followed a regular pattern: purification and sacrifice followed by the pythian response and translation by the priests, where necessary, into Greek hexameters. (Sometimes the pythia, it seems, herself spoke directly in verse.) Consultations took place during nine months of the year, for Apollo was said to be absent in winter, and though the god Dionysus took his place for these three months, the oracle was closed.

Scholars now believe that it was in full session, with the pythia presiding, no more than once a month, i.e. nine times a year, and that on all other occasions there would be consultation by lots, the sort of ritual yes-no tombola (or divination by cleromancy, as we call it today) that was practised at Dodona and elsewhere.

Interpretations of the pythia's response were usually – but not always, as we've seen in Apollonius' case – made orally to enquirers by the priests, who may well have acted as something more than mere interpreters. Through their contacts with pilgrims and legations from all over the central and eastern Mediterranean, there is no doubt that the priests were a great deal more knowledgeable than the pythia about events in the world; they could well have bent their answers to what they themselves thought or what they believed the enquirer wanted to hear. (Suspicions of bribery attached themselves to the priesthood at Delphi – and to the pythia herself – even in ancient times.) If an enquirer could not be present himself for some reason – being a king or a city-state, for example – then the answer was written down and given to the supplicant's representatives in a sealed package.

KING CROESUS' USE OF ORACLES

This is what seems to have happened in the case of a question posed by Croesus, king of Lydia in what is now northern Turkey in the middle of the sixth century BC. Croesus was legendarily rich and his country prosperous. But he was anxious about a possible invasion by the Persians who had recently conquered his neighbours the Medes.

He decided to consult an oracle – but only after he had established which one was the most reliable. He sent emissaries to the oracles at Delphi, Abae, Dodona and Siwah and to those of Trophonius, Amphiarius and the Branchidae at Didyma, putting to them all precisely the same question at exactly the same time, a hundred days after each of his messengers had set out: "What is King Croesus doing at this very moment?" He was, as it happened, cooking a lamb and a tortoise together in a brass pot, probably the most outré thing he could think of.

The pythia at Delphi got the answer exactly right, as did the oracle of Amphiarius, although nothing more is heard of its success. This was not actually a demonstration of prediction (which was what Croesus was really after), but only of what might be called telepathy. But the pythia, before delivering Apollo's reading of the distant present, had laid claim to the god's omniscience, in words very similar to those used to Appius some centuries later:

I count the number of grains of sand on the beach and measure the sea;
I understand the speech of the dumb and hear the voiceless.

This was enough for Croesus. When he heard the news of the pythia's success, he sent back to Delphi a fortune in gold and silver, including a golden wine bowl which, according to Herodotus, weighed half a ton and could hold over five thousand gallons of wine or water. He also subsequently sent three famous questions.

The first asked for advice: 'Should Lydia [i.e. Croesus's own armies] attack the Persians?' The second concerned the future: 'Will Croesus's reign be a long one?' And the third was more personal: 'Will Croesus's son [deaf from childhood] ever speak?' The pythia's answers were for the most part deeply ambiguous. To the question about taking the war to the Persians, the pythia responded: 'After Croesus crosses the Halys [the river that marked the border between the Lydians and the Persians], a great empire will be destroyed'. It never occurred to Croesus that the 'great empire' might be his own.

The same applied to the second answer about the length of his reign, which was: 'When a mule becomes king of the Medes, then flee, soft-soled Lydian by the pebbly Hermus [another river of Lydia]! Stay not, nor feel shame for feeling cowardice!' Croesus took for granted that a mule becoming a Median king was a rank impossibility: i.e. he himself would

King Croesus devised a truly bizarre test for oracles throughout the Mediterranean

thus rule Lydia forever, or at any rate for a very long time. He didn't know that the 'mule' in question was simply a metaphor for a crossbreed, or that Cyrus, the Persian king, was of mixed Persian and Median parentage.

As for the answer to the third question about his son ever speaking again – "Croesus, you prince of fools! Hope to be away from home when your son finds his voice. Be far away on that day, for it will not be propitious for you' – he could safely, he believed, let that lie, for the other answers seemed to guarantee victory and long life. So in 547 BC he crossed the river Halys with an army to take on Cyrus' troops.

There was a bloody encounter from which Cyrus ultimately withdrew, allowing Croesus to return to Lydian territory to muster new forces. But then Cyrus struck during the winter season and rapidly pushed on to Sardis, the Lydian capital, where his soldiers fought their way into the throne-room to capture Croesus. This was when Croesus' son at last found his voice, as the pythia had said he would. 'Swine!' he's said to have shouted out. 'How dare you lay hands on King Croesus?' Though Herodotus says that Croesus later became a valued adviser at Cyrus' court, there is archaeological evidence that he was struck down on the spot.

Whether the pythia's answers to his questions were in fact designed to lead on Croesus and foment the resulting war between the Lydians and the Persians – both of them, in theory at least, potential threats to the city states developing on the Greek mainland – can only remain a matter of speculation. But it is certainly true that a number of Delphic oracles did have the effect of successfully directing – or at least underwriting – state policy. As Damon Wilson writes:

The Delphic Oracle played a major part in the peaceful spread of Greek civilization, for her word was automatically sought whenever a new Greek settlement was planned. It was on the Pythia's advice that the Cretans colonized Sicily, Archias founded Syracuse, the Boeotians built Heracles in Pontus, the Spartans created another Heracles in Thessaly, and the city of Byzantium (now Istanbul) was constructed on the Hellespont. These colonizing projects owed much of their success to the belief that Apollo protected them.

The Oracle also did much to protect the Greek mainland against invasion from the very same Persians who had swamped Croesus' kingdom of Lydia. In 480 BC, the Athenians, hearing that a massive Persian army, led by king Xerxes, was marching against them, hurried to the pythia to ask Apollo's advice. 'Hence from my temple! Prepare for disaster!' came the reply of the god.

The Athenians pressed further, only to be told that the fortress of Cecrops – at the heart of the city – would surely fall, but that wooden walls, 'unshaken', would nevertheless save the citizenry. Once more the Athenians demanded a clearer answer, and the pythia announced: 'Stay not to meet the advancing cavalry and infantry that swarm over the land, but turn and run to fight another day'. She added: 'Oh, blessed Salamis! How many children of women wilt thou slaughter!'

The Athenians concluded that the pythia's 'wooden walls' meant ships, so they abandoned the city and took to the sea. They also had a battle plan, straight from the god's mouth. After making feints in open sea they finally managed to lure the enemy's larger and less manoeuvreable galleys into the place he had indicated, the Bay of Salamis, where they had the advantage of greater skill in close-quarter fighting. Two hundred and forty ships were sunk, two hundred of them Persian; and Xerxes, deprived of a support fleet, was forced to retreat back to Asia Minor.

When it came to wars and diplomacy between the Greek city-states themselves, though, the Oracle was more or less even-handed. It was called on for advice, after all, by virtually every one of them, as well as by embassies from Egypt, Asia Minor, north Africa and eventually Rome. It was, it itself proclaimed, the *omphalos* or 'navel', the centre of the whole known world. It had the same sort of overriding spiritual and political status that medieval Europe was later to accord St. Peter's seat in Rome.

The meaning of the pythia's cryptic reference to 'wooden walls' soon became clear to the Athenians

It gave advice to the Epidamnians on whether to hand over their city to Corinth – and they took it. It directed Sparta towards republicanism and away from tyranny; it encouraged Athens to purify the island of Delos; and on another occasion distantly warned the inhabitants of another island, Syphnos, of a pirate raid. It even backed the Spartans in the invasion of Athens' home territory in Attica which sparked off, in 431 BC, the Peloponnesian War. 'If you press the war with energy', the pythia said, 'then victory will be on your side'. She even allowed that she, speaking as Apollo (the god of healing – and hence of disease), would help them. After Athens had won early victories at sea, a plague obligingly broke out in the city which wiped out a quarter of its population.

THE DECLINE OF ORACLES

The internecine Peloponnesian War, which dragged on for twenty-seven years, as the Oracle on another occasion predicted – to the ironic applause of the historian Thucydides, who was not a natural believer – bled all those

who were involved in it more or less dry. The power of the Greek city-states was fatally eroded, leaving them open to conquest, first by the Macedonians under King Philip and his son Alexander the Great, and then by the armies of the rapidly expanding Roman Empire.

The oracle at Delphi gradually fell into decline. An intriguing remark made by the Roman historian Plutarch, who himself became a priest at Delphi in the first century AD, suggests that the number of pythias on active duty there – two working, one kept in reserve – had by the time of his arrival shrunk to just one. Even earlier than that, though, both the temple and the sanctuary, though still revered, had lost their importance. When the people of Nicaea went to consult with the god in the first century BC, they were told that he no longer had a voice:

Pytho's oracle can no longer find its talkative voice,
For now, destroyed by passing time
It has locked itself in a silence without predictions.
Offer to Phoebus [Apollo], as is the custom, the sacrifices which lead the gods to make known their wishes.

The Oracle at Delphi, today nothing more than a ruin, began to slip into decline as early as the first century AD

The source of this story, in which all that is left to the Delphic priests, it seems, are the perks, is the Christian apologist Eusebius – and is part of a polemic against the ancient oracles. Part of the same propaganda campaign – almost certainly – is the account of the Roman emperor Augustus' personal consultation of the Oracle a few years later.

On this occasion, the pythia is supposed to have announced: 'A Hebrew boy bids (he who rules as god among the blessed) that I leave this house and go to Hades [the underworld]. Depart therefore from our halls and tell it not in the future'. Augustus immediately went back to Rome and placed in the Capitol, according to Michael Wood, an altar inscribed with the words: 'To the firstborn god'.

For all this, though, the Oracle managed to limp on. It was consulted by the first-century AD emperor Nero, who was anxious, it seems,

about his future. He was told to beware of the age of seventy-three. He took it for granted that he would live until that age at least, and blithely continued on his psychopathically self-regarding way, burning down Rome, among other things, and viciously persecuting the Christians. Then in 68 AD, facing rebellion all across the empire and even in Rome, he was either killed or committed suicide. His successor was a Spanish general called Galba, who had been holding his army in readiness. Galba was at the time in his seventy-third year.

It is possible that this story was made up after the event, though some scholars believe it has the ring of truth. And for all the later Christian conviction that the oracles of the ancient world must have died with the birth of Christ, there is evidence that they still persisted. The future Roman emperor Hadrian is said to have visited Delphi, and to have been told that he would one day take up the purple. When he ultimately did so, in 117 AD, he sent emissaries, it is said, to close down the Oracle and to fill up the fume-producing cleft, so that no-one else would be encouraged as he had been. Even so, this wasn't the end of the story.

Fully two hundred and fifty or so years later, the emperor Julian – called 'the Apostate' because he favoured paganism over Christianity – sent his personal physician to Delphi. He came back with this poignant message, quoted by Michael Wood in his *The Road to Delphi*:

> *Tell the king the fairwrought hall has fallen*
> *   to the ground.*
> *No longer has Phoebus a hut, nor a*
> *   prophetic laurel, nor a spring that speaks.*
> *The water of speech even is quenched.*

Thirty years later, the emperor Theodosius still had to issue an edict against oracles because their influence remained so pernicious.

The Christian propagandists who eventually won the day against the oracles were in a long line of earlier sceptics – among them Thucydides, who wrote of "the vulgar, who… when visible hopes fail them in extremity, turn to the invisible, to prophecies and oracles, and other such inventions that delude men with hopes to their destruction," and the Roman orator Cicero who spoke of "the obscure, ambiguous and fantastic speech of prophetic jargon". Nevertheless, the records of the Delphic Oracle were carefully preserved by this same Christian world: they were housed in Constantinople for centuries. They only disappeared, when Constantinople was captured and sacked by the Ottoman Turks, in 1453.

The Oracle at Delphi gave Nero a false sense of security, until his murderous behaviour brought him face to face with certain death

II
THE PROPHETS OF YAHWEH

ONE OF THE CENTRAL BELIEFS of the peoples surrounding the eastern Mediterranean in the period before Christ was that human life was preordained. Oedipus, for example, was fated to kill his father and marry his mother – and there was nothing he could do about it. The audience which went to see Sophocles' play *Oedipus Rex* knew the inevitable outcome, so it is hard to see, where the drama in the piece could have lain – or indeed why oracles, one of which Oedipus himself consulted, could contrive to alter a future that had already been set down.

The answer, in the case of *Oedipus Rex*, is that, though the audience did indeed know from the beginning what would happen, Oedipus himself believed that his fate could be avoided – indeed, he did everything possible, to the audience's evident approval, to escape it. He had freedom to act, in other words, and the drama lay, in Sophocles' hands, in the intricate trap that this very freedom of his contrived for him. The attempt to escape fate, then, was not in itself in any way foolish. It was noble. It was acquiescence that was base, even if the result of both acquiescence and the exercise of contrariness was the same – even if all of Oedipus's nobly-taken roads led inexorably, for all his ducking and diving, to the crossroads where he killed his father and to his mother's bed.

This tension between predestination by the gods and the operation of free will – however illusory free will might be – was what lay at the heart of a staggering amount of early western and middle-eastern literature. (It is the central theme, for example, of the *Epic of Gilgamesh*, written in what is now Iraq over three thousand years ago.) Obviously the master plan of the gods did leave humans some room for manoeuvre. Otherwise it would make no sense to attempt to propitiate them with sacrifices, and no sense at all to consult one of their oracles in an attempt to foresee and alter what was to come.

This room for manoeuvre was provided by the sheer number of gods who were available for worship in the early pantheons of the eastern Mediterranean bowl. In Homer, for example, the Greek gods on Olympus are portrayed as a sort of dysfunctional heavenly family, endlessly scheming and conniving and squabbling amongst themselves, pushing the fortunes of their own earthly favourites or else doing their best to cast others' protégés down. As Damon Wilson points out, Odysseus, the hero of *The Odyssey*, spent nine years making a journey by sea that should have taken him a matter of weeks on land, simply because two gods were locked in arguement about what should ultimately happen to him.

The capricious gods on Mount Olympus decided the fate of many mortals

Given this, there were clearly opportunities for individuals to intervene: to butter up with sacrifices or pleasing behaviour a particular heavenly patron, to read omens, and to propitiate one way or another any other god or goddess in the pantheon who was perceived to be inimical or downright hostile. That way – with 'Nothing too much' (inscribed on the temple at Delphi) as a guiding principle – some influence might indeed be exerted by human decisions over future outcomes.

The gods were capricious, yes – they toyed with human destinies. But the future wasn't written in stone. Some gods were more powerful or more kindly than others. They brought victory in war, for example, if they were treated with the right respect and/or obsequiousness. And victory in war clearly underwrote the rightness of the fealty their worshippers had shown to them: it meant that they were more influen-

tial in the celestial halls where decisions were negotiated than those the enemy laid claim to.

This is precisely what makes, in retrospect, the arrival of what we today call Judaism such an extraordinary and epochal event. For Judaism was the first monotheistic religion: it announced that Yahweh ('I am') – whose name was too sacred to speak and who had to be described in circumlocutions like 'Adonai' and 'Jehovah' – was the one and only true god, responsible for all human destinies.

In what seems a sudden coup – but was almost certainly a gradual process that took centuries – this article of faith caused a profound sea change in the nature of prophecy and in the community's stance vis-à-vis the future. For the single God of the Hebrews allowed no competition. There could be under his aegis no more wrangling in heaven. He alone was omniscient; he alone was all-powerful. What he

Following consultation with Yahweh, the prophet Abraham moved his followers to Canaan

said, stood. All that remained, in Damon Wilson's words, "was for a chosen 'Prophet of God' to tell the people just what God had ordained".

THE ORIGIN OF THE HEBREWS AND THE FIRST PROPHETS

According to Wilson's excellent account in his *The Mammoth Book of Prophecy*, the Hebrews can almost certainly be identified with the 'Habiru' referred to in an Egyptian papyrus of around 1207 BC – the first reference to them, if this is so, that we know of outside the Bible. By their own account in the Pentateuch (the first five books of the Old Testament), their founding father was a nomadic trader called Abraham, who was the direct descendant of Shem, one of the sons of the ark-builder Noah, who had ensured the survival of mankind (and the animal kingdom) from the devastations of the Great Flood. According to the Book of Genesis, Abraham was a native of Ur in Sumeria on the river Euphrates; and he was probably born there around 1800 BC.

ABRAHAM

It was Abraham who first proclaimed Yahweh to be the one true god, and pronounced him his own family's special tutelary deity. He instructed the members of the family never to marry outside the clan; in so doing he founded not only a new religion, but also, in effect, a new race (kept pure by endogamy over generations). He also had direct unmediated communication with the deity, who advised him to take his growing tribe to the land of Canaan (present-day Israel and Palestine), where, after initial difficulties – which involved the wholesale destruction of Sodom and Gomorrah – they finally settled. It was then that Jehovah, speaking through Abraham, pronounced that Canaan was 'the Promised Land': theirs to rule over in perpetuity (Genesis 13:14 *et seq.*):

And the Lord said… lift up now thine eyes, and look from the place where thou art northward, and southward and eastward, and westward.

For all the land which thou seest, to thee will I give it, and to thy seed forever.

And I will make thy seed as the dust of the Earth: so that if a man can number the dust of the Earth, then shall thy seed also be numbered.

Because the deity spoke directly to and through Abraham – and because he spoke of a future time when Abraham's descendants would, in effect, rule over the earth, Abraham should be seen as the first in what was to become a long line of Hebrew prophets – and the original generator of one of the main themes of Jewish prophecy: the arrival of a warrior Messiah who would lead the Jewish people towards the inheritance (of dominance) that Jahweh had promised them.

The story of Abraham's immediate descendants is more or less well-known: the almost-sacrifice of Esau; the hardships of Jacob (which earned him the title of *Israel* ('struggler with God'); and the family feud which saw his brothers selling Joseph, Abraham's great-grandson, into slavery in Egypt. (Joseph eventually became a much favoured high court official there after he successfully predicted a future famine on the basis of the Pharaoh's dreams.) At some time thereafter, the whole extended family followed Joseph from Canaan ('Promised Land' or not) to Egypt, perhaps compelled to

migrate there because of the famine Joseph had predicted (as the *Book of Exodus* records) or as camp-followers of the armies of a mysterious people called the Hyksos, who invaded Egypt around 1630 AD and ruled there for a hundred years.

For whatever reason they arrived in Egypt, though, the Israelites, as they became known, settled into a new life as traders, prospered and significantly increased in numbers – such numbers, ultimately, that they came to be regarded as a threat. Some time after the Hyksos had been driven out, they were enslaved and forced to work in the fields and on the spate of new temple-building launched by the restored (and revivified) Egyptian rulers. Their degradation persisted for some two hundred years – until the arrival of the second great prophet of the Hebrews, Moses.

MOSES

Moses, according to the Bible, was an Israelite foundling who had been discovered as a baby by the Pharaoh's daughter floating on the river in a basket of reeds; she adopted and raised him. He had, then, as a young adult a high position at court – and had largely forgotten the inheritance of his blood. Then, though, he was persuaded by the famous vision of the Burning Bush to use his power and influence to have his people set free.

The Pharaoh, however – who may have been the sneeringly proud Rameses II, who ruled from c. 1304 to 1237 BC and built the larger temple at Abu Simbel – was unmoveable, until, that is, Moses called down on the Egyptians ten successive plagues, and thereby moved the business of prophecy up a notch. He became, as he announced each one to the still-unbending Pharaoh, something more than the mouthpiece of Yahweh. He became His embodiment, the expression of His wrath.

The ten plagues represented – in modern

The plague of hail, one of the ten plagues visited upon the Egyptian people by Yahweh

interpretations, at least – a rolling tide of eco-
logical disaster. The first plague – in which the
Nile turned red and all its fish died – may have
been caused, according to an American public-
health epidemiologist, by a bloom of toxin-pro-
ducing freshwater algae called physteria,
unleashed, if very rarely, in extremely hot
weather. From this would more or less inevitably
have followed the second, third and fourth
plagues: those of frogs, of lice and of flies.

The frogs would have rapidly abandoned the
river to avoid the toxins and would have died in
the desert or have been exterminated in vast
numbers by the human population. This would
then have left a yawning gap in the food chain
and led to an enormous proliferation of both
lice and flies (which were normally preyed on by
amphibians). These in turn might well have
produced the sixth plague – the death of
Egypt's cattle and horses – brought on by
swarms of a livestock-attacking Egyptian midge
called coolacoides; and perhaps even the seventh, the plague of boils, which may be a
description of a disease called glanders, which
was spread by the African stable fly.

Only with the eighth plague do we enter a
different kind of territory. For this was a plague
of hail and of fire – neither of them, of course,
unknown in Egypt, but hard to interlink.
Locusts, the ninth plague, are much more
expected and routine, particularly in the sort of
boiling weather that may have scared up the
bloom of physteria on the river – and they in
turn may be connected to the tenth, in which all
the first-born children of the Egyptians died.

It is at least possible that in the face of the
invading plague of locusts, the Egyptians
buried their supplies of grain underground,
where they were contaminated by a mould
called *Stachybotrys atra*, which produces toxins
capable of causing death, if eaten in sufficient
quantities, by a haemorrhaging of the lungs.
The first-born, according to this theory, being
specially favoured by their parents (and larger

than their siblings) would have eaten more of
this toxin than both their siblings and their
indulgent parents, and so would have been singled out. The Israelites, of course, as slaves,
would have been unlikely to have been fed
much precious grain, if any – and would have
remained unaffected.

It was this final plague – whether inflicted by
Yahweh or merely successfully predicted by
Moses – that finally broke the back of the
Pharaoh's resistance. The Israelites were manu-
mitted and allowed to pass over the Sea of
Reeds that separated the delta of the Nile from
the Sinai Desert. Moses, as we learn in the Old
Testament, subsequently brought down the
tablets of the Ten Commandments from the top
of Mount Sinai and his people spent forty years
wandering in the wilderness, before finally
resettling in Canaan.

THE EGYPTIAN CONNECTION

There's one thread in this story, however, that
makes little sense. For if the worship of Yahweh
had been successfully instituted by Abraham
and had remained resolutely in place during his
descendants' long exile in Egypt, why did it
take so long to establish (via the Ten Commandments) its central credoes and basis in
ethics? Is it at all possible that the monotheism
of the Israelites was not in fact born fully
fledged in ancient Sumeria, but had its most
important tap-roots in Egypt?

No less an authority that Sigmund Freud, in
his *Moses and Monotheism*, believed that it might
have. As he pointed out, a monotheistic state
religion had existed for a brief moment in
Egypt during the reign of Amenhotep IV, also
known as Akhenaton. Akhenaton had come to
the throne in c. 1372 BC (i.e. less than a century before the beginning of the reign of Rame-

ses II, Moses' probable pharaonic adversary), and he was, no doubt, a religious revolutionary.

He threw out the Egyptian pantheon and instituted instead the worship of a single god, the sun-god Aton, who was pictured as beneficent and humane, spreading his rays and essential goodness equally to all men, just as Akhenaton himself, Aton's embodiment upon earth and his physical son, did to his subjects. For some seventeen years, Aton and Akhenaton (together with Akhenaton's queen Nefertiti) seem to have reigned in almost perfect harmony. A new capital was built to enshrine the new worship; and a new school of Egyptian painting arose, celebrating nature.

It wasn't long, though, before the ousted priests of the old gods fomented a revolution, backed by the common people, who had taken offence at Akhenaton's defacing of the old gods' images and statues. He was first forced to share power with his own son-in-law, and then shortly afterwards he died, probably murdered. The traditional Egyptian pantheon and polytheism were soon restored.

In musing over the possible connection between Akhenaton's worship of Aton and the worship of Jehovah, Freud first suggested that Moses might not have been an Israelite at all, but a member of the Egyptian royal family, quite capable of confronting, because of his own status, the living godhead of the Pharaoh. His name, he said, suggested as much, since 'Mose' in ancient Egyptian meant 'son of' – it would have formed part of a characteristically Egyptian patronymic, perhaps shortened in Israelite traditions to disguise his true origins.

Proceeding by a process of intuitive speculation, Freud then opined that Atonism might well have survived in Egyptian court circles in much the same way that Roman Catholicism did in the aftermath, in England, of Henry VIII's reformation of the Church; and that, with its benign message of equality under the sun, it might well also have been the preferred religion

of Egypt's slaves, just as Christianity was later to be in the days of the Roman Empire.

From here it was but a short step for Freud to maintain that Atonism and Jehovahism might therefore be one and the same, but that the original Atonism of the Egyptians (and Israelites) had become slowly contaminated, after the escape from Egypt and Moses' eventual death, by the forms of worship of the Semitic tribes the migrants encountered, fought and assimilated before their re-arrival in Canaan. Thus, though the practice of circumcision (an ancient Egyptian custom) survived, the softness of the sun and its imagery in the end disappeared, to be replaced by a fierce god of vengeance more suited to prosecuting the wars in which they were by now involved as they fought their way back to their homeland.

Freud even suggested that the result was an abiding fault-line running through what might be called the Jewish mind-set: with the eye-for-an-eye brutality of the Old Testament (and Zionism), on the one side, and the mysticism, quietism and ruefulness, that were (perhaps) the residual legacies of Atonism, on the other. He believed that there was something profoundly contradictory at the heart of Judaism; and that Christianity and the Kabbala, both born out of it, were attempts to reconnect, perhaps, to the Atonist side of the divide.

All this, of course, was mere speculation on Freud's part. There was no actual evidence given in *Moses and Monotheism* to connect the origins of the Hebrews' one god to Egypt. His theory, however, is not by any means as far-fetched as it may seem. The Ten Commandments and the covenant sealed with the deity at Sinai (i.e. the promise that Israel would from then on would be a holy nation, dedicated exclusively to one god) have a strong similarity to certain passages in *The Egyptian Book of the Dead*, which predates their pronouncement; there are also passages in both *The Book of Proverbs* and *The Psalms* which seem almost to be

Vengeful Israelites under the direction of Joshua destroyed several Palestinian cities, including Jericho

quotes from *The Wisdom of Amenemope*, a book of advice that some scholars believe may have been written by Akhenaton himself.

If the monotheistic cult of the Hebrews, though, did indeed have its roots in Atonism, this still leaves open the question of how on earth an essentially peaceful religion – Akhenaton notoriously neglected wars and foreign conquests – was so quickly transformed into a belligerent one. For there is no doubt that by the time the Israelites arrived in Canaan after being condemned to forty years in the wilderness as a punishment from their god for their disobedience and backsliding, they were very belligerent indeed.

Archaeological evidence in Palestine points to a brutal invasion of the area in about 1250 BC; and the Old Testament also makes it clear that under the leadership of the prophet Joshua, Moses' successor, the Israelites razed to the ground a number of the towns and cities (like Jericho) they found there. They also either killed or expelled the inhabitants and waged a particularly venomous war against the gods that the inhabitants had worshipped: Baal and Ashtaroth.

BAAL AND ASHTAROTH

The name Baal (meaning 'master') the people of Israel had already come across, when the men had been seduced by the women of the Midianites into forsaking God and worshipping him instead, in rites that were clearly both ecstatic and sexual. It was also the name given by the Canaanites to their god of weather and fertility who, with his wife Ashtaroth, the goddess of love and war, ruled the Canaanite pantheon. *The Lion Handbook to the Bible* says of them:

> *These gods did not set laws (like the Ten Commandments), although they might make cruel demands like child sacrifice – so people could behave much as they pleased. This, and its close link with good crops and fertility, made Canaanite religion easy and attractive.*

It also meant that the Canaanite religion must have been a source of considerable temptation to a nomadic people tethered in by sexual taboos. For sex was central to the operation of Baal and Ashtaroth's temples. Virgins were ritually deflowered by strangers in the temple precincts for money that went to the priests, who seem also to have presided over orgies and other sexual rites. Werner Keller, in his *The Bible as History* (quoted by Wilson) describes the impact this must have had on the Israelites:

> *What temptation for a simple shepherd folk, what perilous enticement. More than once the Baal religions got a firm foothold and penetrated right into the temple of Yahweh, into the Holy of Holies…*
>
> *Without its stern moral law, without its faith in one God, without the commanding figures of the prophets, Israel would never have been able to survive this struggle with the Baals, with the brothel religions of the fertility goddesses.*

Wilson continues:

> *And this, Keller explains, is why the Hebrew prophets habitually denounced "the abomination of the heathens" over the centuries. When Isaiah denounced Jerusalem as having become "a harlot", he did not mean that the people had slackened their morality and become licentious, he meant that they had gone back to the religions of Baal and Astarte [another name for Ashtaroth].*

KEEPING TO THE STRAIGHT AND NARROW

Moses and Joshua were both prophets with a capital 'P'. They were the mouthpieces of Yahweh to his quarrelsome people and therefore its God-appointed leaders. There existed, however, within the ranks of the wandering Israelites another prophetic tradition, and this seems to have come into prominence with their arrival in Canaan.

This tradition is first mentioned in *The Book of Numbers* when, shortly after the departure from Mount Sinai and with the Israelites already complaining of their never-ending diet of manna, Moses called together seventy tribal elders and gave them a taste of the 'spirit' (or 'wind') of God that had inspired him. The seventy men began to prophesy, says the Bible, "and did not cease". Later, Moses received complaints that two other men – not in this privileged inner circle – had also begun prophesying without any sanction. He refused to punish them, saying that he wished all the children of Israel had the same gift. "Would that all God's people were prophets!" he announced.

With the colonization of Canaan by the twelve tribes and after the death of Joshua, this

kind of ecstatic – some might say, shamanic –
prophesy seems to have become the norm. The
settlements of the Israelites were by now under
constant attack, particularly from the so-called
Philistines (or Phoenicians) from the coast, and
there was no longer any central leadership of
the kind exemplified by Moses and Joshua.
Instead the people were ruled by a loose con-
federation of so-called 'judges'; the prophetic
function was taken over by individual seers and
by prophetic guilds, which may have had their
origins in Canaanite practices.

These seers and prophetic collectives worked
for money and gifts and were associated with
sanctuaries such as Samaria, Bethel, Jericho,
Jerusalem and Gilgal – and dance-induced
trances may have been the most important part
of their repertoire, for the Levitical guilds and
singers who operated in the Jerusalem Temple
were said to "prophesy with lyres, with harps
and with cymbals" (I Chronicles). Elsewhere
there are references to prophets dancing or
rolling on the ground in ecstasy as they uttered
oracular chants. On one occasion, Saul, the first
king of Israel, met a group of these dervish-like
nabis (or 'called ones') and joined in their dancing, ending up frenziedly proclaiming prophecies of his own.

It is with the appearance of Saul as the uni-
fier of the Israelite tribes in the 11th century
BC that we meet the next generally-accepted
Prophet (in the sense of a man speaking with
the direct, unmediated authority of Yahweh):
Samuel.

SAMUEL

Samuel was a priest, seer and judge (or ruler)
who was also head of a *nabi* guild and his part
in Israelite history was short but crucial.

It was he, speaking as the god himself, who
approved the idea of appointing a king to bring
political and military unity, even though he
warned of its considerable dangers. (It was a

*With the Witch of Endor's help, a jealous Saul attempted to raise
Samuel from the dead*

small but crucial step away the ideal of God
alone as Israel's King.) Saul, a farmer and
guerilla leader, was thus duly anointed by
Samuel.

However, he proved unreliably religious and
prone to fits of violence; and God's favour soon
moved elsewhere, to a shepherd-boy called
David, who was secretly anointed to take his
place. David single-handedly killed with a sling-
shot the Philistine champion, Goliath, and
became the only person who could soften King
Saul's increasingly black moods with his harp-
playing.

Eventually, though, Saul grew jealous of
David's popularity, and David was forced to flee
for his life. Samuel died, and Saul himself was
killed in a last-ditch battle against the
Philistines, together with all his sons (including
David's friend, Jonathan) – though not before
he had tried to raise Samuel from the dead with
the help of the Witch of Endor.

DAVID

David, though God's chosen successor, was backed only by his own tribe of Judah, and now faced civil war. However, he early on captured the Jebusite city of Jerusalem and made it his capital and moved to it the Ark of the Covenant, which he enshrined there upon a hill. Gradually the other tribes responded, and united now into a nation, they fought off their enemies (including the Philistines and the Ammonites) and extended the area under their control from the Sinai peninsula northward towards the Euphrates.

David, who ruled for forty years, was refused permission to build the Temple by the prophet Nathan – he had become too contaminated by war and was also fatally indulgent to his children. But he was promised by Nathan that God would build *him* a house, a dynasty, which would be "for ever" – and on this promise there came to rest a hope which echoes right through the remainder of the Old Testament: the hope for a Messiah.

David's era was a golden age, to which the children of Israel ever after looked back with immense nostalgia. His legacy was almost immediately eroded by his successors.

SOLOMON AND REHOBOAM

His son Solomon – though he built the Temple and beautified Jerusalem – instituted taxation and created a new class of urban building-labourers to do so. He created a huge bureaucracy and he also lived in considerable luxury, with a massive palace that dwarfed the Temple. He also had a considerable harem of foreign wives and concubines who seem to have seduced him back to the worship of Baal. The tiny building, the Temple itself, when finally constructed, bore a strong resemblance to Baalist temples and its architect, Hiram of Tyre, was himself a Baal-worshipper.

Solomon's son, Rehoboam, fared even worse. Asked by the northern tribes to lessen their tax burden, he announced that, on the contrary, he intended to increase it. The tribes rebelled and then seceded, taking with them the name Israel, instituting their own king (Jeroboam) and even setting up religious centres of their own, centres that soon degenerated, says the Bible, into idolatry and fertility-cult worship. As for what was left, Rehoboam's kingdom of Judah, its capital Jerusalem was invaded by the armies of an Egyptian pharaoh in 922 BC, and the Temple's treasury looted. Samuel's prophecy had come true: Human kingship had indeed led to disaster; God's kingdom had been almost fatally compromised.

It became the duty from this point on of the Old Testament prophets to keep the worship of Yahweh as uncontaminated as possible, and the two kingdoms undivided in their attention to the one God's purposes. In the northern kingdom, for example, when King Ahab (c. 874-853 BC) married Jezebel of Tyre in a strategic marriage, she brought with her in her retinue the religion she favoured: that of Baal (or the Phoenician god Melqart).

ELIJAH

Elijah, who was later regarded as the greatest of the prophets – his name means 'My god is Yah(weh)' – almost immediately made a dramatic appearance, and predicted a coming punishment from Yahweh, a prolonged drought, which the so-called Phoenician weather-god would be totally unable to prevent.

He also challenged Baal's priests to a contest, a demonstration of which of the two gods would be able to kindle fire on an altar unassisted. "The living Lord" won easily and the priests of Baal were soon put to death by the people, whereupon the drought came to an end.

For all this, though, Elijah was forced into hiding in the southern desert of the Sinai

His work on earth complete, Elijah ascends to heaven in a fiery chariot

peninsula (where he was fed by an angel, performed miracles and was spoken to by the small voice of God "out of the stillness"); he returned to the northern kingdom only once, to predict publicly the ruin that faced both Ahab and Jezebel. Ahab was subsequently killed in battle against the Syrians; and Jezebel, who survived him for ten years, was ultimately defenestrated by her own servants. Elijah, though, was not there to see her downfall. He had been by then, says the Bible, wafted up to heaven alive in a fiery chariot, after passing on his mantle to his successor, Elisha.

Elisha went on to perform miracles of his own, especially among the poor and excluded. He foretold the future, led the coup against

Jezebel, rooted out the worship of Baal, bro-kered a peace agreement and even saved the life of a Syrian general. He and Elijah – whose return to earth he prophesied (in what may later have served as a model for predictions of the Second Coming of Christ) – exemplified, in other words, a new and important role for what scholars now call 'the classical prophets'.

They and their successors combined their watchfulness over what might be called the community's 'religious correctness' with a strong sense of social injustice and a willingness to enter the political arena whenever necessary to combat it. The prophet Amos, for instance, not only decried the religious practices of the northern kingdom (on the grounds that Jerusalem had been God-ordained as the only true site of His cult), he also attacked tyranny, the irresponsible luxury of the rich and the reduction of religious practice to no more than by-rote rituals and elaborate sacrifices (or 'burnt offerings'). He proclaimed, harking back to an earlier and more simple age, that justice, mercy and charity were much more important than these.

This thread of nostalgia for the past was combined with a particular interpretation of the nation's history, which held that the people of Israel were – and indeed had been from earliest times – apostates: they had, in other words, consistently rejected a faith they had once embraced and had persistently fallen into the worship of other gods, thus rejecting the future that Yahweh, out of love, had offered them. The result would be, they proclaimed, that He would ultimately judge – even perhaps destroy – them, just as He had done their enemies.

What this judgment would consist in was variously described by the classical prophets. But some basis for hope was usually allowed: the idea that, whatever ultimately happened, a remnant of the chosen people would somehow remain. Many would fall away, but the future of this remnant would be placed in the hands of

an ideal future king – as described, for example, by the prophet Isaiah.

The divine blessing would never be wholly withdrawn, and the kingdom of "the annointed one" would be (re-)established in the Holy Land, with Jerusalem at its centre. The classical prophets' foreshadowing of the future of this remnant is precisely what has given the word 'prophecy' its predictive meaning.

PROPHECIES FULFILLED

In 720 BC, after more than a century, it seems, of paying tribute to the kings of Assyria, the northern kingdom of Israel finally reaped the whirlwind for its attempts to enter an alliance with Egypt.

After a three-year siege by the army of King Sennacherib, the capital Samaria was captured and destroyed; most of its inhabitants were dragged away into slavery in what are today north-eastern Syria, Turkey and Iran. (Sennacherib's successor speaks of deporting "27,290 of its inhabitants, together with their chariots… and the gods in whom they trusted".)

What became of them (assimilation? extinction?) is unknown. But they were cast retrospectively as sinners, disrespecters of God's law, and became known as 'the Lost Tribes', still imagined as waiting to return to their birthright from under the heels of the gentiles.

Sennacherib next turned his attention to Judah and Jerusalem, where the prophet Isaiah, mostly ignored by his own people, had long warned against the Assyrian threat. With Isaiah's help, though, the city was finally saved – assisted, almost certainly, by a hefty bribe. A clay prism, found buried in the foundations of one of Sennacherib's palaces, records events in what are seemingly the King's own words, directed at his successors:

[Hezekiah of Judah] *I shut up in Jerusalem, his royal city, like a bird in a cage. I encircled him with watch towers and made it impossible for him to leave his city by the gate. His towns which I had captured I detached from his kingdom… and so reduced his land. In addition to their previous tribute payments, I imposed upon them a further payment as a due to my lordship… To Nineveh, my lordly city, he had brought after me 30 talents of gold, 800 talents of silver, precious stones, antimony, large blocks of carnelian, ivory beds, ivory chairs, elephant hide, ivory, ebony, whatever was very valuable, his daughters, his royal women, singers male and female…*

Isaiah, despite his role in seeing off the Assyrians, appears to have been less than enthusiastic about the eventual outcome. He saw the destruction of Jerusalem as inevitable – he once walked naked through the city as a practical demonstration of how it would one day be stripped. One of his successors, Ezekiel, wore a rotten girdle as an emblem of the city's decay

Josiah attempted to institute religious reform during his reign

and, in the words of Winwood Reade in his *Martyrdom of Man*:

> *... buttered his bread in a manner we would rather not describe as a sign that* [its people] *would eat defiled bread amongst the gentiles. Jeremiah* [he goes on] *wore a wooden yoke as a sign that they would be taken into captivity...*

Beset by enemies on every side, Josiah, king of Judah between roughly 640 and 609 BC, did his best to institute religious reform after a book of the law (perhaps a copy of the text of *Deuteronomy*) was found during repair-work on the Temple. With the help of a prophetess called Huldah, he renewed his people's covenant with Yahweh, purged his country of pagan worship and ordered the celebration of the neglected Feast of the Passover.

It was too little, too late, though. Josiah was ultimately killed in an unnecessary battle with the Egyptian Pharaoh Necho (at Megiddo – or Armageddon) in 609; soon afterwards, when the occupying Egyptian army was in turn defeated by the rising power of Babylon (as foreseen by Isaiah), his royal grandson, installed as a puppet but of dubious loyalty, was summarily removed by King Nebuchadnezzar to his own capital, along with Jerusalem's Temple treasures and leading citizens, including the unfortunate prophet Ezekiel.

Another prophet, Jeremiah, who had constantly warned of the dangers of political intrigue and of the threat posed by Babylonia, was witness to the final disaster. King Zedekiah, the next puppet installed by Nebuchadnezzar, also rebelled; and in 587 BC, after an eighteen-month siege, the city was taken and burned to the ground (as recorded in *The Book of Ezekiel*).

The Temple was looted and razed; and as for Zedekiah, his sons were killed in front of him, and he himself was blinded. Every citizen of Judah of any substance was then dragged away

into captivity, leaving behind only the rural poor. Jeremiah, who had been arrested and thrown down a well as a suspected Babylonian sympathizer because of the accuracy of his predictions, was invited to Babylon by Nebuchadnezzar as an honoured guest, but declined. Instead, after the Babylonian-installed governor was assassinated, he made his way with those escaping retribution to Egypt, where he died.

THE BABYLONIAN CAPTIVITY AND ITS AFTERMATH

Jeremiah had predicted, correctly, that his people would be deported to Babylon. The prophecies of what scholars call today Deutero-Isaiah ('the second Isaiah', contained in chapters 40-45 of *The Book of Isaiah*) seem to have been aimed at the exiled community and outlined its responsibility for preserving Yahwism in captivity.

Jeremiah had foreseen that their stay in Babylon would last seventy years, a period in which, he said, the Jewish people would be separated, good from bad, like healthy figs separated from rotten ones by a farmer. After that, he announced, the gentile peoples of the north – among whom he listed the Medes – would rise up and free the children of Judah from captivity. They would then return to the Promised Land and enter a golden age, in which Yahweh would create a new (and renewed) Israel. Purified by their ordeal, the Judahites – or 'Jews', as they would later become known – would there come together in a perfect theocracy. The Lost Tribes would return from wherever they had ended up after their transplantation by the Assyrians, and join them.

As it turned out, their exile in Babylon lasted

just forty-eight years. For in 539 BC, Cyrus the Great – who was half-Median, half-Persian – took Babylon, annexed it to his burgeoning Persian empire, and freed the Jews from captivity. Many, however, did not return – and those who did were not enough to restore any great lustre to the new Persian province of Judea and to its capital, Jerusalem, even after the gathering-in of those who had remained. The Temple was finally rebuilt and the city walls were re-erected. But neither the Lost Tribes nor any *mashiak* (Messiah or 'Anointed One') appeared. The role of prophets and prophecy in the ordering of Jewish society and right direction of its worship diminished.

In the article *Prophecy in the Ancient Middle East and Israel*, included under *Doctrines and Dogmas, Religious* in *The Encyclopaedia Britannica*, the author G.W.A. writes:

> *Why prophecy died out in Israel is difficult to determine, but Zecariah offers as good an answer as any in saying that the prophets "in those days" told lies. Prophets did appear, but after Malachi none gained the status of the classical prophets. Another reason may be found in Ezra's reform of the cult in the 5th century BC, in which Yahwism was so firmly established that there was no longer any need for the old polemics against Canaanite religion.*

The prophetic heritage was channelled instead through the teaching of the classical prophets' words. But the impulse towards prophecy, thwarted of its hoped-for end – the arrival of 'the Anointed One' – found another outlet in a new form of (prose) literature. G.W.A. says of this literature:

> *There is a tendency in prophetic preaching to spiritualize those aspects of religion that remain unfulfilled; herein lie the roots of eschatology, which is concerned with the last times,*

and apocalyptic literature, which describes the intervention of God in history, to the accompaniment of dramatic, cataclysmic events.

G.W.A. argues that the visions of the classical prophets which remained unfulfilled were transformed into historical apocalypses like *The Book of Daniel*. The writers took the names of ancient figures like Adam, Enoch, Abraham, Daniel and Ezra, and saw themselves as taking over and carrying on the prophetic task.

The events they described had usually occured long before, but they retold them in order both to hint at and to predict the future. Dominant in this apocalyptic literature is the theme of God's ultimate rule over all the universe; and the message is twofold: of the doom to come at the end of time, and of hope in a new age beyond it under the rule of God, when the righteous would be vindicated.

The apocalyptic literature which G.W.A. describes seems to have arisen after a long period of stagnation in the Jewish state under the benevolent rule, first of Persian governors, and then of Alexander the Great.

With the break-up of Alexander's enormous empire, however, Judea came under the hegemony of the Seleucid kingdom of Syria. Though it was mostly left alone to go its own way, in 175 BC, a new king of Syria, Antiochus IV, decided to drag it out of the past and introduce it, willy-nilly, to Hellenistic civilization and religion.

CAUSES OF JEWISH UNREST

Under his influence, the High Priest was assassinated, and two successfully Hellenized Jews called Jason and Menelaus (one a gradualist, the other a vicious root-and-branch reformer) fought it out for control of the city and the Temple, progressively outraging Orthodox Jews. Jason introduced Greek schools and a gymnasium.

The refusal by Orthodox Jews in Jerusalem to follow Menelaus' orders to eat forbidden pork led to many deaths

However, Menelaus, in two separate periods of rule, went much further. He installed a statue of Zeus in the Temple's empty inner sanctum, which had once held the Ark of the Covenant. He forbade circumcision, the ownership of sacred Jewish texts and the observance of the Sabbath, and later tried to force plates of (forbidden) pork on Orthodox Jews in front of the Greek God's statue. Those who refused, so called *Hasidim* or 'holy ones, were tortured to death, as later Christian martyrs were.

The whole of Judaea soon erupted into a civil war between Menelaus' Hellenized followers and an Orthodox faction of *Hasidim* led by Judas Maccabeus and his brothers. Antiochus, known vaingloriously as Epiphanes ('the manifestation of god'), was prevented from intervening because of campaigns elsewhere. Eventually, in 164 BC, the Maccabees took back the capital and relit the holy lamps in the Temple which had been extinguished by Menelaus (thereby instituting the festival of lights, Hanukkah).

For a hundred years after that, the Maccabees ruled Judaea with little intervention from Antioch, Syria's capital, or indeed anywhere else. But in 63 BC, a schism developed within the ruling family which once more threatened general civil strife, and one of the factions made the mistake of inviting the Roman army in to settle the dispute. General Cnaeus Pompeius Magnus ('Pompey the Great') promptly invaded Judaea, put down both factions of the Maccabees and declared the nation a Roman province. Twenty-six years after that, with the collapse of the Roman republic, the new emperor Augustus made a foreigner, an Edomite called Herod, its king.

It was this succession of attacks on the integrity of Jewish traditions and on the right of the Jewish people to rule themselves as they saw fit that provoked the efflorescence of a literature that claimed knowledge of the divine purpose and offered speculations about the different eras through which history was passing as the world approached the end of time. Only one of the books, *The Book of Daniel*, was finally thought worthy of inclusion among the sacred works of the Old Testament. But what is clear in all of them is the influence, partly of Hellenistic, but particularly of Persian, thinking about the relationship between the human and the divine.

These books are the record, at least in part, of the sort of dreams and visions which were characteristic of the scriptures of Zoroastrianism, the official religion of the Persian empire. They are concerned with a struggle, not between the Jews and their enemies, but between absolute spiritual good and evil, darkness and light, just as Zoroastrianism was.

Instead of looking back, moreover, towards an ancient ideal – the Kingdom of David – they looked forward to a glorious new world in which an everlasting Israelite kingdom would be founded by Yahweh upon the ruins of the gentile kingdoms which had long held it in thrall. This future was not simply historical, for it existed outside and beyond time. It was a future – as in the post-battle resurrection, 'the time of making wonderful', the universal judgment and punishment of the wicked promised by Zoroastrianism – that belonged firmly to the supernatural. Damian Thompson, in his book *The End of Time*, comments:

> It was a shift of emphasis which was to change the course of human history. Christianity would not have been possible without it.

THE BOOK OF DANIEL

The Book of Daniel, almost certainly written during the revolt of the Maccabees against the Menelaites and their Seleucid allies, is sometimes described as the first piece of Jewish propaganda to be included in the Bible and it is a very curious work. It purports to have been written by Daniel, a Judaean exile (probably a hostage) at the court of Babylon four hundred or so years before the book was actually written. Daniel and his friends in the book are held in high favour. They graduate from the King's school. But they follow a vegetarian diet (to avoid eating meat not slaughtered in accordance with Jewish law), and are secret but obstinate worshippers of Yahweh.

The first part of the book concerns an ongoing competition between Daniel and his companions and the priests of Babylon's state religion, a competition always won by the superior Yahwists. Daniel is first called on to interpret a dream had by the King, Nebuchadnezzar – which he does so successfully that the King is converted. The King, though, is an unreliable Yahwist and later sets up a golden image of himself, which he calls upon every one of his subjects to worship.

Daniel's companions refuse and are cast into a 'fiery furnace,' which they survive unharmed. Daniel himself regains favour as a dream-interpreter and is given a high position at court – he is also called on to interpret "the writing on the wall" that appears at the feast of a later king, Belshazzar.

His religion makes him vulnerable, though. He continues to pray to his God in defiance of a royal edict, and is thrown into "the lion's den", emerging from it, like his companions, unharmed.

DANIEL'S VISIONS

At this point in the narrative (after chapter 6), the whole tone of *The Book of Daniel* changes. A vision had by Daniel himself is now introduced: a vision echoing and underwriting the dream had earlier by Nebuchadnezzar. In it, Jahweh is

seen as casting judgment on five creatures –
four of them winged beasts and the fifth a
resplendent human being. The four monsters
represent the successive "evil empires" of Babylon, the Medes, the Persians and the Greeks,
while the fifth, human, figure is both 'one like a
son of man' (Jesus' later description of himself)
and the future everlasting kingdom of God on
earth centred in Judaea (7: 13-14):

*And behold, with the clouds of heaven there
came one like the son of man, and he came to
the Ancient of Days and was presented before
him. And to him was given dominion and
glory and kingdom, that all peoples, nations
and languages should serve him; his dominion is an everlasting dominion, which shall
not pass away, and his kingdom one that shall
not be destroyed.*

Daniel's vision of the winged beasts echoed Nebuchadnezzar's earlier dream

Other visions follow. After a prolonged sequence of dynastic struggles, an evil 'King of the North' appears who pollutes the temple and sets up 'the abomination of desolation'. Finally though, at 'the time of the end', there is a culminating battle in which the tyrant is destroyed. A prince called Michael emerges who, in the Book's words (12: 1-3), ushers in

a time of trouble such as never has been since there was a nation till that time: but at that time your people shall be delivered, every one whose name shall be found written in the book. And many of those who sleep in the dust of the earth shall awake, some to everlasting life and some to shame and everlasting contempt. And those who are wise shall shine like the brightness of the firmament: and those who turn many to righteousness, like the stars for ever and ever.

The 'King of the North' is clearly Antiochus Epiphanes, and 'the abomination of desolation' the statue of Zeus he set up in the Temple's Holy of Holies. (This passage, at least, was clearly written between the start of the Maccabee rebellion and its final, successful conclusion.) But what is most startling here (like the reference to 'the son of man', above) is the prospect of eternal life being held out to faithful Jews – like those *Hasidim* currently fighting in the name of Orthodoxy against the Menelaites.

Up until this point, the Old Testament has shown little interest in the idea of the afterlife. The dead are simply seen as gathering in a dark and dreary underworld called Sheol and maintaining a shadowy existence there, regardless of their goodness or badness in life. In the new order, on the other hand – to be ruled by Jews, and covering the whole world – the resurrected and the living both play an equal part. This idea goes far beyond the idea of the restored kingdom envisioned by the classical

prophets – and looks forward both to Christian doctrine and to the *Revelation* of St. John the Divine.

It is clear from the text of *The Book of Daniel* that it was at least partly designed to demonstrate the abiding superiority of Yahweh over the brutal, flawed and transient empires of the world, and to encourage the Maccabee rebels to face death with equanimity, in the knowledge that the dead would be gathered together with the living in the final achievement of His perfect rule. This – crucially – was seen as imminent.

In a passage much scoured over by Christian believers in the idea of 'the time of the end', Daniel recalls in chapter 9 a prophecy of Jeremiah about the Chosen People going through seventy years in Babylonian captivity. However, the angel Gabriel, appearing to him in a vision, reinterprets this (in the light of the long period since, in which the Jews have achieved no peace) as really meaning "seventy weeks of years": i.e. (70 multiplied by 7) = 490 (rather than 70). After sixty-nine of these seven-year periods, he says, an "anointed one' is to be "cut off", or killed; and in the week following, there will be war and chaos, with Jerusalem suffering at the hands of "the prince who is to come".

The "anointed one" is usually interpreted as being the High Priest Onias, murdered by one of King Antiochus's fellow-Hellenizers – thus setting up the rivalry between Jason and Menelaus and the Maccabean revolt. The problem is that it is impossible to fit the 490 years cited into the time period between Jeremiah and Antiochus. However, the author of *Daniel* provides an alternative. He announces that the 490 years should begin "from the going forth of the word to restore and build Jerusalem". This did not in fact happen in Jeremiah's time, but almost a century later, when King Artaxerxes gave a commission to Nehemiah to do exactly this in 445 BC.

A recalculation of the time-period suggested by the angel Gabriel, then, means that the "cutting off" of "the anointed one" now takes place (in the sixty-ninth week) between 31 and 38 AD, during most of which time a man called Pilate was procurator of Judaea…

THE BOOK OF ENOCH AND OTHER APOCALYPTIC LITERATURE

Another work, *The Book of Enoch*, was written, like *The Book of Daniel*, long after its central character had passed away. (Other apocalytic books were assigned to Ezra, Abraham and even Adam) Enoch had been the seventh patriarch of the Hebrews, but his prophecies were probably written during the period of Maccabee conflict before the Roman invasion.

By that time the Jewish state had been independent for almost a century, yet all hopes of the arrival of God's kingdom on earth had been disappointed. 'Enoch' believed that the reason must lie in a supernatural conflict that derived from Babylonian and Persian myth but had never appeared earlier in Jewish literature. It is thus in Enoch that we first hear of the War in Heaven, the rebellion of the archangel Lucifer and his attempt to take the throne of Yahweh, of the defeat of the rebel angels and their casting down from Heaven.

Elsewhere in the literature Satan, hitherto a minor demon, was assigned a major role in the troubling of God and his chosen people. A dragon-monster called Beliar was also invoked. Against these powers of evil, a panoply of protective angels came to be ranged – among them Michael, the special protector of Israel. Human agency, it was implied, was no longer enough.

The intervention of God himself was required. *The Testament of Naphtali* announced:

> *God shall appear on earth to save the race of Israel, and to gather the righteous from among the Gentiles.*

The arrival of God on earth, however, was generally regarded as a cataclysmic event, one that would involve the activity of a special divine champion. Some authors, following up Daniel's image of the 'son of man', made him a new Israelite king. *The Book of Enoch* described him as the Righteous Elect One, a celestial viceroy who would sit enthroned in judgment over all and bring enlightenment to the Gentiles. But it also went further: it connected Daniel's 'son of man' directly to the older idea of 'the anointed one', the Messiah.

All this increasingly fevered and desperate speculation, fuelled in large part by the failure of the Maccabee dynasty and the Roman occupation, looked forward to an imminent golden age in which the enemies of the chosen people would vanish into history, where the sun would shine brighter, deserts would bloom and living creatures would live in harmony with each other. Water would flow from Mount Zion and a rebuilt Jerusalem would become the world's capital. God would pronounce judgment upon all humanity and each would receive his just deserts. There would be, as 'Daniel' had predicted, a resurrection of the dead, perhaps of a select few, perhaps of the dead in general. If the latter, the good would dwell in an eastern paradise, Gan Eden; the wicked, in a western land called Gehinnom.

The stage had been set, in other words, for the teachings of Joshua, known in his name's Greek form as Jesus, of Nazareth – also popularly called 'Christos', or (again in Greek) the anointed one.

III
THE LAST PROPHETS

AMONG THE FOLLOWERS of Judas Maccabeus there seem to have been people who could foretell the future, and prophets continued to appear and to be looked for in the aftermath of the successful rebellion. Simon Maccabeus, who secured political independence for Judaea in c. 140 BC, was chosen, according to *I Maccabees* chapter 14, as "leader and high priest forever, until a trustworthy prophet should arise"; one of his successors, the Maccabean prince John Hyrcanus, was generally reckoned to have met the necessary criteria and was pronounced a prophet by the 1st century AD Jewish historian Josephus. Josephus also mentions in passing a number of Jewish revolutionaries also regarded as prophets, and a man called Menahem, who prophesied in the 1st century BC, as another.

Several prophets are also identified by name in the New Testament, among them Simeon, the prophetess Anna and Zechariah. Zechariah is described in Luke as having perished "between the altar and the sanctuary", and is singled out as having been the last prophet before Jesus to have been killed by the Jews.

It was Zechariah who, under the influence of the spirit, uttered the prophetic song, the so-called 'Benedictus' (or 'Blessed', after the first word in its Latin version); his wife Elizabeth is said to have been similarly inspired. He was, furthermore, the father of another prophet who played an important role in the story of the New Testament, John the Baptist.

THE TEACHINGS OF JESUS AND JOHN THE BAPTIST

Josephus, writing perhaps seventy years after the event, characterized John the Baptist as a political demagogue executed for sedition by Herod Antipas. (There is no mention of the roles of Herodias or Salome in his downfall.) But John, in the New Testament's version at least, is a far more interesting figure than this.

A hermit and itinerant preacher, he was in a sense the heir of the apocalyptic writers who had preceded him – preaching, as he did, the imminent judgment of God upon mankind and the absolute necessity for his hearers to turn their backs on the world, to repent, and to be washed free of their sins immediately, before the Kingdom of God arrived. Jesus himself seems to have recognized this. He described John, his cousin – and by extension the others who had preceded him, like Zechariah, John's father – as the culmination of Old Testament prophecy.

It is worth remarking, in this connection, on the ways in which Jesus' teachings differed from those of both John and of the apocalypticists who seemed desperately to long for God's intervention in, and cancellation of, human history. Jesus, first of all – after his baptism by John and his forty days spent in the wilderness considering his future and being tempted by Satan – took his mission largely to townspeople, rather than to the countryside, as John had.

John the Baptist urging sinners to repent

He also differed from John in suggesting that embracing the world as it was and living a just life were not incompatible. There were other ways, too, in which his teachings followed a new path. He stressed, for example, that the will of God was an everyday presence in the world, acting on every single human being, in a way no earlier prophet had and insisted that surrender to this will, in the heart of every individual, was the only road to salvation.

His message, it is true, did insist, like that of John, that the Kingdom of God was imminent. But Jesus' Kingdom was rather different from that probably envisaged by many of those who heard him. It did not involve the coming of a great warrior who would sweep aside the empires of the Gentiles which continued to oppress them, nor did it mean the sweeping up *en masse* of the Chosen People into a state of bliss and/or dominance over the whole earth.

Pre-eminent in his thinking, as in that of the prophet Amos, was man's realization of God's will through justice and through care for the poor and damaged. His new Kingdom, therefore, was to be a place in which the evils and injustices of the world had been finally vanquished: a heaven on earth made by men and women who had completely submitted themselves to God's purpose.

Jesus further embraced the idea (in contrast to John) of a bleak and terrible future for those who refused to submit themselves to the divine programme for the perfection of the physical world – and in this, too, he went much further than his prophetic predecessors. He announced that they would burn in hell for eternity. Thus he not only preached the continuation of existence after death, a revolutionary idea to most Jews, accustomed only to the idea of a kind of zombiedom in Sheol, but he also combined notions of the afterlife that belonged to two different cultures: the Persian and the Greek.

THE GRECIAN AND PERSIAN INFLUENCES

The Greeks had long taken the view that the dead passed over into a realm called Tartarus, which was ruled over by Hades. Though most lived there in the sort of suspended animation characteristic of Sheol, some, who had offended the gods, were tortured (in full consciousness) in perpetuity by the presiding deity. The rest were granted the small consolation of being allowed to drink the water of the stream Lethe – or 'Forgetfulness' – which blotted out all memory of their previous lives on earth. The Zoroastrians, for their part, reserved a similar fate for those who had lived in wickedness and sin: they were consigned to a stinking pit and condemned to remain there until they had been purified by fire.

It was from these two sources that Jesus appears to have drawn the picture of the (Christian) Hell that awaited those who set their face against God's will: i.e. the malodorous pit full of flames and torments presided over by the Devil (or Satan). It is not surprising that it was conflated in contemporary minds with the valley of Gehenna, south of Jerusalem, which had become the city's festering rubbish-dump. Earlier, Gehenna had been the site of the immolation of children by Baal-worshippers – a practice that the Jews had followed for a time, it seems, in their 'burnt offerings.' It had an association already, then, with death and flames.

Given these borrowings from the cosmologies of other religions – capped, if you like, by the positively Greek assumption that a god could (and did in Jesus' case) beget a child in human form – in what sense can it be said that Jesus was a prophet, part of the long line of Old Testament prophets who had done their best to steer the Chosen People towards God's Kingdom?

The answer is that he undoubtedly met all the relevant and necessary Biblical qualifications. He performed miracles like Moses, spoke out for social justice like Elijah and Amos, used visionary language and parables like Daniel, and correctly predicted the destruction of Jerusalem (after an insurrection by revolutionary Zealots, in 70 AD), just as Jeremiah had before him. He also addressed God directly and claimed to speak with his direct authority: a claim also made by the so-called 'classical' prophets.

Any presumption, though, that Jesus was a prophet in any conventional sense is, of course, undermined by the additional claim that he was not only the Messiah foretold by earlier prophets, but also the son of God. And it may be instructive here to draw a comparison between Jesus and a later prophet, the founding father of another religion: the prophet Muhammad.

In the Old Testament, the Semitic peoples of the Arabian peninsular are described as having stemmed from Ishmael, the child by Abraham of his seemingly barren wife's servant, Hagar. During her pregnancy, Hagar had been driven out into the desert by wife Sarah's mistreatment of her. However, an angel had appeared to her to announce that her forthcoming son would be "a wild ass" of a man, hard to tame, independent – and would provide her with descendants too numerous to count. She returned to Abraham's household.

Fourteen years later she was once more expelled, when Sarah herself became pregnant. She left Ishmael under a bush to die, but God called out to her, reminding her of his promise that he would make Ishmael into a great nation. From that point on, says *The Book of Genesis*, God watched over Ishmael, and saw that his promise was kept.

At this point in the Bible, the nation of Ishmael, the Arabs, locked in a million square miles of unforgiving territory between North Africa and Iran, simply disappear from the story of the Israelites. By the 6th century AD, when they re-emerge again into ours, the Arabs

Banished to the desert, Hagar received assurance from an angel

were a group of scattered tribes, clan-based, polytheistic and tolerant of those in their midst who had converted to Zoroastrianism, Judaism and Christianity. Like the Israelites, they also had a tradition of prophecy.

According to G.W.A. in *The Encyclopaedia Britannica*, there were two types of prophets called oarraf and kahin ("seer," cognate to Hebrew kohen, "priest"). The kahin was an ecstatic, considered to be possessed by a jinni ("spirit"), through whose power miracles could be performed and predictions made. Seers and diviners of this sort were of very high standing. The answers they gave to those who consulted them were regarded as having divine authority. Kahins often became sheikhs, i.e. temporal leaders, and there were instances in which the position of kahin was hereditary.

MUHAMMAD

It was against this background that Muhammad, the founder of Islam ('Surrender'), appeared. He was born in about 570 AD in Mecca, the most important of Arabia's inland trading-towns, which was watered by a famous well called Zemzem and marked by a temple, the Ka'bah, which contained a black stone said to have been owned by the first human, Adam. (The Koran later asserted that the Ka'bah had been built during the time spent by Abraham in Arabia with his son Ishmael.)

A member of the Hamish clan, he was orphaned at an early age, and travelled widely as a young man with his uncle's merchant caravans, before creating a trading business of his own and settling down in marriage. He had a reputation among his tribesmen, the Quraysh, as an ecstatic, a *jinni*-inspired *kahin*. However, there was nothing in particular to mark him out from other such prophetic figures.

Then, though, at the age of 40, he began a series of retreats into the mountains, where, feeling an increasing spiritual unease, he began to think deeply about religious questions and the state of the society in which he found himself. The fundamental problem he faced was that, though the Jews and Christians had sacred scriptures of their own (in Hebrew and Greek respectively), the Arabs had no written knowledge of the divine against which could be measured his gatheringly strong sense that the Day of Judgment was at hand.

Finally, though, he received a call from God in the shape of a terrifying figure, whom he later identified as the Archangel Gabriel, seen in a vision as announcing to him:

> *Recite: In the name of Allah, the Merciful and Compassionate. Recite: And your Lord is most generous. He teaches by the pen, teaches man what he knew not*

The Archangel also made clear that from that time on Muhammad was to be something more than just a prophet: he was to be the messenger (*rasul*) of the god Allah, the final messenger in a long line that had begun with Adam and had continued through Noah, Abraham, Isaac, Jacob, Moses, David and Jesus.

A subsequent series of auditions (as against visions) arrived, usually consisting of the Archangel reading the divine message from a book to the ecstatic Muhammad, who repeated them, as he listened, to his faithful wife. These successive revelations made it quite clear to Muhammad that Allah was the one and only true God: He who had created the universe and had inspired both the Israelite prophets and Jesus.

None of these, however, had revealed Allah's message in full, since they were spokesmen only to one nation. Muhammad, by contrast, was to be spokesman to all the nations of the earth and even to the spirit-world – and this time, the message would be complete, sometimes correcting, sometimes confirming the preachings of the earlier prophets. He was to represent "the seal of the prophets", the end of all prophecy.

TEACHER AND DIPLOMAT

Muhammad's first mission was to preach the imminence of Allah's Final Judgment (a concept no doubt borrowed from Judaeo-Christianity). Eternal damnation could only be avoided, he taught, by protecting the poor and joining in the community (*ummah*) of Moslems ('those who had surrendered to God'), transcending all clan and tribal ties. This soon set him at odds with the traders and merchants of the Quraysh and even with the members of his own clan, who saw no reason not to continue their manipulation of the markets and their stranglehold over Mecca's poor. In 622 AD he fled to Medina, where many of his followers had settled – ostensibly as an arbiter in a dispute between its polytheistic and Jewish clans.

Muhammad was a remarkable diplomat and negotiator, a thoroughly practical and pragmatic man. Interestingly, after his arrival in Medina, ecstatic revelations played a lesser part in his prophecies – and poetry gave way to prose – as he became more concerned with political and social issues. He placated the Jews by proclaiming that they, like Moslems and Christians, were all fellow believers in the Old Testament and equally, therefore, "people of the Book."

Furthermore, since his wife and two sons had recently died, he was free to appease the polytheists by marrying into their families – and incorporating their practice of polygamy into Islam. He also took charge of the spoils from the town's main industry, caravan-raiding, and not only divided them fairly, but also organized a tithe of five per cent to be given to the Moslem poor.

By these and other means he gained large numbers of converts to his version of monotheism, and he was soon in a position to exile the most powerful Jewish clan in Medina and to demand that Christians and Jews should from then on pay the *ummah* a protection fee as the price for continued residence in its midst. He also announced that his followers, when praying to Allah, should no longer face Jerusalem, as they had at the beginning (together with Jews and Christians), but towards Mecca and the Ka'bah; pantheism, as still celebrated in the Ka'bah, remained his (and Allah's) most important enemy. With it still in place, there could be no Arab unity. Clan squabbles and tribal in-

fighting would continue in the absence of a shared faith.

This is not the place to give a detailed and prolonged account of Muhammad's remarkable 20-year career as the unifier of the tribes of the Arabian peninsular under Allah. Suffice it to say that he finally broke the back of an anti-Islamic confederacy raised against him by the Meccans and won the right for his followers to make pilgrimage to the Ka'bah. He insisted that Moslems should deal only with other Moslems (or, at the worst, with other "people of the Book"), and forbade his co-religionists from raiding or making war on other Moslems.

This in turn encouraged more and more tribes in an ever-widening circle around Medina to convert, and ultimately led to the surrender of Mecca, where the idols of the polytheists were removed from the Ka'bah and only the Black Stone was left. Finally, Muhammad defeated the last remnants of the pagan tribes in the area, and then led an army of 30,000 northward in what seems to have been an attack on the southern outposts of the Byzantine Empire.

Old age was, finally, the only thing which defeated him. In the end he turned back at the border with Syria, and returned to lead the by-now annual *haj*, or pilgrimage, to Mecca. A few months later, he died in Medina at the age of 62. His successors, the caliphs, or 'deputies', were to spread the word and power of Allah from India to Spain, and from central Africa to the Balkans.

SIMILARITIES AND DIFFERENCES WITH JESUS

Now the first thing to be said about the career of Muhammad is that, like Jesus, he clearly believed himself to be in direct communication with God. He was – also like Jesus – God's messenger, whose duty was to prepare the world for the day of Final Judgment, before which it was

necessary for every single individual to surrender in his heart to God's will, if he wished to be saved. He furthermore preached, exactly like Jesus, that the first concern of a merciful God was to see that the poor were cared for and that social justice was promulgated.

Where he differed from Jesus, of course, was that he made no claim to having a closer relationship with God than that of simple messenger, and, as a practical man, he laid down exactly how the life of the poor could be ameliorated and social justice observed – he placed a religious tax on every Moslem's goods and income. He performed no miracles. But he did do something that Jesus seems to have made little effort to achieve: he insisted that God's word – transmitted directly to him and therefore inarguable – should permeate every corner of secular Islamic life. As Damon Wilson points out in his *The Mammoth Book of Prophecies*, "Muhammad's teachings intertwined religion and state in a way not seen since the dissolution of Judea".

He left behind him no priestly class and no religious hierarchy. (Imams, as Wilson points out, are not like Catholic priests: they have no special relationship with Allah.) There were, in other words, to be no admonitory guardians of souls. It was enough for each individual to acknowledge in his life the presence of Allah, with his (or her) neighbours as witness.

What Mohammed left behind him, in fact, was a blueprint for a fully functional religious state, ordained by Allah. There was room in special circumstances for interpretation of the Koran. *Ijma* ('consensus') of the contemporary Islamic community was allowed to play a role. But where Allah had been specific, there could be no bucking of the law – and *ijma*, all too often, lay in the hands of the authorities, both secular or religious, following their own agenda.

As for the future of Islam, there was a thun-

Mecca, the most holy place of the Muslims

derous verse in The Koran, the received word of God (61:9), that announced in no uncertain terms that:

> He [Allah] *it is who has sent his Messenger* [Muhammad] *with guidance and the Faith of Truth, that He may make it* [Islam] *conqueror of all other religions, much as the idolaters may dislike it.*

JESUS

The character of Jesus in The New Testament, by contrast – told in the stories of the four gospel-writers and interpreted and embellished by the books that follow – is of an entirely different order. It is possible, of course, that he too might have laid down the template for a theocratic state, had he lived longer. The indications are that he would not have.

He speaks in the gospels – mostly a collection of episodes and anecdotes, with few historically identifiable landmarks – of his Church's enlargement via no more than conversion. This was to take place among Gentiles and women and those such as tax-collectors – with whom he seems deliberately to have consorted, in the manner of Gandhi with India's 'untouchables' – as well as among Jewish males.

Christ also seems positively to have courted his own death. Already known, it seems, as a descendant of King David, he told his disciples, for example, to find him an ass and a colt for him to ride into Jerusalem on his final journey, thus consciously fulfilling a prophecy of Zechariah about the 'just' king who would come (riding in this way) and 'bring salvation'. He next 'cast out the moneychangers' from the Temple forecourt, an act that was again seemingly devised to show that a warrior Messiah had arrived. Then, when asked by the High Priest, after his subsequent arrest, whether he was in fact Christ, Son of the Blessed, he did

not dissemble answering tersely: "I am".

His case was then passed on to the Roman authorities, which had little option but to execute him by crucifixion, even though procurator Pilate publicly expressed his disgust at the way he had been forced into a corner by symbolically washing his hands.

The death of Jesus set nothing in stone. It finalized nothing, as Muhammad's had done. Instead it can be said to have been the beginning of the spread of a Church still bemusedly obsessed with what had happened after Christ's death and gradually coming to terms – under the direction of Paul of Tarsus, one of the most gifted publicists who ever lived – with what exactly had transpired.

SPREADING OF THE WORD

It was Paul's contention that Jesus, the Son of God, had died upon the cross to redeem mankind from the consequences of original sin, the eating of the Fruit of Knowledge by Adam and Eve which had condemned mankind to inevitable suffering and death. In the act of resurrection he had held out an alternative to all men if they seized upon it: eternal life in a democratically accessible Heaven – which was, accommodatingly for Gentiles, not much different from the Elysian Fields that had hitherto been reserved for Graeco-Roman heroes.

The Word was soon spread, first among the Jews, then among the colonized peoples of Asia Minor and Greece, and finally among slaves and the oppressed across the whole of the Roman empire. This was considerably helped, no doubt, by the fact that it early lost its focus in the Holy Land. Alternative sects like the Messianists – those still waiting for the Messiah – said to have been led by Jesus's brother James, were soon expunged. Then, in 70 AD, after an

Jesus expelling moneychangers from the temple. His actions played into the hands of his enemies

uprising against the Romans by revolutionary Zealots, Jerusalem itself was razed and the Temple looted and destroyed. Christianity joined the Jewish diaspora.

The Church of Christ, then, resting on the assumption that Jesus had been the Son of God and would come again, ceased abruptly to be the expression in any sense of a nation's aspirations, as Islam was to be. It became a universal work in progress, which continued many of the traditions established in the Near East, but altered and adapted them. Among these was the tradition of prophecy.

PROPHECY AND THE NEW TESTAMENT

Several people in the early Church are mentioned in the New Testament as being blessed with prophetic gifts; indeed the term 'prophet' seems to have been used of a particular office in the Church different from (and higher than) that of 'teacher' and 'evangelist'. His or her role appears to have been the revelation to the congregation of esoteric knowledge: of divine mysteries and of God's plan of salvation.

Paul gave instructions as to the correct use of prophecy, which he regarded as the greatest spiritual gift from God. However, he made a distinction between prophecy proper and 'speaking in tongues' via ecstatic trances, which he described as being of doubtful worth. He also warned against the problem of false prophecy, which would cause chaos and lead congregations astray. Clearly all prophetic activity had to be carefully watched.

For a while, so-called prophets continued to play an important role in the Church: they were sometimes referred to as 'high priests' and were the only people allowed to speak freely during the liturgy, because of their inspiration by the Holy Spirit. Gradually, as the liturgy became more and more fixed, though, their role diminished and ultimately disappeared. Not, however, before one last great work of prophecy had been added to the canon: *The Revelation of St. John the Divine*.

THE BOOK OF THE APOCALYPSE

Revelation was almost certainly written towards the end of the 1st century AD, during a time of major persecution of the Church by the Roman emperor Domitian who had demanded universal worship as the 'Master and God' inscribed on his coinage. Christians, convinced that the arrival of God's Kingdom was imminent, refused, and thousands were martyred as a result.

Its author introduces himself as John, currently living in banishment or refuge on the Aegean island of Patmos; early tradition identifies him as the apostle John, the writer of the Fourth Gospel. 'John' addresses his book to his fellow-Christians in Asia Minor, organized into seven bishoprics – seven is a number that recurs throughout the text – and suggests that they read it aloud together.

At the beginning of *Revelation*, Christ appears to John and tells him to write what he is about to see, "what is and what is to take place hereafter." Then, after the message to John's co-religionists, the visions begin. Christ opens a door to Heaven, to reveal God enthroned and holding in his hand a scroll covered with writing and sealed with seven seals, which only Christ is worthy to open.

CHRIST OPENS THE SEALS

Described as "the Lamb that was slain", he opens the first four, and four men on horseback appear, the first an armed conqueror, the other three representing war, famine and death (though only death is actually identified by

John). These 'Four Horsemen of the Apocalypse', as they were later called, are followed by another personage, Hell; "and power was given unto them over a fourth part of the earth".

The Lamb then opens the fifth seal, and John sees the souls of all those who have already died as martyrs, clamouring to know how long they must wait for the end of persecution and God's ultimate vengeance. They are told that they must be patient "for a little season" until yet more have have suffered: "a great number," says John later, "which no man [can] number, from every nation, all tribes and peoples and tongues".

At this point John is moving into a future world in which the Church has become international, and with the opening of the sixth seal he arrives among future portents. This seal unleashes the first signs of God's anger. There is an earthquake and an eclipse of the sun. The Moon becomes as red as blood and the stars fall from heaven. There follows a mighty wind, after which the sky rolls up like a scroll and the mountains and islands of the earth are shifted.

With the opening of the seventh seal, there is a "silence in Heaven about the space of half an hour". Then seven angels carrying seven trumpets appear. The first six sound their trumpets

The opening of the seventh seal inflicted new catastrophes upon the earth

in turn, and with each fanfare a new catastrophe is inflicted on the earth: fire, darkness, water pollution and a plague of giant locusts followed by an invasion of diabolical cavalry.

At some point in this sequence, two fierce 'witnesses' (presumably representing the Church) appear and try to convert the defiant survivors of these disasters to God's path. They are killed by "the beast that ascendeth out of the bottomless pit", and their corpses are left to rot in the streets of a town "called Sodom and Egypt, where also our Lord was killed". Eventually, though, they are resurrected and 7,000 people are killed in the town by an earthquake in revenge. At last the survivors begin to repent and give glory to God, at which the seventh trumpet sounds. Christ returns to rule over the earth and heavenly voices cry: "The kingdom of the world has become the kingdom of our Lord and Christ, and he shall reign for ever and ever".

With the sounding of the final trumpet, the story – if that is what it is – seems complete. But an angel has already told John that he must prophesy again – and so he does in chapter 12, going back this time to the beginning of Christianity and taking a new route to the ending of the world in Christ's triumph.

THE ENDING OF THE WORLD

'John' describes "a great portent" in the sky: "a woman", about to give birth. "clothed with the sun, with the moon under her feet, and on her head a crown of twelve stars". She clearly represents both the twelve tribes of Israel and the Virgin Mary; the child she bears is, equally clearly, Jesus. A huge red Dragon, with seven heads and ten horns, then appears and attempts to devour the child, who is swept up to heaven. The woman, now given eagle's wings, also escapes the Dragon, who is identified by 'John', first as "that old serpent, called the Devil, and Satan" – and later as the rebel angel Lucifer

referred to in *The Book of Enoch*. The Dragon assaults Heaven, is thrown down and, in 'John's' words, "his angels were cast out with him".

This three-in-one supreme enemy of mankind – Snake, Devil and Lucifer – then gives way to a great "beast" which rises up from the ocean with the same seven heads and ten horns as the Dragon: it is obviously the Dragon's earthly spawn. It is described as chiefly resembling a leopard, but having the feet of a bear and a mouth like a lion's; these features, along with the horns (of a goat?), immediately bring to mind the four winged beasts in the vision of the prophet Daniel, and suggests that it therefore represents a superpower, containing all the worst aspects of the four successive empires Daniel conjured up: those of Persia, Media, Babylon and Alexander the Great.

In a later chapter, 'John', allowed a closer look, sees a woman riding on the beast, identified (by a sign on her forehead as "Babylon the Great, the Mother of Harlots and the Abominations of the Earth" – and this clearly identifies the beast as Rome. For 'Babylon' was a code word among early Christians for the city of Rome; the beast's seven heads are later described by 'John" as "the seven mountains" – i.e. the seven hills of Rome – "on which the woman sitteth".

The seven mountains, however, as 'John' explains, also stand for the seven ackowledged emperors of Rome prior to the accession of his own contemporary, Domitian: i.e. Augustus, Tiberius, Caligula, Claudius, Nero, Vespasian and Titus. He adds that one of the beast's heads "seemed to have a mortal wound, but its mortal wound was healed, and the whole earth followed the beast with wonder… saying 'Who is like the beast, and who can fight against it?' "

This wounded head seems to be a symbolic reference to the aftermath of Nero's death in 68 AD, when imperial pretenders fought for the throne, and the Roman empire was in danger of falling apart. Vespasian finally took control –

and the crisis passed. Furthermore, Nero's legacy – of vicious persecution of the Christian Church – was also passed on, "healed", to his successors, particularly to Titus' son Domitian. 'John' describes the beast itself as being "an eighth" in the line: i.e. personalized anew in Domitian.

In the same chapter (13), he speaks of the way in which the beast's subjects worship it, a reference to the official cult of empire and emperor – a cult of which many Christians, under Domitian, fell foul. But he also appears to look further ahead. He introduces a second beast – also called the False Prophet – who organizes the worship of the first and makes it compulsory and universal, under pain of death.

This is unlikely to refer to the persecution of 'John's' own time, since the persecution of Christians was by no means universal – the churches in Asia whom 'John' was addressing were apparently thriving. So it is at least possible that he is referring to some totalitarian future under Roman rule, perhaps the same future in which, as described earlier, an unnumbered multitude would die "from every nation, all tribes and peoples and tongues". He then gives a clue to the beast's identity, in what is perhaps the most famous verse in the Bible:

> *Here is wisdom. Let him who has understanding reckon the number of the beast, for it is the number of a man; and its number is six hundred and sixty-six.*

THE NATURE OF THE BEAST

It is universally accepted that this strange verse invokes a simple sort of code called a *gematria*. In ancient languages, Greek and Hebrew for example, letters of the alphabet had to do duty as numbers – our Arabic numerals had not yet come into use. Every letter, therefore, had, and was, a number. So the letters of a person's name could be added together to give a total representing it. The name of Jesus, for example, transliterated into Greek as 'Iesous' with a long 'e', gives the numbers 10, 8, 200, 70, 400 and 200, or the total 888. This can be said to be 'his' number. Any internally coherent numerical system (i.e. A=1, B=2 etc.) can be applied to any language on earth to get a result.

As of course it has been. Muhammad has been more or less satisfactorily fitted to the number 666. So has 'L'Empéreur Napoleon', as has Hitler (based in his case on A=100, B=101 etc.). However, this sort of fantastical theorizing ignores the fact that the beast had to be recognizable to John's audience and its name had to be in a language with which it was familiar (rather than one with an alphabet as yet not invented). Another clear candidate for the beast was the name 'Nero Caesar' which, when transliterated from the Greek *Neron Kaisar* into Hebrew, did indeed give the right value. Yet another, noticed by the earliest commentator on *Revelation*, the second-century Bishop of Lyon, Irenaeus, is 'Lateinos', the Greek word for "the Latin" or 'the Roman', one of those, Irenaeus says helpfully, "who now reign".

Irenaeus, who claimed that his mentor Polycarp, Bishop of Smyrna, had known John personally, also, however, noted a third possibility, 'Teitan', a Greek word for the sun and, more specifically, for the sun-god Apollo. Though this may once more refer to Nero – who was praised during his lifetime as a 'New Sun' and as a reincarnation of Apollo – Irenaeus was disposed to believe that the identification of Teitan carried a warning about the future – and if this is so, then it was a remarkable one indeed. For it wasn't until a hundred or so years later that the Sun began to play an important new role in Roman imperial politics; and it wasn't till more than another century had passed that it led to a new wholesale slaughter of Christians.

WORSHIP OF THE SUN GOD

In 193 AD, Septimius Severus became emperor of Rome and brought with him to Rome a new cult, that of Sol Invictus, 'The Unconquered Sun', which had been part of his wife Julia Domna's religious upbringing. Her father had been a hereditary priest of the sun god of Emesa (now Homs in Syria) on the river Orontes. Septimius had made him his patron deity, likening his own light-bringing rule to the rays of the sun, just as Akhenaton had in Egypt. Septimius' sons then kept the cult alive, and when Heliogabalus, Julia Domna's great-nephew and himself a priest of the sun at Homs, ultimately became Caesar, he took some tentative steps towards making worship of Sol Invictus the official religion of the empire.

The debauched Heliogabalus didn't last long enough to get very far with his quest. However, in about 270 AD, a remarkable man called Aurelian did. Aurelian, who came to the throne in about 270 AD, inherited an empire that was falling apart at the seams, constantly eroded by barbarians and ambitious local princes. In short order, though, he regained Britain, Gaul, Spain, Egypt, Syria and Mesopotamia and restored the realm to its former glory. The success of his Syrian campaign, at least, he ascribed to the sun god of Homs and once back in the city of Rome, he announced that Sol Invictus was now 'Lord of the Roman Empire'.

Aurelian built a temple in his honour and appointed a special college of priests to supervise his worship. The Sun was transformed in the process from a Syrian godlet into the official bolsterer of imperial unity, combining elements of the ancient Greek god Apollo and of the Persian god Mithras, who was immensely popular among the empire's soldiers. He became the focus of a new paganism acceptable to all the

Worship of the sun-god became part of everyday life for Diocletian's subjects

empire's far-flung subjects and the guarantor of loyalty to successive emperors, his representatives on earth.

It should perhaps have been clear from the beginning that the new Lord and Master of Rome would not be able to tolerate for long the existence of a rival Supreme Being. So, when Diocletian reorganized the empire at the end of the third century into four autocratic and heavily-taxed fiefdoms, he soon decided that the Christians who inhabited them were too powerful, too intractable and too independent-minded to be allowed to survive.

In 303 he authorized a concerted attack on their assemblies. Congregations were broken up, buildings razed and sacred books confiscated. The following year he went further: he announced that anyone who refused to sprinkle incense on the altar of the emperor – himself a god, as the Sun's representative on earth – should be put to death. Many thousands of Christians, across the whole empire, were subsequently executed.

If 'John' did foresee the rise of 'Teitan', a Syrian sun-god, to pre-eminence in official late-Roman religion, shortly before the final victory of Christianity, it was a remarkable prophecy. But did he see any further? There are some indications that he may have. For the beast, it will be remembered, is depicted as having ten horns; and an angel in chapter 17 of *Revelation* explains what they represent:

> *The ten horns that you saw are ten kings who have not yet received royal power, but they are to receive authority as kings for one hour together with the beast… They and the beast will hate the harlot* [i.e. Rome]: *they will make her desolate and naked, and devour her flesh and burn her up with fire.*

This seems to state that kings given authority by, and within, the Roman empire (the beast) will in the end turn on Rome (the harlot) and

destroy it – and this is more or less exactly what happened. In the late fourth and early fifth centuries AD, various tribes of (so-called) barbarians were given the right to carve out their own independent territories at the borders of the empire, and became increasingly hungry for land and power.

Under leaders like Attila, Alaric and Gaiseric, the Huns, the Visigoths and the Vandals (originally from Germany and eastern Europe) pushed their way across the Alps into France, north Africa and the Western Mediterranean. Attila invaded Italy; Alaric sacked Rome with his Visigoths in 410 AD; and the Vandal Gaiseric led an expedition from north Africa in 455 which virtually destroyed the city – and with it the Roman empire. In the same chapter, 'John' says of these kings – and it is eminently possible to round up their number to ten – that they were ultimately conquered by Christ, as indeed they were. The Vandals were finally defeated by Christian Byzantium, for example, and the Visigoths in southern France and Spain were ultimately converted to Christianity and disappeared among the local populations.

THE END OF TIME

In chapter 19, after visions of plagues and damnation and the destruction of the harlot city of Rome, 'John' envisages a feast held to celebrate the final marriage of Christ to the bride of his faithful followers (the fine linen of her wedding dress made from "the good deeds of God's people"). This is the moment at which, based upon a passage in St. Paul's *Letter to the Thessalonians*, fundamentalist Christians believe that they will be carried up to heaven in what has become known as the Rapture, leaving everyone else to face what are called 'the last days' without them. 'John', however, fails to mention this; and indeed he later makes it plain that no souls are actually allowed into

According to John, the barbarian hoards that ravaged Rome would ultimately be conquered by Christianity

heaven until later in his sequence.

At this point – where we would expect to see the bridegroom – we are given a vision of a figure on horseback, with eyes like flames of fire and wearing a robe dipped in blood. Behind him are the armies of heaven, "arrayed in fine linen, white and pure", ready finally to take on the beast and all his followers.

This, then, is the great war at the end of time that has come to be known as the Battle of Armageddon ('the hill at Megiddo'). The beast and 'the false prophet' are both captured and cast alive into a lake of fire and brimstone. Satan's earthy followers are put to the sword, their bodies left to be eaten by birds; Satan himself is finally taken by an angel and thrown in chains into a bottomless pit.

For a thousand years thereafter, says 'John', Christ and his saints reign in peace. But then Satan escapes for a final battle with God. He gathers a great army from "the four quarters of the earth" and attacks "the beloved city", but is finally beaten back when God sends down fire from heaven. This time, Satan is thrown into the burning lake, alongside the beast and 'the

false prophet', to be tormented there "day and night for ever and ever".

God himself appears; the physical world comes to an end; the souls of the dead appear from their graves or from Hell to be judged "according to what they had done". "Whosoever was not found written in the book of life was cast into the lake of fire", along with Hell and Death, now both outmoded. A new heaven and a new earth then replace the old order, and a new Jerusalem comes down from heaven, "prepared as a bride adorned for her husband". 'John' writes:

> I saw a new heaven and a new earth… And I saw the Holy City… coming down out of Heaven from God… Now God has his dwelling with mankind… He will wipe every tear from their eyes. There shall be an end to death, and to mourning and crying and pain.

There are many such passages of considerable beauty in *Revelation*, as well as scenes of almost surreal terror and horror. However, none have created such difficulty – or spawned so many

both elaborate and spurious theories – as 'John's' conception of the beast and his description of Christ's and his saints' reign as lasting for a thousand years.

'John's' given length of a thousand years is unprecedented in the Bible, and in the Christian era it eventually chimed with the counting of years from Christ's birth (the suggestion of a Scythian monk called Dionsius Exiguus in 525 AD). This gave rise to much prophetic anxiety and speculation surrounding the passing of the first and second millennium AD, by which time in any case millenarianism was in full swing. Damian Thompson in his *The End of Time* described its origins:

> Some Jewish radicals of the first century AD believed in a Great Week which would be brought to an end by the arrival of the Messiah 5,000 or 6,000 years after the Creation. The early Christians slotted the Millennium of Revelation neatly into a seven-day Great Week. The Epistle of Barnabas, written around AD 120, puts it succinctly. 'Listen carefully, my children, to these words: "God finished his work in six days…" That means that in 6000 years God will bring all things to completion, because for him "a day of the Lord is as 1000 years…" Therefore, my children, in six days, that is in 6000 years, the universe will be brought to its end [and the thousand years of Christ's reign with his martyrs will begin]. "And on the seventh day he rested…"' Here, in a nutshell, is the idea that over the centuries was to launch a thousand different theories about the date of the Second Coming.

There was also an early Christian tradition among the Gnostics that the world had been created 5,000 years before the birth of Christ.

So the world was set to end in 500 AD and at various (recalculated) times thereafter. The timing of the Second Coming has been looked for ever since, even though in *Revelation* 'John' said nothing that connects his thousand years to anything of the sort.

As for the beast, the Church later came to identify it as the Antichrist. Damon Wilson, for example, writes of the Antichrist:

> This is a figure who emerged in the later books of the New Testament (2 Thessalonians and 1 John) and, although never mentioned by Jesus himself, was quickly taken up as Christian doctrine. The Antichrist, as the name suggests, is – or rather will be – the direct enemy of Christ: Satan's attempt to create an avatar on earth and beat God at his own game, so to speak… The Antichrist is described as "the lawless one" in 2 Thessalonians, and is prophesied to be a worker of false miracles and a spreader of false doctrine.

Other writers invented a fuller Antichrist scenario. They predicted that human history would come to a climax with a powerful ruler, a 'Last Emperor', who would bring universal peace and the final triumph of the Church. However, after his death, the Antichrist would appear and unleash upon Christians the worst persecutions ever, prior to the second coming of Christ.

Since then, the coming of the 'Last Emperor' – and therefore of the Antichrist – has become part of a huge body of eschatological speculation that is still being added to today. For a while, Mikhail Gorbachev in Russia was regarded as a prime candidate for 'Last Emperor' and the Antichrist has been identified with everyone from the Emperor Napoleon to each successive incumbent of the Papacy.

Satan's arguments with God led to the Battle of Armageddon

IV
PROPHECY AND THE FUTURE

WITH THE ESTABLISHMENT of a more or less fixed liturgy the role of prophecy in the Christian Church took very much a back seat. For all the continued speculation about the timing of the Second Coming, a network of bishops began to enforce orthodoxy of belief, and warnings about false prophets abounded.

These found a particular focus in the second century AD in the rise of a cult called Montanism, led by Montanus, a self-styled prophet, and his priestess Maximilla, who preached that the new Jerusalem was about to descend, literally, onto an obscure region of Phrygia. Montanism briefly threatened to supplant orthodoxy. It certainly promised a future of doctrinal anarchy, dominated by End-time speculation. It wasn't long before all charismatic prophecy in the Church was suppressed (after Montanus' new Jerusalem failed to arrive) and ecstatic inspiration was pronounced demonic.

The appearance in the third century AD of another 'last messenger' of God, Mani – the founder of a dualistic religious movement called Manichaeanism which spread widely in the east – merely underwrote the decision. All so-called prophets were in future to be outlawed. Some, however, did survive – not in the hierarchy of the Church, but in holy orders. Mystically-oriented holy men would sometimes appear as prophets with a special message, and even ecstatics found their places within the monasteries and convents.

HILDEGARD OF BINGEN

One of these was Hildegard of Bingen, an extraordinary 12th-century abbess who wrote the earliest surviving scientific work by a woman (a treatise on natural history, physiology and medicine), was a voluminous composer and corresponded widely with popes, emperors and

Hildegard of Bingen, musician, poet and mystic

kings. She also recorded a series of visions – perhaps brought on by migraine – in a book called *Scivias*, mostly concerning disasters that would ultimately befall the church because of its corruption.

ST JOACHIM OF FIORE

Another was St. Joachim of Fiore, a 12th-century Italian abbot who, like Hildegard, made prophecies about what would happen to the world (and the Church) before the Second Coming. Well known during his own time (wrongly) as a successful predictor of future events – he was once consulted by King Richard Coeur de Lion – Joachim's legacy lay rather in a grand scheme of history derived from the Bible.

He took the doctrine of the Trinity and applied it to the movement of time, with the past (the age of God the Father) and the present (the age of God the Son) inexorably leading to the future (the age of God the Holy Spirit) in a manner which could be predicted. The third age, he believed – an age in which the Church and society would be transformed after a time of tribulation – would be expressive of John, the "beloved disciple" to whom the fourth Gospel and *Revelation* were attributed.

New religious orders would be founded, unmarred by power and wealth. Communities would replace hierarchies. Universal love and enlightenment would reign. All this was backed up by meticulous cross-referencing to events in the Bible and by an elaborate numerical symbolism; and though it may seem quaint to us now, Joachim's theory of the passage of history has been called 'the most influential known to Europe until the appearance of Marxism'.

ST MALACHI

An example of a prophet of a rather different kind can be found in the case of St. Malachi,

who became abbot of Bangor in Ireland in 1123. Malachi was a friend of the hugely influential churchman, St. Bernard of Clairvaux, who described him as having the gift of second sight, the ability to foretell the future – though he failed to give any very convincing examples of this.

Some years later, however, *The Prophecies of St. Malachi* appeared, purporting to be a previsionary list made by St. Malachi of the Popes (in the form of brief Latin mottos) who would appear after his time (up until about the year 2000). Lists of this kind in the Middle Ages were not uncommon – all of them looking forward to a time when a so-called 'Angelic' Pope would cleanse the Church and bring about universal peace (ushering in St. Joachim's age of the Holy Spirit). But Malachi's list, which was quoted for the first time in 1595, was probably a contemporary confection, designed to influence a Papal election, with the mottos for known past Popes included to give it authenticity. The only extraordinary thing about it is the accuracy in which the characters of future Popes (i.e. after the 1590s) are nevertheless sketched out.

These three examples of what might be called medieval Church prophets – one an ecstatic because of a physical/mental impairment, one a proto-scientist using the Bible as his source of inspiration, and the third the pseudo-author of prophecies written in fact much later – are closely mirrored in the lay community. One could, for instance, invoke as a lay equivalent of Hildegard (though she was eventually to become a nun) Elizabeth Barton, "the Holy Maid of Kent", who was famous in England during the time of Henry VIII.

ELIZABETH BARTON

A domestic servant in Kent, she had a long illness and began to show what some thought to be supernatural powers. She was visited by a monk called Edward Bocking, who accepted

The challenging nature of Elizabeth Barton's prophecies ultimately led to her demise

her word that she was inspired by the Virgin Mary; and she later, under Bocking's spiritual guidance, entered a convent, where she continued to have visions and to go into trances, sometimes lying on the floor, her whole body thrashing.

Most of her visions concerned the supreme authority of the Church, at the time under attack from Henry VIII for refusing him permission to divorce Catherine of Aragon and marry Anne Boleyn. But because Bocking wrote a book about her – and others, pamphlets – she became a political figure of some importance, with the support of a number of religious houses. She was interviewed by Sir Thomas More and John Fisher, the Bishop of Rochester (both later executed); she even had an audience with the King.

Finally, though, she went too far. Encouraged by those who had taken her up, she wrote a letter to the Pope urging him not to comply with Henry's request, and she prophesied that if the King did indeed marry Ann, he would only live one month longer. She was soon arrested – along with the monk John Bocking – and later hanged for treason.

MOTHER SHIPTON

A contemporary of Elizabeth Barton's, Ursula Shipton, can be seen as the rough equivalent of St. Malachi: i.e. as someone whose name and reputation was later used for political or myth-making purposes. Old Mother Shipton, as she was called, was a hunchbacked and famously ugly Yorkshire 'wise woman' and fortune-teller who seems to have been regularly consulted by both the gentry and the aristocracy in the middle years of the sixteenth century.

She was said to have predicted the stabbing

of the Mayor of York, the trial for treason of Cardinal Wolsey and the eventual fate of leading figures in the Cardinal's party. But how many of her recorded prophecies are authentic it is now impossible to say. Certainly she remained an important part of English folklore until well into the seventeenth century. Samuel Pepys recorded in his diary in 1666 during the Great Fire of London:

> [Sir Jeremy Smith] *says he was on board the Prince when news came of the burning of London' and all the* [crew of the] *Prince said now that Shipton's prophecy was out.*

The prediction ran, it is said

> *Triumphant Death ries London through*
> *And men on tops of houses* [i.e. firewatchers] *go.*

Mother Shipton was, then, both a real historical character and, apparently, a predictor of future events. But she was also extremely useful as someone who could be later invoked as authorizing a particular political stance or view of history. Furthermore, her name sold books long after her death. One of her most famous predictions, for instance, seems to describe astonishingly accurately the developments of the industrial era:

> *Carriages without horses will go*
> *And accidents fill the world with woe…*
> *Around the world thoughts shall fly*
> *In the twinkling of an eye…*
> *Through hills men shall ride,*
> *And no horse or ass be by his side,*
> *Underwater men shall walk,*
> *Shall ride, shall sleep, shall be seen,*
> *In white, in black, in green…*
> *Iron in water shall float,*

> *As easy as a wooden boat. .*
> *All England's sons that plough the land*
> *Shall be seen book in hand.*
> *Learning shall so ebb and flow,*
> *The poor shall most wisdom know…*
> *The world to an end will come*
> *In eighteen-hundred and eighty-one.*

Apart from the lamentable miss on the final arrival of Armageddon, this is a fairly accurate description of Victorian England – and no wonder. It was written by a man called Charles Hindley in 1862, to boost the sales of his *Life, Prophecies and Death of the Famous Mother Shipton*.

COINNEACH ODA

Scotland has its own version of Mother Shipton (and of St. Malachi) in the so-called 'Brahan Seer', one Coinneach Oda, born somewhere in the Highlands or Scottish Islands in the second half of the sixteenth century or at the beginning of the seventeenth. He may possibly be the man of the same name who was arrested for witchcraft in the estates of the earl of Seaforth in 1577.

He is said to have predicted that the last of the Seaforths would be deaf and dumb and that his sons would die before him – as happened during the lifetime of Sir Walter Scott. It is also claimed that he foretold the battle of Culloden and even the coming of the railways. But though an account of his life was recorded by Alexander Cameron of Lochmaddy soon after his death, stories about him were not written down in any great detail until the nineteenth century.

What about the third category of prophet, though, laid out in this schema: i.e. that represented by St. Joachim, the proto-scientist using old manuscripts for inspiration? For this we need look no further than the most famous lay prophet of them all: Nostradamus.

V
NOSTRADAMUS: SAGE OF SALON

Le lion jeune le vieux surmontera,
En champ bellique par singulier duelle,
Dans cage d'or loeil il lui crevera,
Deux plays une puis mourrir mort cruelle.

[The young Lion will overcome the old one
On martial field in single combat
In a golden cage he shall put out his eye,
Two blows in one, then a most cruel death.]

WITH THIS little four-line verse, or quatrain, first published in France in May 1555, Michel de Nostradame, known as Nostradamus, established his credentials as the most remarkable and enduring secular prophet the world has ever known. There were 352 other verses in this first collection of his (later to be organized, added to and marshalled into 'centuries', or groups of a hundred each). He produced twelve 'centuries' in all, two of which survive only in fragments. Out of a total of 1,013 surviving *Prophéties*, this one was to have the most immediate impact. Four years later, in July 1559, the French King Henri II, whose unofficial badge was a lion, was mortally wounded in a jousting tournament by a younger man called Gabriel de Lorges who, as the commander of Henri's Scottish guard and the Count of Montgomery, also carried on his coat the lion of Scotland.

Henri had already fought and won two ceremonial bouts that morning. However, he was honour-bound as champion of the field, he said, to fight a third. So the two men, with blunted lances, thundered down the lists towards each other at full tilt in the name of honour, each seeking to unhorse the other and end the day. Two unsuccessful passes were made, but then, at the third pass, to everyone's horror, the Count's lance smashed into the King's breastplate and shattered; the sharp broken end careened up through the barred visor of his gold-embossed helmet and entered his brain just behind his right eye. He died, blind and in agony, ten days later.

Every single detail in Nostradamus' prophecy, it seemed, had been borne out: the old and young lions, the 'martial field' and 'single combat', the eye 'put out' in its golden cage (the barred visor), even the two blows in one (sometimes translated as 'two passes, then one:' the fatal final encounter). His reputation soared, and guaranteed his collections of prophecies, as they emerged from his home at Salon in Provence, best-seller status – to this day they have never been out of print.

It was fortunate, perhaps, that by the time of the King's death, Nostradamus had already

Nostradamus' quatrain concerning Henri II proved to be eerily accurate

secured the patronage of his wife, Queen Catherine de' Medici – and that she bore him no grudge for not having been more specific about the application of the prophecy to her husband. Otherwise there is no doubt that he would have been rapidly brought to book by the Catholic Church's feral watchdog, the Inquisition, for sorcery, invoking the Devil's aid to read the future. That he wasn't in fact tried for witchcraft and burned at the stake seems in retrospect astonishing, for the little that we know of Nostradamus' life should have marked him out as a potential threat to Mother Church from the very beginning.

EARLY LIFE

Michel de Nostredame was born in Provence in December 1503 to a family of Jews which, two generations before, had converted to Christianity in order to escape the options of emigration or execution handed out to France's Jewish population – and converted Jews were prime objects of mistrust.

More than that, though, he was educated privately by one of his own grandfathers, who taught him not only Latin and Greek, but also – and much more suspiciously – Hebrew, astrology and perhaps even the body of esoteric

Jewish (and therefore deeply anti-Christian) lore known as the Kabbala.

In 1522, after studying mathematics and astronomy in Avignon, Michel was sent to Montpellier, then one of the greatest universities in the Western world, to train as a doctor, a profession which was barely condoned by the Bible; one of his contemporaries there was a well-known suspected heretic, the great Renaissance writer and notorious free-thinker, François Rabelais.

Even at this early stage of his life, and at almost every subsequent step of the way, in fact, the man with the almost defiantly Catholic name – Nostredame means 'Our Lady' – seems to have flown in the face of orthodoxy and 'right' thinking.

When plague broke out in Montpellier and the university was closed, he stayed in the city to help battle it and, though the medicines he concocted were the usual useless nostrums of the period, he appears to have introduced sanitation and treatment methods which were well before their time.

He recommended that patients should be kept in sunlit and well-ventilated rooms, for example, that they should be bathed as often as possible, and that they should drink only boiled water. He abandoned the universal 'cure-all' of bleeding and had the mattresses and personal property of dead victims burnt. So famous did he become as a result of these highly unorthodox and, to some, dangerous practices that when plague eased in Montpellier, he was sent for by other affected municipalities, and became a celebrated – and extremely well-paid – itinerant scholar-doctor even before he had fully graduated.

For four years the young Michel campaigned against the plague before returning to his studies, winning a laureate in medicine with honours in about 1530. He took the Latin name of Nostradamus and though he was offered a place as a teacher at the university, he refused

it. Instead, he went back on the road travelling from township to township, finding time along the way, according to his later pupil Jean de Chavigny, to translate *The Book of Orus Apollo, Son of Osiris, King of Egypt*, a work that might well have attracted the beady eye of the Inquisition – suggesting, as it did, a preoccupation with ancient mysteries – had it not been dedicated to the Princess of Navarre. Dr. Nostradamus apparently, even at the age of not much more than 27, already had protectors in high places.

DEVELOPMENT

Sometime in the first half of the 1530s, he finally settled in the town of Agen in Aquitaine with his wife, by whom he was to have two children. Agen, on the face of it, was a curious choice although it did have two particular distinctions. First, it had been until comparatively recently an English possession – and England had become a Protestant country in 1529. It may well have provided, therefore, a more international, more religiously tolerant atmosphere than rigidly Catholic, Inquisition-ruled Montpellier.

Second, and perhaps more significantly, it was the home of a celebrated scholar called Jules-César Scaliger, who is known to have had a strong interest in esoteric lore. It seems unlikely that two such well-known men can have lived in the same relatively small town without knowing each other and there have been suggestions that Scaliger was Nostradamus' guide to secret magic practices, inducting him into a circle of occultists and introducing him to the arcana of both alchemy and the lost art of precognition.

There is no actual evidence – as so often in what little we know of Nostradamus' life – for any of this. All that we do know, via Jean de Chavigny, is that his wife and two children died some time in the late 1530s, either of plague or

Michel de Nostradame (1503-1566)

of diphtheria, about which nothing was then known. There is a tradition that almost immediately afterwards he quarrelled with Scaliger, was sued by his wife's family for the dowry it had given him, and was finally accused of heresy, it is said on the basis of some chance remark he had made some years earlier.

Summoned to appear before the Inquisitor in Toulouse, he is said to have escaped trial only by once more taking to the road, though again there is no coherent account of what exactly constituted this heresy of his – and no documentary evidence of any kind.

THE BEGINNINGS OF THE PROPHECIES

The same is true of his life over the next ten or so years – which he is said to have spent travelling through France, Italy and Sicily. De Chavigny says that it was during this period that he began to develop his prophetic skills; there is a well-known story that they first became manifest when somewhere near Ancona in Italy he passed a group of mendicant friars. He immediately dismounted from his horse and knelt at the feet of a young novice, an ex-swineherd, addressing him as 'Your Holiness'. Everyone present was mystified. However, years later the young swineherd became Cardinal Peretti and, in 1585, long after Nostradamus had died, Pope Sixtus V.

Another famous tale is that during this time Nostradamus correctly predicted the fate of a pair of suckling pigs found in the courtyard of a château in Lorraine where he was a guest. "The black one will be eaten for dinner, the white one will be eaten by a wolf", he said blithely. His host, a Monsieur de Florenville, immediately ordered the chef to prepare the white one for dinner, but it was stolen from the kitchen by a pet wolfcub and – the chef confessed later to the assembled company, who had hoped to trick Nostradamus into a false prediction – he had been forced to cook the black one instead.

Nostradamus' presence in Lorraine has been seized on by some over-eager followers of his to claim that he must have been inducted there into the Priory of Sion, a secret and deeply heretical (so-called) Rosicrucian order, with which François Rabelais may also have had some connection. Interestingly enough, the Rosicrucians were said to be heirs, not only to a tripartite doctrine of man's relationship to the cosmos, but also to ancient Egyptian mysteries.

Once more, though, there is not the slightest real evidence of this. All in fact that is known for sure of Nostradamus' long wanderings is that he remained active as a doctor-for-hire. In 1544, for example, he was in Marseilles, helping to control an outbreak of plague; two years later he worked at the same task in Aix-en-Provence so effectively that he was awarded a pension-for-life by the city fathers. Finally, in 1547, soon after fighting an epidemic of whooping-cough in Lyon, he returned to prosaic domestic life, his travels now over. He settled in the Provençal town of Salon-en-Craux (now Salon-de-Provence), where he married a rich widow and moved into a house on a dark narrow street from which he never long strayed for the rest of his life. It was from here, as the so-called 'Sage of Salon', that his fame began to become more or less universal – not as a doctor but as a writer.

THE PROPHÉTIES

He began in 1550 by producing for a new, print-hungry audience the first of a series of yearly almanacs, which set out events in the coming year, together with astrological tables of the stars' conjunctions. Then, in 1552, he branched out into medicine with an account both of his pharmacological researches and of his novel – and much-scorned – attitudes to patient treatment. Within this treatise of his, he included recipes for cosmetics and jams, which he later expanded on in a further book, a particular favourite of Catherine de' Medici. Finally, in 1555, he produced the first volume of his *Prophéties*, which rapidly became a runaway best-seller.

The reasons for this are not by any means clear, for the quatrains, written in medieval Provençal French mixed with occasional Greek and Latin, are at first almost laughably obscure. The first two, for all this, do make some kind of sense, and seem to describe his method of divination:

> *Seated at night in my secret study,*
> *Alone, resting over the brass tripod,*
> *A thin flame leaps out from the solitude,*
> *Making me proclaim what it's not vain to*
>   *believe*

and:

> *With divining-rod in hand, placed in the*
>   *middle of the branches,*
> *I wet both limb and foot.*
> *In fear I write with trembling hand;*
> *Heavenly Splendour; the Divine is seated*
>   *nearby.*

Nostradamus is clearly in his study here, at the top of a (still-existing) spiral staircase, looking out over the rooftops of Salon, gazing by candlelight into a brass bowl full of water, which is divided up into a kind of grid (the 'branches') and may be reflecting the night-sky above. He is using a dowsing-rod to indicate particular areas (or visions) of interest, and is writing down, in a kind of trance, his impressions.

In the third quatrain of the century, though, he immediately abandons any further account of his ways and means and takes on the dark, mystagogic tone that is familiar to anyone who has studied these deeply strange short poems:

When the litter's turned upside-down by the
   whirlwind
And faces are covered with their cloaks,
Then shall the Republic be vexed with new
   people
And Whites and Reds make judgment
   conversely.

This is seen by some as a prophecy of the post-Revolutionary Russian Civil War, with its conflicting armies of Whites and Reds. It is, however, more likely to refer to the French Revolution, in which republicans and monarchists were also known as 'reds' and 'whites'. This would make the 'new people' men like Marat, Robespierre and Danton, who indeed arrived after the birth of the Republic with new ideas about a permanent revolution, and who overturned assumptions – and made new enemies – on both sides.

CAUTIOUS BEHAVIOUR

Why, though, the determined obscurity of the language? Was it that Nostradamus himself failed to make much sense of what he saw in his eyrie? Or was he deliberately covering his tracks? In a long letter to his son César, which acts as a preface to the *Prophéties*, Nostradamus announces that his 'gift of occult prediction' will die with him and cannot be passed on to his son. He says that his knowledge derives from 'astronomical effects' or 'Judiciary astrology,' revealed to him 'through occult sources' – first, 'through supernatural light... through the science of Stars'; and second, through 'inspired Revelations... a communication from divine eternity' combined with 'natural instinct'.

He has been preoccupied with divination, he goes on, for many years. He has been reluctant to put 'all this in writing' because 'of abuse, not only in current times' and among 'those of the present Reign, Sect, Religion and Faith... but also in the greater part of [the] future.' It is for this reason that he now prefers, he says, to "use abstruse and perplexing sentences to explain future causes, as well as more immanent ones", and to ignore Christ's advice about not casting 'your pearls among swine, lest they trample them under their feet, and turn again and rend you'.

It is clear from this preamble that Nostradamus feared, above all, the long arm of the Inquisition and any future version of it that might pursue his son César even after his death. In a fascinating aside, he acknowledges that he has consulted "numerous books that I have come upon that have been hidden for long centuries", but he claims that he has already burned them. He even makes it clear that he has at least dabbled in alchemy: "I made a gift [of the books] to Vulcan, and while he was devouring them, the flame that was licking the air had an unusual brightness brighter than a natural flame... So, in order that in future they not be misused, *observing the principles of perfect transformation... and that of the incorruptible subterranean metals subjected to occult waves,* I reduced them to ashes."

The preface is a tantalising performance: owning up to a vast knowledge of the occult on the one hand, and claiming on the other that the evidence for it has been destroyed; constantly invoking the Christian God as his inspiration, while at the same time underlining the fact that his son cannot possibly be involved. It has simultaneously a defiant and a wheedling quality. It says to 'them': 'Come and get me if you can'. Of course in the end 'they' couldn't, for by that time he was protected by one of the greatest in the land.

When he finally died, he died at home in Salon, two years after Catherine de' Medici and her son, King Charles IX, had paid him a special visit, in exactly the way he himself predicted in the last quatrain of a further collection of his verses, published posthumously, called *Présages*:

> On returning from Embassy, the King's gift
>   safely stored,
> No more will he labour, he will have gone to
>   God.
> Close relatives and friends, blood brothers,
> Will find him quite dead, near bed and
>   board.

Nostradamus had just returned from a mission to Arles on behalf of his town; he still had in his possession the 100 gold écus Catherine's kingly son had given him in Salon two years before and he was found between his bed and the bench he used to help him heave his gout- and dropsy-ridden body into it. He died on July 2nd, 1566, despite, according to his disciple Jean de Chavigny, cheerfulness and apparent good health the night before.

He left behind him a long sequence of messages direct from the late-medieval mind to future generations, as we shall see…

WAS NOSTRADAMUS A ROSICRUCIAN?

The picture that has been passed down to us of Nostradamus the prophet is of a man already famous in France as what we would call today an epidemiologist and hygienist. He was also an accomplished astrologer and astronomer – there was little distinction made at the time between the two disciplines – and an experimenter in what might loosely be described as pharmacology (medicines, decoctions of various kinds, and ointments). He seems, for all this, for most of his life to have studiously avoided the limelight. He turned down a teaching position at a great university (where the empiricist philosopher John Locke later studied). He settled instead in small provincial towns and he spent long periods as a wanderer. For years he was – in the language of the courtroom – 'of no fixed abode'. Why?

Given Nostradamus' background and education, it is tempting to believe that one of his motives was indeed to escape the scrutiny of the Inquisition, which ruthlessly policed the boundaries of permissible enquiry with the threat – and not always just the threat – of torture, excommunication and death by fire. He played down, at the least, his origins within a family of learned converted Jews – and his disciple and biographer, Jean de Chavigny, later flatly denied them. He was also, there is no doubt, in a general sense a seeker of knowledge – and he may well have used his travels, as some commentators have suggested, to visit other physicians and perhaps even esotericists such as Jules-César Scaliger, his fellow-citizen of Agen.

It has also been suggested, based on his stay there and what can be interpreted in the *Prophéties* as general anti-Catholic tone, that he may have been a covert Protestant; it is at least interesting in this regard that his departure from Agen was caused, according to popular tradition, by an accusation of heresy – one which would certainly have led, if the story is true (and had he not disappeared from view), to a full-blown ecclesiastical enquiry.

But what real evidence is there that Nostradamus was a member of some sort of secret society that we might call Rosicrucian? The first thing to be said is that the often-accepted view that he 'must have been' has to deal from the outset with a serious problem. The first manifestos and descriptions of the Rosicrucian order – the *Fama*, the *Confessio* and *The Chemical Wedding of Christian Rosencreutz* – did not appear in print until fifty or so years after his death – and then not in France, but in what is today Germany. Also – despite suggestions to the contrary – there is no concrete evidence in these extremely curious documents that the so-called Brotherhood of 'the Rosy Cross' – and/or, perhaps, 'the Dew of Heaven' – was anything other than an allegorical representation of a complex set of religious and philosophical convictions about the need for change. (The full title of the *Fama* begins with the words: 'Universal and General Reformation of the whole wide world'.) Indeed the man who was behind the publication of at least one of the books described it as a *ludibrium*, a joke, a piece of fictional theatre.

THE ROSICRUCIAN BROTHERHOOD AND TEXTS

Having said this, though, it is clear that Nostradamus shared, at least to some degree, the convictions and concerns laid out in these Rosicrucian texts. What they describe is the career of a mysterious *'illuminatus'* called Rosencreutz, active in the fifteenth century, who became convinced, after travelling to the east to learn magic and Kabbala, that man was on the brink of a new kind of knowledge of the world and of his place in it, but was being impeded by the Catholic Church and by a blinkered adherence to old authorities like Aristotle and Galen.

What Rosencreutz (or Brother R.C. as he was also known) was searching for – via magic, Kabbala and alchemy – was a breakthrough into the light of the world's *harmonia*, which had been glimpsed, says the *Fama*, by such men as Paracelsus, the Swiss alchemist/physician, who had advocated specific remedies for specific dis-

Rosicrucian texts were beautiful and complex in their detail

eases and noted the relationships between such things as cretinism and goitre and paralysis and head injuries.

When Brother R.C. tried, though, to gather the learned men of Spain to his cause, he fared no better than did Paracelsus, who was mocked out of Basle by his medical colleagues and forced to wander through Europe, preaching (to ears that didn't hear) the virtues of clinical observation. Back in his native Germany, however, according to the *Fama*, Brother R.C. had managed finally to set up a Fraternity of the Rosy Cross with, at first, three disciples. Gradually numbers grew. Their prime responsibility was the treatment of the sick, but they also travelled widely 'to spread knowledge', and gathered once a year at their headquarters in the House of the Holy Spirit.

In around 1604 the Brotherhood had discovered, the *Fama* announced, the door to the vault in which Brother R.C. had been buried – and wonders lay behind it. The vault had no windows to let in the light, but was lit by perpetually-burning lamps. It had walls filled with geometrical figures and inscribed with the names of the Brothers; it contained many treas-

Alchemy's complexity and its results were often represented in literature allegorically as a sacred union or marriage

ures, including the works of Paracelsus, and instruments for recording sounds and images.

The opening of this vault is clearly regarded in the text as the herald of a new sunrise which will fill all of Europe with its light, just as the vault's inner sun does. This message of a new dawn is repeated with even greater fervour in the *Confessio*, published together with 'a Brief Consideration of the more Secret Philosophy written by Philip à Geballa', a name which can perhaps be read as a reference to its origins in the Kabbala. Old learning, the *Confessio* reiterates, has been rediscovered and collected by the Brotherhood from 'Magia, Kabbala and Alchemy', learning that is connected with medicine and healing, but also takes in mathematics and geometry – and is also at root profoundly religious and spiritual.

The *Confessio's* alchemical philosophy has nothing to do with 'ungodly and accursed goldmaking', in the words of the *Fama*. Neither founding Father nor any Brother rejoices 'that he can make gold, but is glad that he seeth the Heavens open, and the angels of God ascending and descending, and his name written in the Book of Life'. The author of *The Rosicrucian Enlightenment*, historian Frances A. Yates, says of the *Confessio*:

A powerful prophetic and apocalyptic note sounds through it… When the Trumpet of the Order shall sound with full voice [those] things which are now only whispered in enigmas will come forth and fill the world and the tyranny of the Pope will be overthrown. The world has seen many alterations since Father

R.C. was born and many more are to come. But before the end, God will allow a great influx of truth, light and grandeur, such as surrounded Adam in Paradise, to be poured forth on mankind. New stars [noted by the astronomer Johannes Kepler in 1606] *have appeared in the constellations Serpentarius and Cygnus which are signs of the coming of these things.*

The third document in what might be called the Rosicrucian trilogy, and one which is looked at in some detail here, was published in Strasburg in 1616. This was *The Chemical* [also Chymical] *Wedding of Christian Rosencreutz*, a fantastical piece of fiction described by Yates as:

> *... a romance about a husband and a wife* [a King and Queen] *who dwell in a wondrous castle full of marvels and of images of Lions, but is at the same time an allegory of alchemical processes interpreted symbolically as an experience of the mystic marriage of the soul – an experience which is undergone by Christian Rosencreutz through the visions conveyed to him in the castle, through theatrical performances, through ceremonies of initiation into orders of chivalry, through the society of the court in the castle.*

The action in *The Chemical Wedding* takes place, like the Creation in the book of Genesis, over seven days, one of which is taken up by the discovery of a secret vault similar to that in the *Fama*, and another by work in an alchemical laboratory, during which life, in the form of an alchemical Bird, is created. (Earlier, on Day Four, six persons had been beheaded, and placed in coffins, only to be later resurrected.)

On the seventh day, the company, having earlier attended a theatrical performance culminating in the wedding of the title, is told, prior to its departure on twelve ships carrying the signs of the Zodiac, that all have now been inducted Knights of the Order of the Golden Stone. A procession takes place, with the knights carrying white banners inscribed with a red cross, in which Rosencreutz rides with the King and a page reads out the rules of the order:

> *I. You, my Lords and Knights, shall swear that you will at no time ascribe your order either unto any Devil or Spirit, but only to God, your Creator, and his hand-maid Nature.*
> *II. That you will abominate all whoredom, incontinency, and uncleanness, and not defile your order with such vices.*
> *III. That you, through your talents, will be ready to assist all that are worthy and have need of them.*
> *IV. That you desire not to employ this honour to worldly pride and high authority.*
> *V. That you shall not be willing to live longer than God will have you.*

Finally, the Chemical Wedding concludes when Rosencreutz hangs up his rose-decked hat, as well as a golden fleece earlier given him, in a chapel in the castle as a memorial, and writes his name and motto there:

> *Summa Scientia nihil Scire.* [The highest form of knowledge is to know nothing]
> *Fr. Christianus Rosencreutz.*

Yates, in her revealing account of what might be called the Rosicrucian impulse, sums up *The Chemical Wedding* by saying:

> *Basically, it is an alchemical fantasia, using the fundamental image of alchemical fusion, the marriage, the uniting of the sponsus and the sponsa, touching also on the theme of death, the nigredo through which the elements must pass in the process of transmutation... The allegory is of course also a spiritual one,*

typifying processes of regeneration within the soul. Alchemy has always carried such double meanings, but in this case the theme of spiritual alchemy… is of a particularly subtle kind.

WERE ROSICRUCIAN TEXTS INFLUENCED BY NOSTRADAMUS?

It may seem at first blush that this account of Rosicrucian documents published after Nostradamus' death can have little or nothing to do with him. Although Yates firmly believes that the Brotherhood of the Rosy Cross was in no sense an organized secret society, she does think that the ideas contained in the trilogy were widespread in Europe – particularly Protestant Europe – long before; she even gives some evidence that the documents were circulated in manuscript before being finally published.

The whole atmosphere within the documents is one of 'ardent piety combined with magico-scientific striving' and she believes that they represent 'a religious movement using alchemy to intensify its evangelical piety, and including a large programme of research and reform in the sciences'. The mystical background behind this movement, she goes on, '[was] intensely religious, Hermetic, magical [and] alchemical'. She continues in a later chapter:

Magic was a dominating factor [in the Rosicrucian outlook], *working as a mathematics-mechanics in the lower world, as celestial mechanics in the celestial world, and as an-gelic conjuration in the supercelestial world. One cannot leave out the angels in this world view, however much it may have been advancing towards the scientific revolution. The religious outlook is bound up with the idea that penetration has been made into higher angelic spheres. . ; and it is the angels who are believed to illuminate man's intellectual activities.*

It can be seen from all this that Nostradamus and his *Prophéties* were born out of precisely the same sort of intellectual climate as the Rosicrucian texts. He certainly studied astrology, astronomy and mathematics. He had, it seems, a good knowledge of alchemy, as is clear from his preface to César and he may well have had a profound knowledge, too, of the Kabbala, passed on to him by his grandfather. He was a healer, as the Rosicrucians were, he seems to have believed strongly in the power and efficacy of clinical practice, as Paracelsus (another astrologer-doctor) did and he made use, as recorded in the same preface to César, of both 'inspired revelations' and 'communication from divine eternity'.

It is tempting to believe, from the last line of the quatrain quoted earlier, describing his working methods – 'Heavenly Splendour; the Divine is seated nearby' – that he was in some way involved in the conjuring of angels. Certainly his translation of *The Book of Orus Apollo* shows that he had at the very least a strong interest in the sort of 'Egyptian' or 'magical' religion embraced in Italy by yet another forerunner of modern science, Giordano Bruno.

VI
BRUNO AND THE ROSICRUCIAN WITCH-HUNT

GIORDANO BRUNO, who championed the view of the world of Nicolas Copernicus (1473–1543) – that the earth revolved round the sun – was burned at the stake by the Inquisition in 1600. He had earlier wandered through Europe preaching a coming reformation of the world based on the teachings contained in the so-called Hermetic texts, documents probably collected in the centuries after Christ but widely believed to have been written by a pre-Christian Egyptian God-priest called Hermes Trismegistus (or 'Thrice-Mightiest').

These documents had been rediscovered and had become popular among Italian intellectuals in the early Renaissance, when they had been reconciled with the teachings contained in the Bible via a Kabbalistic interpretation of the book of Genesis. The resulting map – as it might be called – of the universe was one over which Jehovah presided; it consisted of a series of concentric circles – of angels, stars, elements, and man at the centre – all of them linked, one to another, by astral connections. A process of mystical regeneration was seen as absolutely necessary (by Bruno, as by his intellectual pre

decessors) if man, at the centre, were to be able to regain the dominion over the whole system that he had lost at the time of the Fall.

This view of the world, which was that held, roughly speaking, not only by Bruno, but by the Rosicrucianists and the forerunners of modern empirical science (Paracelsus, Copernicus etc.), may seem remote and harmless to a contemporary audience. However, it is instructive to look back – keeping an eye meanwhile on Nostradamus living quietly, out of the limelight – on the way in which it was greeted in France when the Rosicrucian texts first came to general attention there in 1623.

What these texts were offering, after all, was a vision of the world in which Paradise was regainable and all things ultimately knowable, if men of learning would only gather together selflessly, committed to healing, under the Rosicrucian banner. (Some did try to make contact with what they assumed to be a real underground secret society, but to no effect.) Yet when Rosicrucianism appeared in the open in France, it soon scared up a vicious – and in its way very revealing – witch-hunt.

Early scientist Giordano Bruno so upset the authorities with his defence of Copernicus that he was executed by the Inquisition

SOCIETY'S RESPONSE TO ROSICRUCIANISM

The whole affair may well have begun as a kind of spoof. One writer claimed that placards had been put up in 1623 in Paris, announcing the arrival in the city of 'deputies of the principal College of the Brothers of the Rosy Cross… [both] visible and invisible… to draw men from error and death'. Spoof or not, though, the result was a sensation. Rumours swept though France – and various publications immediately followed, with titles like *Horrible Pacts made between the Devil and the Pretended Invisible Ones*.

Rosicrucian representatives were rumoured to have held an assembly and a Black Mass in Lyon in the preceding year, at which it was decided to send six deputies to Paris. They had allegedly vowed to turn their backs on Christianity, and had made a pact with the Devil which allowed them to transport themselves anywhere in the world and to remain there disguised as native residents. The Devil had also given them the gift of eloquence which permitted them, not only to attract men of learning, but also to be held wiser by them than the ancient prophets.

No mention was made in any of this, of course, of the Brothers' mission of healing, nor of their continual invocations of both God and Jesus. They were emissaries of the Devil, faceless infiltrators, pure and simple; their commitment to learning was a front. A noted French Jesuit, François Garasse, wrote in the same year that their teachings were heathen and that a number of them had recently been condemned as sorcerers in Malines. All of them, in his view, eminently deserved to be broken on the wheel or hanged.

A slightly more measured – and more interesting – work also appeared in 1623: *Instruction to France about the truth of the history of the Rose Cross Brothers*, by Gabriel Naudé. Naudé evidently knew the *Fama* well, and Yates says of his book:

> *According to Naudé, the Fama had* [already] *been making a great impression in France, arousing hopes of some impending new advance in knowledge. He says that it is being rumoured everywhere that after all the 'novelties' which surprised 'our parents' – the discovery of new worlds, the invention of cannon, compasses, clocks, novelties in religion, in medicine, in astrology – another age of discoveries is at hand. The new movements are culminating, so runs the rumour, in the Brothers R.C. and the hopes which they raise. Tycho Brahe* [1546-1601: the Danish astrologer who predated the discovery of the telescope and never fully accepted Copernicus' system] *is making new discoveries; Galileo has invented his 'spectacles' (the*

telescope), and now comes the company of the R.C. Brothers announcing the imminent 'instauration' or renewal of knowledge promised by the Scriptures.

Naudé speaks extremely scathingly of these claims. Following more or less the orthodox Jesuit view laid down by Garasse, he declares that the Brothers are pernicious and their publications both 'misleading and useless'. However, in discussing the Brothers' reputation for magic, he reveals a good deal – more than he should have known, perhaps – about their antecedents and allies.

He mentions Robert Fludd, a Paracelsian physician and philosopher living in London who had published defences of the Brotherhood of the Rosy Cross and of the 'good' magic which he saw at the heart of all natural philosophy. He had also dedicated his *History of the Macrocosm* to the English King James I as '*Ter Maximus,*' the title sacred to Hermes Trismegistus. Naudé condemned as belonging to the same Rosicrucian 'labyrinth' Nostradamus' fellow-student François Rabelais, Thomas More's *Utopia* – and even two medieval English mathematicians, John Hentisbury and Richard Swineshead, who were to have a considerable influence on 17th-century scientific thought.

He further made a list of a number of men whom he considered as belonging, in one way or another, to the same school of thought as the Rosicrucians. This list is very revealing indeed for it includes both Paracelsus and Giordano Bruno; François de Candale, who translated (in 1579) Hermes Trismegistus into French; and Trimethius, whose book *Steganographia* is today considered by some to be the main Renaissance manual of practical Kabbala and angel-conjuring. There is one other name in particular that stands out and merits further consideration: that of John Dee.

VII
JOHN DEE

JOHN DEE, variously described as a clergyman, magician, mathematician, astrologer and alchemist, was born in England in 1527, twenty-four years after Nostradamus. He was charged with sorcery in the reign of Catholic Queen Mary, but with the coming to the throne of her Protestant sister-successor, Queen Elizabeth, he quickly came into his own. He advised her on the most auspicious day for her coronation and thereafter became her trusted court physician/astrologer and mage, patiently explaining to her, for example, the comet of 1577 and writing scientific treatises about newly discovered lands.

Dee was, said his contemporaries, the greatest mathematician of his age. He wrote a *Preface to Euclid* and a defence, which to this day has not been found, of Roger Bacon, the thirteenth-century English scientist and philosopher who had been accused at the time (and since) of practicing magic. Bacon, now seen as one of the fathers of natural science, had (like Paracelsus) promoted accurate observation of phenomena. He was a mechanical genius who is sometimes said to have had invented both gunpowder and the use of the microscope. He also (like Paracelsus) had a profound interest in alchemy; it was this that had laid him open to accusations of conjuring and consorting with demons.

Dee is said to have responded to this charge by stoutly maintaining that Bacon's achievements derived, not from any truck with the Devil, but from his extraordinarily profound mathematical skills and from a deep knowledge of nature. (In his *Preface to Euclid*, he wrote a remarkable survey of the mathematical arts – chief among which, he claimed, was architecture – and proselytized for their urgent revival.) Dee, too, was an alchemist – and something more than that, for it was he, more than any other contemporary figure, who added alchemy to the Renaissance synthesis of Hermetic and Kabbalistic teachings and so paved the way towards the scientific revolution of the seventeenth century. He also had a major influence on the philosophy behind the Rosicrucian manifestos.

The *summa* of Dee's work as a writer was the *Monas hieroglyphica*, published in 1564 and dedicated to the Emperor Maximilien II. In it, says Yates:

> He related his study of number to the three worlds of the [Kabbalists]. *In the lower elemental world he studied number as technology as applied science… In the celestial world his study of number was related to astrology and alchemy, and in his Monas hieroglyphica he believed that he had discovered a formula for a combined [Kabbalist], alchemical and mathematical science which would enable its possessor to move up and down the scale of being from the lowest to the highest spheres. And in the supercelestial sphere, Dee believed that he had found the secret of conjuring angels by*

numerical calculations in the [Kabbalist] *tradition. Dee… is thus a figure typical of the late Renaissance magus who combined 'Magia,* [Kabbala]*, and Alchymia' to achieve a world-view in which advancing science was strangely mingled with angelology.*

THE LIFE OF JOHN DEE

Conventional accounts of Dee's life record that he had a crystal 'as big as an egg: most bright, clear and glorious' and that he employed one Edward Kelley as a 'scryer' – an assistant able to see visions in the reflective surface of polished metals, glass, ink, water (Nostradamus' favoured medium, it seems), or the now much-derided crystal ball. This scrying of Kelly's was said to have revealed a consistent and coherent language called Enochian, which angels used to communicate with the two men.

There are also suggestions that Dee was a spy for Elizabeth as well as her astrologer and that Enochian functioned between them as a kind of code; Elizabeth referred to him as her 'ubiquitous eyes', and Dee signed his letters to her with a pair of eyes followed by a seven: i.e. (extraordinarily enough) 007. It is further recorded that Dee foresaw the use of the telescope as an aid in battle; that he predicted the execution of Mary Queen of Scots in 1587 and that he not only foresaw the arrival of the Spanish Armada in 1588, but also advised Elizabeth on the best way to defeat it.

Dee – with his interest in technology, his mathematical orientation, his esoteric mathematical mysticism and belief in angel-guidance – was in fact the dominating figure in the so-called Elizabethan Renaissance. He was a close friend and associate of many of its most brilliant figures, including Raleigh, Sidney and Gilbert. He helped to create the cult of the Queen as Gloriana, and contributed greatly to the mystique which surrounded her court –

which makes it all the more surprising that he should have left England in 1583, as a mob attempted to burn his library, for the court of Emperor Rudolph II in Prague.

Details of Dee's career in Prague and time among the aristocrats and intellectuals who surrounded Emperor Rudolph are extremely hard to find. But Rudolph, there is no doubt, was a very remarkable man. He had moved the capital of his empire to Prague from Vienna, and had kept his distance from his lordly – and extremely intolerant – nephew, King Philip II of Spain. He had sunk himself into abstruse studies and had surrounded himself with adepts and mystics of every kind.

The city, under Rudolph's aegis, in fact, had become a power-house of late Renaissance scholarship. His palace was filled with books and with technological marvels, and scientists like Bruno, Kepler and Tycho Brahe flocked to it from all over Europe. Rudolph's favourite religious adviser was a Kabbalist, and he held at least one interview with an extraordinary man called Rabbi Loew, who was the main conduit

John Dee was for many years a trusted advisor to Elizabeth I

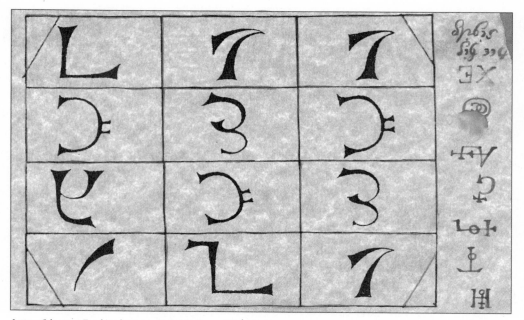

Letters of the secret Enochian language devised by Dee and his assistant

for a new form of Kabbala – marked by intense meditation, magical techniques and the importance of a return to Paradisal beginnings – which had been recently developed in Palestine. He gave imperial protection to the Bohemian church, the first reformed (or Protestant) church in Europe, and he also looked kindly on the Bohemian Brethren, a mystical brotherhood attached to it.

Dee, we know, plunged into this atmosphere of tolerance and intense investigation with gusto. Edward Kelley gave what seem to have been convincing demonstrations of transmutation and Dee himself became a prime influence in this early Prague spring, creating a legacy that was to resurface, according to Yates, after the death of Rudolph in 1610 and the desperate attempt to place on the throne of Bohemia the (Protestant) Palatine Elector Frederick and his new wife, the daughter of English King James I. This legacy took the form of the Rosicrucian manifestos, published just as the dream of Prague was dying with the accession of a new Catholic Hapsburg emperor, Ferdinand of Styria, who had been Jesuit-trained.

Dee himself had returned to England long before this time, and had been well received there by Elizabeth. However, the new King, James I – who was a a great believer in demons – ignored him, and Dee died in extreme poverty, having had to sell his books for food, in 1608. The publication of his *Spiritual Diary* later in the century – which purported to record his conversations with angels – led to him being dismissed as a charlatan and a devil-worshipper, and he had become by that time in any case too dangerous a figure to invoke as an intellectual influence. Even though he seems to have been instrumental at long distance in the institution of both freemasonry and the Royal Society, Dee was, in effect, written out of history – and it is hard again to find him.

There are a number of unanswered questions relating to John Dee. What, for example, had he been doing in Prague? Had he been spying for Elizabeth? Had he been an emissary sent to buoy up the Protestant cause and to gain new scientific knowledge that might be of use to the English queen and her scientist-adventurers? No-one really knows. But his presence in Prague – as well as that of Bruno, Kepler, Brahe and the rest – suggests another account of the Rosicrucian Brotherhood – and of the wanderings, in both Italy and France, of Nostradamus.

VIII
MAGIC, KABBALA AND ALCHEMY

We can do more than we know... Though everything is not permitted, everything is possible.

ROGER BACON (C.1214–94)

THERE WAS, and is, no evidence of the Rosicrucians' existence as an organized secret society. Many, including Robert Fludd, tried to make contact with such a society – and completely failed. But what if the Brotherhood of the Rosy Cross were simply an allegory to explain a situation that was already in existence: i.e. that scattered across Europe were a number of adepts, scholars and proto-scientists who alone, because of their advanced knowledge and exceptional faculties, were able to communicate with and recognize each other? This is in fact not very different from a situation that developed in the twentieth century and continues today.

In late-Victorian times, there was a general agreement that the programme of physics had been completed – there was little that remained to be discovered. However, just a few years later, a new, deeply esoteric physics appeared. Albert Einstein, for example, was said to have been comprehensible only to five or six people in the world, and there are perhaps today no more than a few hundred mathematicians and physicists capable of meaningfully addressing in a mutually comprehensible way such advanced topics as black holes and super-string theory.

This élite, these 'chosen' ones or *illuminati*, do of course regularly openly confer at international conferences and seminars in universities across the world, thanks to the invention of the jet engine. But then they are not hamstrung by the fact that their research is banned, illegal, seen as the work of the Devil, as was that of the proto-scientists of the sixteenth and seventeenth centuries.

To push the analogy further, modern physicists and mathematicians – just like those involved, one way or another, in what might be called the Rosicrucian enterprise (like Nostradamus) – are today convinced that the nature of the universe will finally be understood, that all things are ultimately knowable. (They, too, are readers, as were their predecessors, in the *Liber Mundi*, 'the book of the world'.) They also speak in a language that is almost totally inaccessible, as did the alchemical philosophers, to ordinary, untrained minds.

A number of experimenters today, such as those involved in weapons and human cloning, perforce work, as these earlier scientists did, in secret and more and more have been drawn into questions of ethics and of religion. As Robert Jungk wrote in *Brighter Than A Thousand Suns*:

In order to achieve his aims, the alchemist had to spend a great deal of time experimenting

> *Among the young atomic scientists, some looked upon their work as a kind of intellectual exercise of no particular significance and involving no obligation, but for others, their researches seemed like a religious experience.*

Winner of the 1945 Nobel Prize for Physics Wolfgang Pauli, in his youth an icy advocate of science for science's sake, later wrote something which was even more reminiscent of the Rosicrucian ideal:

> *In view of the division of the activities of the human mind into different compartments which has been strictly maintained for centuries, I envisage a method whose aim would be to reconcile contraries in a synthesis incorporating a rational understanding and a mystical experience of their unity. No other objective would be in harmony with the mythology, whether avowed or not, of our epoch.*

Harmony, unity, the Book of the World, an impulse towards mysticism and spiritual purity: all this begins to seem not at all unlike the philosophy behind the publication of the Rosicrucian trilogy (and earlier of Nostradamus' *Prophéties*). Modern science, too, has become exactly the sort of secret society the Rosicrucians earlier mooted. This was confirmed by Albert Einstein, when he said that "those who have the power to make far-reaching decisions on good and evil" constitute a real 'cryptocracy' – or 'secret rule'.

Were Nostradamus' wanderings across Europe, then – as well as those of Paracelsus and Bruno – simply journeys undertaken for meetings with like minds? And were the later Rosicrucian manifestos merely the first (open, if allegorical) account of the existence of this network, which had found a focus – since lost to history and Catholicism – at the court of Emperor Rudolph in Prague?

Read in this light, the manifestos – with their withering attack on the forces of reaction within the Catholic Church – seem a whole lot less odd; even the placards supposedly put up in Paris in 1623 seem much more rational – the sort of banners, indeed, that might appear at (or outside) a scientific conference. What they announced was the presence of a movement that prefigured the coming of a new world of discovery which necessitated an entirely new approach to moral and social life. As Soviet writer Vladimir Orlov remarked about a conference on radio-isotopes held in Paris in 1957 (quoted in *The Morning of the Magicians* by Louis Pauwels and Jacques Bergier):

The "alchemists" of today would do well to remember the statutes of their predecessors in the Middle Ages… in which it is laid down that no man shall devote himself to alchemy who is not "pure in heart and inspired by the loftiest intentions"

ALCHEMY

We don't have any real idea of what the 'alchemists' and adepts gathered in Prague in the generation after Nostradamus were actually up to. We know that Isaac Newton, the seemingly *ne plus ultra* exemplar of the modern scientific mind, had a profound interest in alchemy and spent much of his time practising it. We know too that René Descartes, who did as much as anyone else to shift the world of science from magic to mechanism, was himself entirely familiar with the Rosicrucian programme and may well have been a Rosicrucian-style adept. So what was it about alchemy that drew such men towards it? What were they, as well as Bacon, Paracelsus, Dee, Fludd – and Nostradamus – actually engaged in?

WHAT IS ALCHEMY?

Any modern account of alchemy – dedicated as it was not only to the transmutation of metals but also to the achievement of spiritual purity – is clearly an extremely perilous enterprise for someone who is not an adept himself. However, it is worth saying at the outset that the alchemical adventure, whatever it was, seems to have occupied the minds of often supremely gifted men – and some women – over at least two thousand years and that the alchemical literature, though obscure and concealed behind esoteric language, is truly vast.

It is worth adding too that alchemy gave rise to a number of extremely important discoveries. Listed below (first cited in Pauwels and Bergier and set out here with some minor amendments) are some of the discoveries, and those who discovered them:

Albert le Grand *(1193–1280)* [otherwise known as Albertus Magnus], [who] *succeeded in producing potassium lye, and was the first to describe the chemical composition of cinnabar, white lead and minium.*

Raymond Lull *(1235–1315),* [who was included among the forebears of Rosicrucianism by Gabriel Naudé and] *who prepared bicarbonate of potassium.*

Theophrastes Paracelsus *(1493–1541),* [the contemporary of Nostradamus, who] *was the first to describe zinc, hitherto unknown. He also introduced the use in medicine of chemical compounds.*

Blaise Vigenère *(1523–96)* [who] *discovered benzoic acid.*

Giambattista della Porta *(1541–1615)* [who] *produced tin monoxide.*

Johann-Baptiste Van Helmont *(1577–1644) who recognised the existence of gases.*

Basil Valentin *(whose real identity is still unknown)* [who] *discovered, in the seventeenth century, sulphuric acid and chlorohydric acid.*

Brandt *(died 1692)* [who] *discovered phosphorus.*

[and] **Johann-Friedrich Boetticher** *(1682–1719)* [who] *was the first European to make porcelain.*

It is clear from this list – as it is from all other sources – that alchemists were (at least in part) metallo-chemists, preoccupied with discovering and seeking to alter the structure of matter. Their quest to unlock, in effect, the secrets of the universe had moral, philosophical and spiritual dimensions – as can be seen in what is sometimes regarded as their overall goal: the creation of gold from other (base) materials.

Gold, with its natural resistance to tarnish, corrosion and fire, was the ultimate metaphor for beauty, purity of substance and endurance. It was the acme of creation and whatever could facilitate its manufacture in the hands of man could also guarantee him immortality and spiritual redemption. The search for this physical and spiritual catalyst – a substance generally known as the Philosopher's Stone – was central. It involved experimentation in the laboratory and utter dedication to the process of purification in the mind of the individual concerned, who looked for guidance through dreams and visions and meditation, anywhere he could find it. He also relied greatly on revelations known as 'gifts from God', brought by guiding spirits or angels.

From this very basic account, it can be seen

that, though alchemy was a unitary enterprise, it can be parsed out into a number of different branches or schools: one preoccupied with laboratory metallurgy (Roger Bacon, Albertus Magnus etc.); another which saw the Philosopher's Stone as a potential cure-all for human diseases and was thus drawn to medicinal chemistry (Paracelsus and Nostradamus); a third, which was deeply engaged in philosophical and metaphysical speculation, attempting to find answers to the most profound questions about the nature of our lives and our rôle in the universe (Giordano Bruno and the Hermetic-Kabbalist sages); and a fourth whose central concern was with what might be called the changing of consciousness via the induction of visions and the conjuring of angels (John Dee). It is a measure, in fact, of John Dee's importance to the whole alchemical movement – and to the Rosicrucians – that he found a way of linking these different spheres of endeavour into one indissoluble scientific enterprise via a new mathematics linked to astronomy.

ALCHEMICAL LITERATURE AND CODES

This, of course, gets us no nearer to what alchemists actually did, what their practices consisted of. The problem here is one that can be readily connected to Nostradamus once more. In the words of André and Lynette Singer in their *Divine Magic: The World of the Supernatural*:

Nothing about alchemy is plain or straightforward, and a typical alchemical document is virtually incomprehensible to the untutored eye. Layers of symbolism, metaphor and allegory protect the knowledge and restrict its use to the initiated, and only a limited amount of information has ever been written down. Because of this deliberate obscurity, and the inevitable curiosity of the greedy, the art and its practitioners have usually been viewed with the suspicion and hostility that accompany all arcane pursuits. Alchemy has been banned at various points in history, beginning with the Roman Emperor Diocletian, who in the 3rd century burned all the available texts (mostly Egyptian) and forbade its practice.

Another reason for this secrecy, apparently, was that the practice of alchemy was inherently dangerous, both because of those who condemned it and because of the nature of the experiments undertaken. The Singers also cite the case of Raymond Lull, a Catalan alchemist and missionary of the 13th century, who was another Gabriel Naudé described as belonging to the Rosicrucian 'labyrinth'. He cautioned his readers: 'If you reveal this, you shall be damned.' Thomas Norton, an English alchemist of the 15th century, went further. He wrote:

This art must ever secret be.
The cause thereof is this, as ye may see:
If one evil man had thereof all his will,
All Christian peace he might easily spill.

The necessity for secrecy often led to obscurity and hidden meanings within alchemical literature.
Represented here is the union of fire and water

This resulted in alchemical literature becoming incomprehensible to the modern reader (in exactly the same way – and perhaps for the same reason – as Nostradamus' *Prophéties* did). They seem to be written, in fact, in a kind of allegorical or symbolic code, and it is not without interest that sixteenth-century alchemist, Blaise Vigenère, was the inventor of a number of codes and methods of cyphering used until comparatively recently. He may have developed this sideline while interpreting earlier texts.

René Alleau's view of alchemical coding as set out in his *Aspects de L'Alchimie Traditionelle* (again quoted in Pauwels and Bergier):

> Consider the game of chess, whose rules and principles are relatively simple but permit of an infinite number of combinations. If we look on the whole body of... treatises on alchemy as so many games annotated in a conventional language, we shall have to confess in all honesty that we know neither the rules of the game nor the cypher employed. Alternatively, we assume that the code language is composed of signs that anyone can understand, which is precisely the immediate illusion that a well composed cryptogram should create. We therefore conclude that it would be prudent not to allow ourselves to believe that their meaning is clear, but to study these texts as if they were in an unknown language. Apparently these messages are addressed only to other players, other alchemists who, we must assume, already possess, by some other means than written tradition, the necessary key to an exact comprehension of this language.

The truth is, of course, that we don't have this key – and have never really looked for it. In fact there has never been any sustained attempt by modern scientists, cryptographers, historians, linguists, mathematicians etc. to rediscover it.

The result is that we may well have lost forever the last relics of the science, technology and philosophy of a whole civilization, one that has in effect disappeared. This is amply illustrated with the case of the Arab alchemist Abu Musa Jabir, cited by the Singers. Jabir, also known as Geber:

> ... was skilled in music, art and mathematics and in the 8th century invented a notation system which was reaching toward the modern system of chemical equations. So difficult and complex was this notation [however] that it gave rise to the word "gibberish".

'Gibberish', in fact, is what almost all alchemical literature remains – and with it a whole swath of art and music. Quite apart from their apparent submersal in Nostradamus' quatrains, alchemical principles are said to have been turned into stone in the building of some of Europe's greatest medieval churches and cathedrals. One of the most significant alchemical texts is Esprit Gobineau de Montluisart's *Most curious explanations of the hieroglyphic enigmas and figures on the great West door of the cathedral of Notre-Dame in Paris*. The figures are said to represent, via allegory and symbol, a complete guide to alchemy's processes.

Some of the world's finest paintings – like those of Botticelli – contain alchemical references, and alchemy has even reached deep into Western music. The philosopher-composer Pontus de Tyard, a member of the French Pléiade, was included in Gabriel Naudé's list of proto-Rosicrucians and in fact the whole of Baroque music is said to have been inspired by alchemical ideas. One of its pioneers, the Italian Monteverdi (1567-1643), is widely believed to have been an alchemist, and to have incorporated into the structure of his music several alchemical principles.

THE MYSTERY OF ALCHEMY

The whole alchemical enterprise, then, remains

more or less a mystery, even though its net was very wide. Only very rarely indeed in history has it advanced into the light. One such occasion, referred to both by the Singers and by Pauwels and Bergier, was a strange encounter between an alchemist and Johann-Friedrich Schweitzer ('the Swiss', known as Helvetius), a seventeenth-century court physician at the Hague in Holland.

Helvetius was a convinced rationalist, well-respected, with a reputation for great learning. He was certainly no alchemical adept. He was, if anything, a profoundly sceptical man. Nevertheless, he was visited on the morning of December 27th, 1666 by a stranger. Pauwels and Bergier take up the story, quoting from an unnamed source:

> After asking Helvetius whether he believed in the philosopher's stone (to which the famous doctor replied in the negative) the stranger opened up a little ivory box "containing three pieces of a substance resembling glass or opal". He then declared that this was the famous stone, and that this very small amount was sufficient to produce twenty tons of gold. Helvetius held a fragment in his hand and, having thanked the stranger for his kindness, begged him to let him have a small piece. The alchemist bluntly refused, adding rather more courteously, that even in exchange for Helvetius's entire fortune he could not part with even the smallest piece of this mineral for a reason he was not permitted to disclose. When asked to prove his statement by performing a transmutation, the stranger replied that he would come back in three weeks' time and would show Helvetius something that would astonish him.

The stranger duly returned on the specified day, but refused to do any experiments, on the grounds that they were forbidden. He did, however, give Helvetius a small fragment of the stone "no larger than a mustard seed"; when the doctor expressed doubts about so minute a quantity having any effect at all, the alchemist broke the fragment in two and gave him back half, saying: "This is all you need".

Helvetius now confessed to the stranger that when he had last visited him he had managed to palm a few particles of the stone which had successfully changed lead, not into gold, but into glass. The alchemist, unruffled, said that he should have covered the particles with yellow wax, and that full transformation would have taken place if he had done so. He said that he would return the next morning to show Helvetius how it was done. But he never came back either then or later; and Helvetius' wife finally persuaded him to try the experiment for himself. Pauwels and Bergier continue:

> Helvetius followed the stranger's instructions. He melted down three drachmas [three-eighths of an ounce] of lead, wrapped the stone in wax and threw it into the liquid metal. It turned to gold! "We took it immediately to a goldsmith who declared that he had never seen a finer piece of gold, and offered us fifty florins for an ounce [of it]". Helvetius, concluding his report, informed us that he still possessed the ingot of gold, a tangible proof of the transmutation. "May the Holy Angels of God watch over him (the alchemist) as a source of blessings for Christianity. Such is our constant prayer, for him and for us".

News of what had happened travelled through the Hague like lightning and the philosopher Spinoza immediately set up his own investigation. He first went to see the goldsmith involved, who showed him some particles of silver that had been present in the mixture and had also turned into gold. He was, Spinoza found out, the official minter for the Duc d'Orange – and a thoroughly reliable witness. He then visited Helvetius…

... who showed him the gold, and the crucible used in the experiment. Some scraps of the precious metal were still adhering to the inside of the receptacle... [Like] the others, Spinoza was convinced that the transmutation really had taken place.

There are a few other examples in the literature of apparently successful transmutations (some performed by John Dee and Edward Kelley), but none at all with such a credible witness. Albertus Magnus is said to have produced an elixir which could cure illness and even bring a statue to life – and Albert was certainly no mountebank: he was a Dominican monk and the teacher of the influential Catholic theologian Thomas Aquinas; he made important contributions to science.

However, Aquinas believed that his elixir was the Devil's work and was said to have destroyed it after his master's death. Later in the same century, an alchemist called Nicholas Flamel claimed success in creating gold from base metals and he acquired a fortune, used in founding hospitals, chapels and churches, which seemed to prove it. The same was said of another alchemist in the early 1600s, one Count Moritz, but though he was surrounded by gossip and rumour and also had considerable riches, once again there was no evidence.

Isaac Newton was a firm believer in alchemical principles

MODERN 'ALCHEMY'

It took, of course, a further three hundred years for a scientist, Lord Rutherford, to demonstrate that one element could indeed be transformed into another, in his case nitrogen into oxygen. Today, manipulations of matter at the subatomic level, via particle accelerators, fission and fusion, are routine. So what generations of alchemists claimed darkly to be doing no longer seems utterly bizarre.

Alchemists spoke, for example, of needing to distil water many thousands of times in order to help prepare their mysterious elixir. Now we know, according to the account given by Pauwels' and Bergier, that processes of a similar sort are required to make heavy water. They spoke of needing almost endlesssly to refine metals and metalloids in order to change their properties. Today we understand, from early work on transistors, that the 'zone fusion' by which the germanium and silicon used were prepared works along similar lines. We know that alchemists were not entirely lunatic when they deliberately introduced small quantities of impurities into their crucibles. For we now appreciate, from the same work on transistors, that introducing into a purified metal selected impurities in minuscule quantities produces in it new – and often revolutionary – properties.

The alchemists did not, of course, have available to them any of the high technology available to the modern scientist. Having said that, they were not necessarily involved, for this reason, in some vain and mad pursuit. Isaac Newton, for his part, certainly did not believe so. He famously said, it will be remembered: "If I have seen further, it is by standing on the shoulders of giants" – the giants in question being the chain of *Illuminati*, going back to earliest times, in which he saw himself as a link.

Newton was extremely well read, in fact, in alchemical literature, and thought that it contained potentially important scientific secrets "there being other things beside the transmutation of metals (if these pretenders brag not) which none but they understand". Elsewhere, he wrote of one of his scientific experiments: "[The] way by which mercury may be so impregnated has been thought fit to be concealed by others that have known it, and therefore may possibly be an inlet to something more noble, not to be communicated without immense danger to the world, if there should be any verity in the Hermetic writings". In many of his scientific discoveries, in other words, Newton believed that he was travelling down paths already taken – and that they led to fundamental secrets that still lay beyond his reach. As a contemporary of his wrote:

Modesty teaches us to speak of the Ancients with respect, especially when we are not very familiar with their works. Newton, who knew them practically by heart, had the greatest respect for them, and considered them to be men of genius and superior intelligence who had carried their discoveries in every field much further than we today suspect, judging from what remains of their writings. More ancient writings have been lost than have been preserved, and perhaps our new discoveries are of less value than those we have lost.

A WORLD OF LOST KNOWLEDGE

We seem now, on the face of it, to have strayed a long way from Nostradamus. But he too, you will remember, had "numerous books that I have come upon that have been hidden for long centuries", which he "made a gift to Vulcan", i.e. burned.

The burning (or destruction) of such old and perhaps unique manuscripts goes back a very long way. The vast library at Alexandria, for example, was destroyed by fire, as was the great collection of books at Pergamum. No-one knows what happened to the Pisistratus collections in Athens or the library of the Jerusalem Temple. Tyrants like the Emperor Chou-Huang Ti in China and Diocletian in Rome, meanwhile, made a habit of consigning vast piles of manuscripts to the flames and there is no doubt that during the so-called Dark Ages huge numbers of texts (each one written by hand, remember, before printing) were lost.

What we know of the ancient world and its thinkers, in fact, is more or less a matter of accident, dependent on chance survival – and we all too often have to rely on references in writings that do remain extant for the tantalizing glimpses we have of knowledge achieved – it seems to us now – well before its time. We know, for example, from the surviving writings of Aristotle and others that the idea that all things are composed of tiny particles called atoms and that their constant motion explains the creation of the universe was first proposed by the pre-Socratic Greek philosopher Democritus – and that even then he was drawing on ideas already in circulation, one of which held that the atom was potentially divisible.

Anaximander, through his notion of the infinite and indefinite, was the first man to propose the indestructibility of matter in the sixth century BC. Thales, his teacher, declared that the

Milky Way was composed of galaxies, each consisting of a sun and its planets, in an immensity of space. He is also said to have correctly predicted a solar eclipse. Pythagoras, another rough contemporary, announced that the earth was round, that it revolved around a fixed object, and also – long before Newton – that the force of the attraction between objects varied inversely as the square of the distance between them. Lucretius, in the first century B.C, clearly understood the theory of the uniformity of speed of bodies falling in a vacuum – and so on, and so on.

How on earth did such Ancients, as Newton called them – fully acknowledging his debt to them and to others like them, perhaps now unknown – gain their knowledge in the absence of telescopes, microscopes or any other modern technological aid? We have no idea, but we do know that they also possessed a good deal of knowledge which we are only now beginning to regain.

'Ancients' worked, for example, with extremely difficult substances like copper oxides, and with alloys with special properties, like electrum. They had a profound knowledge of the properties and uses of glass; they had special compounds for the treatment of burns – and even for application to fabric to make it fire-proof and impenetrable by steel. They used a large variety of plant-products as medicines (now being investigated world-wide by the West's pharmaceutical companies) and they seem to have had knowledge both of immunization and of anti-bacteriological agents. All the great scientists of Nostradamus' period, Copernicus, Galileo and Paracelsus – like Newton – fully acknowledged that their discoveries had been facilitated by ancient texts.

It was in the fields of metallurgy, however, and of what might be called 'catalytic chemistry' that the tradition of the Ancients was most strong. This, of course, brings us back to the laboratories of the alchemists, to their furnaces, alembics, crucibles and retorts, and to the long tradition of their labours, stretching back to well before the time of Christ. It also brings us back to my earlier question: What on earth were they up to?

THE ALCHEMICAL VISION

Pauwels and Bergier, in their book *The Morning of the Magicians*, published originally in Paris in 1960, have been among the very few ever to have attempted a coherent account of the alchemical laboratory programme from a scientific point of view. (Pauwels was a writer/editor with an interest in the occult, Bergier a physical chemist. They had met and corresponded with a number of twentieth-century alchemists.)

They begin in *The Morning of the Magicians* with a preamble pointing out that science doesn't necessarily have to mean 'big' science. Radio-activity and wave mechanics, after all, were both discoveries made by men working in isolation. Rutherford "did some of his fundamental work on the structure of matter with old tins and bits of string" and "Jean Perrin and Mme. Curie before the war sent their assistants to the Flea Market on Sunday to look for material." The writers continue, "In the days when the electron was considered to be the fourth state of matter, extremely elaborate and costly machinery was invented to produce electronic currents. Later on, in 1910, Elster and Gaitel showed that it was enough to heat lime [in a vacuum] to a dull red heat".

THE ALCHEMIST AT WORK

The alchemist, with his similarly primitive tools, starts his career by spending many years deciphering old texts which he begins to understand, despite all the obstacles set in his path,

The alchemist needed to be extremely methodical over the many months his experiments would take him

"with the help of patience, humility and faith". Once this has been achieved, he can begin. He first prepares in a mortar made of agate a mixture of three ingredients:

The first, in a proportion of 95 per cent, is some sort of ore: arseno-pyrites, for example, an iron ore containing among its impurities arsenic and antimony. The second is a metal: iron, lead, silver or mercury. The third is an acid of organic origin, such as tartaric or citric acid.

The alchemist continues to grind and mix these ingredients for five or six months. He then heats the mixture, increasing the temperature extremely slowly over a period of days, being careful to avoid the mercury vapour and arseno-hydrogen that is released.

Finally, he dissolves the contents of his crucible by means of an acid applied under polarised light – "i.e. either weak sunlight reflected in a mirror or the light of the moon" – which vibrates in one direction only, rather than vibrating in every direction round an axis. It was in the alchemists' historical search for a suitable solvent to be used at this stage that they discovered acetic acid, nitric acid and sulphuric acid.

The next step is to evaporate the liquid and to re-calcine the solid residue, an operation that is repeated thousands of times. Pauwels and Bergier ask:

Why? We do not know. Perhaps [the alchemist] *is waiting for the moment when all the most favourable conditions will be fulfilled: cosmic rays, terrestrial magnetism, etc. Perhaps it is in order to obtain a condition of 'fatigue' in the structure of matter of which we still know nothing. The alchemist speaks of 'a sacred patience' and of the slow condensation of the 'universal spirit'. But behind this para-religious language there is surely something hidden... The alchemist repeats his operation*

without any variation until something extraordinary happens.

In Pauwels and Bergier's view, the alchemist, in almost endlessly repeating precisely the same protocol, must believe in something very like Wolfgang Pauli's 'principle of exclusion', for which he won the Nobel Prize in 1945. The 'principle of exclusion' holds that in any given system (like the atom) no two electrons (or protons or mesons) can be in the same quantum state. When a particle is added to a system, it must therefore assume a different quantum state from the other particles within it, and its combination with them must create a new and unique system.

In the same way, the alchemist must trust that no two of his experiments can be exactly the same, since they take place within a system which varies each time for other (cosmological? astronomical? spiritual?) reasons. This is comparable to the process of the detection on earth of cosmic rays, in which there is no alternative to waiting, in the hope of being in the right place at the right time – and no result that is either identical or predictable. What the alchemist is waiting for is equally unpredictable, a 'revelation' like those of Nostradamus – though we have no idea what form this 'revelation' may take.

For all this, say Pauwels and Bergier, something finally happens that indicates that the first phase is completed.

[The alchemist] *then adds to his mixture an oxidizing agent, for example, potassium nitrate. His crucible already contains sulphur obtained from pyrites and carbon from the organic acid. Sulphur, carbon and nitrate: it was in performing this operation that the old alchemists discovered gunpowder.*

Over and over again he continues this operation of dissolving and then re-heating for months and years without respite, always waiting for a sign. As to the nature of this sign, the books on alchemy differ, but this is perhaps because there are several phenomena that might occur. The sign appears at the moment of melting. For some alchemists it will appear in the form of crystals shaped like stars on the surface of the solution, while in other cases a layer of oxide forms on the surface and then breaks up, revealing the luminous metal in which can be seen a reflection in miniature, of the Milky Way, perhaps, or some of the constellations.

On receiving this sign, the alchemist removes his mixture from the crucible and allows it to 'ripen', protected from the air and from damp, until the first days of Spring. When he resumes his operations, these will be directed towards what is called in the old texts, 'the preparation of darkness'.

At this point the mixture is placed in a transparent receptacle made of rock crystal [a vacuum?] and sealed in some special 'Hermetic' way. [The word 'Hermetic' is derived from the name of the Greek god of science and the arts, Hermes, who was identified by the Neoplatonists, mystics, and alchemists with the Egyptian god Thoth, the supposed inventor of a process of making a glass tube airtight by use of a secret magical seal.]

It is then brought very carefully to a temperature at which it will incandesce (give off light), but without exploding – the aim being to produce by another cycle of ceaseless cooling and reheating a blue-black 'essence' or 'fluid' which alchemists sometimes refer to as 'raven's wing' or 'alchemist's egg'. This operation, according to Pauwels and Bergier:

... has no equivalent in modern physics and chemistry, and yet it is not without analogues. When a metal such as copper is dissolved in liquid ammoniac gas it turns a dark blue colour, verging on black in massive concen-

trations. The same phenomenon occurs if hydrogen under pressure, or organic amines, are dissolved in liquefied ammoniac gas to produce the unstable compound [known as 'ammonium'] which has all the properties of an alkaline metal... There is reason to believe [too] that this blue-black colouration... is [that] of electronic gas. What is electronic gas? It is the term applied by... scientists to the whole body of free electrons which constitute a metal and endow it with all its mechanical, electric and thermal properties. It corresponds to what the alchemist calls the 'soul' or the 'essence' of metals [which is precisely what he is after within his 'Hermetically'-sealed receptacle].

The next stage described is the decanting in the dark (by its own light) of the resultant fluorescent liquid, which solidifies and breaks up in contact with air. What has now been created by the alchemist is a substance or substances unknown in nature: in effect a new kind of (decomposed and recomposed) matter, even new elements. This may well seem nonsensical to an orthodox physical chemist, but as Hamlet said: 'There are more things in heaven and earth, Horatio, than are dreamed of in your philosophy".

The alchemist's task now becomes two-fold. First he washes and then rewashes over an extended period the residue or dregs that remain in the receptacle in triple-distilled water, making sure throughout that he keeps the water away from the light and from variations in temperature. "This water," say Pauwels and Bergier, "is said to have extraordinary chemical and medicinal properties. It is the universal solvent, the elixir of tradition that ensures longevity, the elixir of Faust" and they contend that its role – as a solvent, at any rate – is not inconsistent with modern science.

The alchemist's second task is to recombine the solid substances – "the simple elements" –

which he has obtained. He mixes and melts them at low temperature with catalysers unknown to us, and ultimately achieves metals – alchemic gold, alchemic silver and alchemic copper, for example – which are indistinguishable from the forms of these metals that we know, but now have extraordinary new properties. Alchemic copper, for example, has "virtually no resistance to electricity"; it is super-conductive, just like those metals created by physicists today at temperatures close to absolute zero.

Another novel substance is soluble in glass at low temperature: even before it has melted, it suffuses it with a dark red colour, as well as with a mauve fluorescence visible in the dark. (John Dee had just such a piece of glass, which he used for divination – and which Queen Elizabeth once saw at his house outside Richmond.) When this alchemic glass is ground in a mortar, the powder that is the result is the so-called 'projection powder' or 'Philosopher's Stone', capable of transmuting base metals such as copper, aluminium and nickel and perhaps even acting as "a sort of reservoir of nuclear energy, controllable to any degree".

THE ENLIGHTENMENT OF THE ALCHEMIST

What Pauwels and Bergier do not give an account of is the process of purification which the alchemist himself is patently seen as undergoing in the course of his long labours in the laboratory: his parallel personal and spiritual transformation. They speak vaguely of "forces emitted by the crucible (that is to say, radiations emitted by nuclei undergoing changes in structure)", of psychic 'mutations' and trance-states induced by gases.

It is clear that, for Pauwels and Bergier, these

The decanting and breaking up of alchemical fluid is represented here by the birds flying from the tree

– if they are to be given any credence at all – are just side-show epiphenomena, for absolutely central to the alchemist's quest from the beginning, is the conscious search, not only for the ultimate secrets of the universe, but also for complete spiritual refinement. Scientific objectivity as understood today is out of the question in this long process. Total personal involvement is mandatory – so much so that the alchemist is often identified in the texts with the gradually changing substance within his 'Hermetically'-sealed receptacle. What he too is after in the end is the release of his own hidden potentialities, with the ultimate goal – precisely that offered in Buddhist teachings – of 'enlightenment' or 'awakening' of inherent powers.

What this 'enlightenment' or 'awakening' consists of we have, of course, no idea. But the analogy with Buddhism suggests that it involves a gradually achieved, or else instantaneous, perception of the Oneness of the universe; a fusion, if you like, in the individual of the two worlds of Heaven and Earth that are connected, in one of the most enduring symbols of the Kabbala, by the tree of the soul. And it brings within its gift, according to alchemical tradition, immortality: the ability to stand outside time and be connected to both past and future.

That this 'enlightenment' was the ultimate goal of the alchemist was ultimately confirmed in an extraordinary interview the physical chemist (and co-author of *The Morning of the Magicians*) Jacques Bergier once had with an anonymous man to whom he had been introduced by his laboratory chief, the celebrated nuclear physicist André Helbronner (later to die in Buchenwald).

THE FULCANELLI INTERVIEW

The meeting took place one afternoon in June 1937 "in the prosaic surroundings of a test laboratory at the offices of the Gas Board in Paris"; and Bergier believed that the person sitting

The Hermes bird, representing enlightenment, the ultimate goal of the alchemist

opposite him – though he could never confirm this – was someone who had written two important books on alchemical themes, *Les Demeures Philosophales* and *Le Mystère des Cathédrales*, under the pen-name of Fulcanelli (derived, perhaps, from the Roman god Vulcan, whose fire burned Nostradamus' books).

The man known as Fulcanelli began by referring to the work Helbronner (with Bergier) was doing at the time on nuclear energy. He said, in what is described as an exact account of their conversation:

> 'M. André Helbronner, whose assistant I believe you are, is carrying out research on nuclear energy. M. Helbronner has been good enough to keep me informed as to the results of some of his experiments… You are on the brink of success, as indeed are several of our scientists today. May I be allowed to warn you to be careful? The search in which you and

your colleagues are engaged is fraught with terrible dangers, not only for yourselves, but for the whole human race. The liberation of atomic energy is easier than you think, and the radio-activity artificially produced can poison the atmosphere of our planet in the space of a few years. Moreover, atomic explosives can be produced from a few grammes of metal powerful enough to destroy whole cities. I am telling you this as a fact: the alchemists have known it for a very long time.'

At this point Bergier attempted to interrupt but 'Fulcanelli' continued:

> 'I know what you are going to say, but it's of no interest. The alchemists were ignorant of the structure of the nucleus, knew nothing about electricity and had no means of detection. Therefore they have never been able to perform any transmutation, still less liberate nuclear energy. I shall not attempt to prove to you what I am now going to say, but I ask you to repeat it to M. Helbronner: certain geometrical arrangements of highly purified materials are enough to release atomic force without having recourse to either electricity or vacuum techniques.'

Fulcanelli then quoted from Frederick Soddy's *The Interpretation of Radium*:

> "I believe that there have been civilizations in the past that were familiar with nuclear energy, and that by misusing it they were totally destroyed".

He went on:

> 'I would ask you to believe that certain techniques have partially survived. I would also ask you to remember that the alchemists' researches were coloured by moral and religious preoccupations, whereas modern physics was created in the eighteenth century for their

amusement by a few aristocrats and wealthy libertines. Science without a conscience... I have thought it my duty to warn a few research workers here and there, [though] I have no hope of seeing this warning prove effective'.

Bergier had himself developed an interest in alchemy within the past year and had found himself "surrounded by impostors" and "fantastic explanations". He could not believe that 'Fulcanelli' spent his time in the pursuit of fabricating gold. He asked him: "Can you tell me, sir, what is the nature of your researches?" 'Fulcanelli' replied:

'You ask me to summarize for you in four minutes four thousand years of philosophy and the efforts of a lifetime. Furthermore, you ask me to translate into ordinary language concepts for which such a language is not intended. All the same, I can tell you this much: you are aware that in the official science of today the role of the observer becomes more and more important. Relativity, the principle of indeterminacy, show the extent to which the observer today intervenes in all these phenomena. The secret of alchemy is this: there is a way of manipulating matter and energy so as to produce what modern scientists call "a field of force". This field acts on the observer and puts him in a privileged position vis-à-vis the Universe. From this position he has access to the realities which are ordinarily hidden from us by time and space, matter and energy. This is what we call "The Great Work"...'

'The Great Work', "realities which are ordinarily hidden from us". Once again there are echoes of Nostradamus.

The above account of the alchemical enterprise may be both speculative and inconclusive. Perhaps it should be stressed once again that men of the highest intellectual quality, men indeed like Nostradamus, seem to have com-

mitted their lives to it over countless generations. Because it seems bizarre and virtually inexplicable does not mean that it was deluded. John Dee was regarded as the most brilliant mathematician of his day and the fact that his mathematics was dedicated to uniting all spheres from the earthbound to the celestial – for all that it involved the conjuring of angels – seems in retrospect to presage the contemporary search for a similar mathematics capable of explaining within its formulaic thickets both molecular and cosmic events.

Extraordinary scientific experiments, moreover, such as the recently claimed virtually desktop demonstration of nuclear fission, have used little more equipment than the alchemists had available to them. Who is to say that it has failed to be replicated in other laboratories because of a now unknown variable – like terrestrial magnetism, say – of which the alchemists had a better understanding? This is at least suggested by a remark made to Jacques Bergier by Fulcanelli's publisher and disciple, Eugène Canseliet, after Bergier had written, as part of an introduction to an anthology of sixteenth-century poetry, about the alchemists' perhaps necessary cult of secrecy:

It is most important that this remark [of yours] should not be dismissed as a mere pleasantry. You are quite right, and I am in a position to state that it is possible to produce an atomic fission by means of an ore, which is relatively common and cheap, and that this can be done with no other apparatus than a good stove, a coal-fusing oven, some Meker burners and four bottles of butane gas".

Whether we believe this or not, it is becoming increasingly clear that the cosmos we inhabit today – with its anti-particles and parallel universes – is at least as rum as the secret world of 'magic, Kabbala and alchemy' from which Nostradamus' *Prophéties* emerged.

NOSTRADAMUS: THE CAUTIOUS ALCHEMIST

That Nostradamus was indeed involved in this complex lost world of 'magic, Kabbala and alchemy' cannot now seriously be doubted. He had all the necessary tools of the trade: a deep knowledge of mathematics and astrology and also, according to many commentators – basing their evidence on a close reading of his texts as well as tradition – of the Kabbala.

He was a doctor in the mould of the alchemist Paracelsus, whom it is not too far-fetched to believe he might have met during the latter's wanderings in Europe. He was certainly (perhaps intimately) acquainted with at least one of the most famous esoteric philosophers of his time. He translated a book that was part of the Hermetic tradition and he travelled widely in Italy, where Hermetic lore was intensively studied and where some elements of what was later to culminate in the vehemently anti-Papist Rosicrucian movement were already taking shape. He may indeed have been referring to the Rosicrucian movement, to its first emergence in Germany and to its gathering influence when he prophesied in century III, no. 67:

> *A new sect of Philosophers*
> *Despising death, gold, honours and riches:*
> *They shall not be limited by the mountains of*
>   *Germany,*
> *They shall have a host of followers and much*
>   *support*

We know that Nostradamus also seems to have been anxious for the major part of his career to avoid attention. He quit Montpellier University rather than accept a chair, as noted earlier, and he settled, instead, in relative obscurity, in an ex-English territory where the chances of detec-tion and denunciation may have been signifi-cantly smaller. He subsequently left his retreat in Agen, after the death of his first family, per-haps in the wake of a heresy charge, and he committed himself to a life, as both Paracelsus and Bruno did for different periods, of constant movement.

Somewhere along the way, he amassed his library of books 'that have been hidden for long centuries' – which he later, *"observing the principles of perfect transformation… and that of the incorruptible subterranean metals subjected to occult waves"* consigned to the flames (of Vulcan). There is no question that he was at the least entirely familiar with the programme of the alchemical quest, that he knew and used the obscure imagery of the 'ancient' texts – and was, perhaps, in consequence an adept of the sort of codes and cyphers used by that other contemporary French alchemist, Blaise Vigenère. It is tempting to believe, too, that his methods of divination involved the conjuring of angels.

Any and all of this would, of course, under normal circumstances, have brought him to the attention of the Inquisition – and it is worth stepping aside for just a moment to consider what he would have been up against.

THE HOLY INQUISITION

The Holy Inquisition had originally been set up in 1233 by Pope Gregory IX to combat the Albigensian heresy. With the spread of the Reformation, however, and its considerable and ongoing threat to the authority of Mother Church, the institution was given a new importance, and moved (in 1542, twenty-four years before Nostradamus' death) to the Holy Office. This was more than half a century after the investigations of heretics and infiltrators, in Spain at any rate, had been ratcheted up a notch with the foundation of the (separate) Spanish Inquisition, set up by the country's rulers in the first instance to measure the sincerity, by the harshest methods, of converted Muslims and Jews.

In 1484, a Papal Bull, emanating from Rome, had announced that no-one but members of the Catholic Church could claim truly to be in contact with divine powers. The only miracles were those sanctioned by God and his Church; anyone else having any truck at all with the supernatural must be doing so through the direct intervention of Satan. There could be no such thing as neutral or mechanical (i.e. Godless) magic. It was approved either by God (i.e. by the Church) or by Satan – and that was that.

A further two years after the Papal Bull of 1484, a book appeared, the *Malleus Maleficarum*, which laid down the ground rules for hunting out magicians and witches, who (in the words of the Bull), "at the instigation of the Enemy of the human race… do not shrink from committing and perpetrating the foulest excesses to the peril of their souls, whereby they offend the Divine Majesty". It was quite clear from this book that, once within the net of the Inquisition or witch-finder, there was no real escape. Alibis were not acceptable, since those who worshipped the Devil had the power to be in – at least – two places at once.

Even confession was not necessarily a recourse, since Devil-worshippers could not be expected to confess everything willingly – if they confessed without torture, then they had to be hiding something even worse. Torture was actually regarded as helping its victim, since "suffering led to purification, a partial expiation of sin. The confessed and repentant [even though broken in body]… could expect at least some mercy in the afterlife. The torturers thought of themselves as doing their victims a favour". Once accusers arrived at a victim's door, in other words, his or her fate was sealed. As the French juror Jean Bodin wrote in *his Demonomania of Witches* of 1580:

The names of all informers are to be kept secret. Children are to be forced to testify against their parents… Suspicion is sufficient ground for torture… A person once accused must never be acquitted, unless the falsity of the accuser… is clearer than the light of day. No punishment is too cruel for witches, including hot irons to their flesh. The judge who does not roundly execute a convicted witch should himself be put to death… Better to burn the innocent than let one guilty [person] escape.

It is no wonder, given all this, that Nostradamus fled Agen, if the tradition is true, at the first suggestion of heresy, and that he later, in his preface, went out of his way specifically to exonerate his son César from any possible accusation of being involved in what his father was up to. As for himself, he had by that time acquired a powerful defence that made him virtually immune from attack: the protection of the wife of the king of France.

PROTECTION IN HIGH PLACES

We know Nostradamus dedicated the Hermetic book he had translated to the Princess of Navarre – the equivalent of taking out insurance against an adverse reaction to its publication. The patronage of the wife of Henri II, Catherine de' Medici, was, however, infinitely more important.

Nostradamus seems to have received a summons to Paris some time in the middle of 1555, shortly after the appearance of the first of his *Prophéties*, which had gained the praise of the courtier and poet Jean Dorat. (Dorat went on to arouse the interest of one of his pupils, Jean de Chavigny, who had been mayor of Beaune. De Chavigny later made pilgrimage to Salon and stayed there, becoming Nostradamus' assistant and first biographer.) The invitation must – it is generally agreed – have come from Catherine, since Henri was much more given to hunting and sexual conquest than he was to astrology, which was one of Catherine's greatest interests. A Spaniard at the French court, Francisco de Alova, later remarked that she always quoted Nostradamus' words with utter confidence, "as if she was citing St. Mark or St. Luke."

What exactly happened during Nostradamus' visit to the court we simply do not know. What we do know is that he stayed at the town house of the Archbishop of Sens (another form of insurance), and that he was called on for consultations there by a steady stream of French nobles – his reputation obviously having preceded him. He is also said to have had an interview with Henri II, during which he offered to translate into plain language his quatrains – a gift which the King, bored with such things, did not accept. Whether he made

the same offer to Queen Catherine is again not known for sure, although he is said to have shown her a magic mirror (or perhaps a crystal) in which she made out three of her seven children occupying the throne of France – as they subsequently did.

If he did decode the first collection of *Prophéties* to her, then she would have known in precise detail the fate of her little-loved husband – and a great deal more besides, for the tenth quatrain of the first century reads:

> *Sergeants sent into the iron vault*
> *Where the seven children of the king are*
>   *placed:*
> *The ancestors and forefathers will emerge*
>   *from hell*
> *Lamenting to see the death of the fruit of*
>   *their line.*

Catherine de' Medici with Nostradamus. Her great interest in astrology is thought to have led to his invitation to visit her court

Catherine and Henri II had seven children (just as in the quatrain) and they must have expected their sons to have male children of their own to continue their line – but they didn't. Of the three of them who came to the throne, François II died within a year at the age of seventeen; Charles IX, his successor, died after fourteen years at the age of 28; their brother Henri III ruled for a further fifteen years before being finally assassinated. Nostradamus had already written of this last event (I, 97):

> *What neither fire nor iron could achieve*
> *Shall be done by a smooth tongue in council.*
> *In a dream in sleep the king shall think*
> *The enemy more in fire and military blood.*

This prophecy, too, came true. Three days before he died, Henri III had a dream in which he saw the royal regalia being trampled underfoot by a mob. Then, on August 2nd 1589, he was approached by a young monk called Jacques Clement who claimed to have knowledge of a secret letter. As he whispered in the King's ear, Clement produced a dagger and stabbed him in the stomach. Henri died the next day. His sister, Queen Margot of Navarre (by marriage), died twenty-six years later, in 1615, five years after the death of her husband, Henri IV of Navarre, the first of the Bourbon dynasty. The Valois line thus came to an end.

A year before his death, Henri III had done his desperate best to maintain the balance of power in France by having the Duc de Guise assassinated – and even this, in almost the last quatrain in his first collection (III, 51) Nostradamus had already prefigured:

> *Paris conspires to commit a great murder;*
> *Blois shall make it come to pass;*
> *The people of Orléans will want to replace*
>   *their leader,*
> *Angier, Troyes and Langre will make them*
>   *pay the price.*

The de Guise family were vehemently anti-Protestant and the third Duc, Henri of Lorraine, whose father François had virtually ruled France during the reign of the boy-king François II, had played a leading role (along with Catherine de' Medici) in the 1572 slaughter of Protestants in Paris known as the St. Bartholomew's Day Massacre.

Furthermore, Henri – though a supporter and friend of Henri III – had decided that the king was becoming 'soft' on Protestants and had formed a 'Holy League' of militant Catholics. Shortly after war broke out between the League and the Protestant Henri of Navarre, Henri of Lorraine was assassinated by the royal guards at the palace at Blois as Henri himself looked on from a hiding-place.

The citizens of Orleans, when they heard of the Duc's murder, overthrew their royal governor and appointed in his place a Guise relative and Angiers, Troyes and Langre, among other towns, soon threw in their lot with the League. Henri III was later excommunicated by the Pope, and formed an alliance with Henri of Navarre, the Protestant ruler of a small kingdom on French territory who was ultimately to succeed him.

Whether Nostradamus revealed any of this – *en clair*, so to speak – to Queen Catherine is unknown. If he did, perhaps she didn't care. Better to have three sons rule France than not – she was an extremely ruthless woman. It is said that he cast the horoscopes of the royal children and that Catherine later offered him the post of Royal Astrologer several times – a post which he declined. She also went out of her way to visit him in Salon, alongside her son Charles IX, while on a royal progress and persuaded Charles to present him with a very large sum of money. She, at any rate – whatever the Church might have thought of Nostradamus' background in 'magic, the Kabbala and alchemy' and however difficult the code he used in his *Prophéties* – was a believer.

IX

THE
PROPHECIES
OF
NOSTRADAMUS

THE TIME-SPAN AND END-POINT OF THE PROPHECIES

There are suggestions in several of Nostradamus' quatrains, as well as in the letter he addressed to his son César, that he wrote a straightforward and undisguised version of at least some of his *Prophéties*, a version he believed would either come to light at some time in the future or would be made available in the form of a finally successful translation. In the letter to César, for example, he speaks of a future disaster involving "the waters of the earth and continual rains", and then adds almost as an afterthought:

. . as I have set down in writing more extensively in my other writings, which are composed in free speech and which define the places, times and the pre-determined limit in which future mankind will unerringly recognize the events when they happen… When the obstacle of ignorance has been removed, fate will be easier to see.

Also, in century III, no. 94, he writes:

More than five hundred years will be taken into account,
Then he who was the ornament of his age
Will all of a sudden give so clear a light
That he will make glad the people of that century.

This suggests that the *Prophéties*, found *en clair* (or successfully interpreted), will provide a beacon of hope: that they will finally emerge – probably before the "more than five hundred years" are up – in a time of seeming catastrophe, and will be a comfort to people facing what seems to be a hopeless future. A further

quatrain (II, 27) appears to announce that this will happen during a time of great irreligiousness, and that efforts will be made to cover up the discovery:

The divine word shall be struck from the sky
And will not be able to proceed further.
The secret of the close-mouthed one will be stopped
And marchers will pass behind and before it.

Elsewhere (in VIII, 66 and 1, 27), it it is suggested (at least) that this prose version of Nostradamus' will be found as a result of some sort of archaeological expedition, and there may even be a clue as to its whereabouts:

When the writing D.M. is found
And an ancient lamplit cave discovered,
Law, King and prince Ulpian will be proved,
With Pavilion, Queen and Duke under the cover.

and

Beneath a Guian chain broken from the sky,
Not far from there is hidden the treasure
Which for long centuries has been gathering.
Once found, he shall die, his eye put out by a spring.

The 'ancient lamplit cave' of course brings to mind the burial vault of Brother R.C. with its many wonders, and D.M. immediately suggests Nostradamus himself, Doctor of Medicine (*Doctor Medicinae*), a degree held also, on the face of it, by the Brethren of the Rosy Cross in the *Fama*.

One must assume, however, that the Indiana-Jones-style adventure to retrieve the manuscript, with its overtones of dangerous traps, secrecy, suppression and a battle between the forces of good and evil, has not yet taken place – or else has been successfully covered up.

The struggle to interpret Nostradamus' own

Nostradamus' wish was that the Prophéties *should bring comfort to a turbulent, unhappy world*

language, according to different formulae, still continues without let-up, leaving in its wake the failed attempts of those who have come before. I have in front of me as I write, for example, 'solutions' which variously announce, on the basis of the quatrains, that George Bush Senior will be re-elected in 1992; Prince Charles and Princess Diana will take the throne of Britain in the same year; Israel will be defeated by her Arab neighbours around 1996 and that scientists will reverse the processes of ageing in 1998.

How, then, should we today go about the astonishingly difficult business of interpreting the *Prophéties*? What sort of time frame, for example, do they cover? In two of his quatrains (X, 74 and I, 48), the Sage of Salon suggests the beginnings of an answer:

At the turn of the great number the seventh,
It shall come to pass at the time of the
  Hecatomb games,
Not far from the great age of the millennium,
That the buried shall leave their graves.

and

When twenty years of the Moon's reign have
  passed,
Seven thousand more will hold its monarchy,
When the sun reclaims its leftover days,
Then is my prophecy accomplished and ends.

We will pass over for the moment the suggestion made by some that the second quatrain prefigures the end of the world as the result of some sort of solar explosion. Important here are two things: first, the possibility that the first quatrain refers to the Olympic Games in Athens in 2004 ('not far from the great age of the millennium'), when an apocalyptic event (or the first successful cloning of a human, or the reappearance of people believed dead) will occur, and second, the reference in both quatrains to a period of seven thousand years (perhaps plus twenty) representing some sort of final fulfilment of the *Prophéties*. This theme is taken up by Nostradamus in the letter to his son César:

> *Though we are at the seventh number of a thousand which completes everything, we are nearing the eighth, where the firmament of the eighth sphere is in a latitudinal dimension where the great eternal God will come to finish the revolution…*

One of the most creditable attempts at discovering the end-point of the *Prophéties* has been undertaken by respected Nostradamian commentator Luciano Sampietro.

LUCIANO SAMPIETRO'S INVESTIGATIONS

Using the letter to César as a starting point – i.e. arguing that Nostradamus in 1555 is saying that the eighth millennium is due to arrive relatively soon, some time within the next five hundred years , say – Sampietro in *Nostradamus: The Final Prophecies* turns his attention to some extremely baffling calculations of the passage of time in the Bible that Nostradamus introduces into his letter to César.

Extrapolating from these, Sampietro then manages – not without some *légerdemain*, it has to be said – to establish a tentative starting-point for Nostradamus' successive millennia with the beginning of Egyptian civilisation around 5000 B.C. He also establishes an end-date for the prophecies of c. 2025-6 AD.

He also makes an an extremely interesting

analysis of a dedication Nostradamus wrote for the full edition of the *Prophéties* published in 1568, two years after his death. This dedication is on the face of it addressed to the French King Henri II; and it is divided into short numbered sections, which sometimes begin in the middle of a sentence. All in all it is a very puzzling document indeed, with a large number of internal contradictions.

Sampietro plays a game of cut-up and collage with some of the dedication's most mysterious sections, in a way that Nostradamus himself seems to suggest, For he says that here too "in these discourses" he is laying down his "predictions in… a confused way". Putting together section 91 with sections 40 and 41 (all headed by Roman numerals in the original), for example, Sampietro captures what could be a prediction of the invention of the propeller and ships' engines. Further, by removing section 106 from the context of its preceding section, he suggests that Nostradamus had in mind a disastrous event occurring in a particular year, the culmination of a steady erosion of the authority of the Church and of human values. He translates Nostradamus as saying in section 105:

> *Putting the tail in the place of the head* [i.e. beginning at the end], *on the basis of a conjunction of Jupiter with Mercury, with a quadrature of Mars and Mercury, while the Dragon's head* [the north mode of the Moon] *with a conjunction of the Sun and Jupiter, the year shall be peaceful and without eclipse, but not altogether, and will be the beginning which will allow for an understanding of what then will come.*

This year – "near the end of his prophecies," Sampietro concludes Nostradamus as saying – can be identified as 1994: the only year in which the astrological and solar conditions – as well as that of relative world peace – can be met. During this particular year the war in Bosnia was already past its peak. However, the United States intervened, economic sanctions were imposed on Serbia, and for the first time NATO planes attacked Serbian-Bosnian lines. Sampietro continues:

> For the first time since the end of the Second World War, Western countries were involved in war activities in Europe. Subsequently, the war broke out in Kosovo… and in 1999 [NATO], as it had done in Bosnia, decided [to bombard] Belgrade and other cities in the Yugoslav Federation.

The other decisive event of 1994, maintains Sampietro, was the birth of an autonomous Palestinian state under Yasser Arafat. This was supposed to create a lasting peace between the Palestinians and the Israeli state, but its subsequent consequences have been dire: terrorist attacks and escalating retaliation, the 'Intifada', the destruction of villages and refugee camps, open military conflict. Sampietro concludes, after a sideways glance at Russia's continued ambition to preserve its super-power status and its disastrous war in Chechnya:

> If… the Balkan conflict in its various phases has brought about a substantial change in the rules governing international military intervention within a state for declared humanitarian reasons, the Middle Eastern question, with all its political, economic and religious implications, has created a situation of permanent conflict due to the simple impossibility of resolving the problems arising from irreconcilable claims by both parties and to the perennial presence of tension and violence in the daily life of these territories.

All this was written before the events of 9/11 and the successive retaliatory invasions of Afghanistan and Iraq. So Sampietro's notion that 'beginning of the end' lay in a conflict which pitted Muslims and Christians against one another for the first time in the modern age and in the increasing animosity between Palestinians and Israelis, is extremely plausible. Nostradamus in his view (pre-9/11) was predicting a gathering war between Islam and the other 'religions of the Book' (Christianity and Judaism), a war whose result would be what Nostradamus calls 'conflagration' – i.e. a Third World War.

It is of note that the war is described by Nostradamus, in both the dedication to César and in a number of quatrains, in terms very similar to those used by St. John the Divine in his Book of Revelation, also known as the Book of the Apocalypse.

PREDICTIONS OF PAST EVENTS

It is now time to take a look at those predictions of Nostradamus which are generally considered to have already been fulfilled – and see whether they offer a clue to his methods and to the way in which he uses anagrams, codes and mystification to cover his tracks. In this, I shall largely follow the schema (and many of the interpretations) laid out by Damon Wilson in his excellent *The Mammoth Book of Prophecies*. I will take the prophecies in temporal sequence, as he does, beginning in Nostradamus' own century.

ROYAL REVELATIONS

> The marriage they will celebrate will be
> unhappy;
> Great will be the joy, but the result will be
> misery.
> Husband and mother will despise the
> daughter-in law
> The Phybe dead and the daughter-in law
> most pitiful.

The unfortunate Mary, Queen of Scots, who was possibly the subject of Nostradamus' quatrain X, 55

This quatrain (X, 55) has often been taken to refer to the marriage of Prince Charles and Diana Spencer (and/or the marriage of Prince Andrew to Sarah Ferguson). However there is at least a possibility that the word usually translated as 'husband' (the old French form, *mary*, given at the beginning of the line a capital letter) actually refers to a foreign woman called Mary – rather than the French form Marie.

The best candidate under these circumstances is Mary, Queen of Scots, whom Nostradamus may have met, since both visited the French court in 1556. Mary was married to the doomed young man who became François II, and whose name may well be concealed in the curious word 'Phybe'. Phy is extremely close to the classical Greek F (*phi*), and the suffix '-be' suggests *beta*, the Greek alphabet's second letter – thus giving us F2, or François II.

The difficult part of the translation is line 3, if the identification of Mary is accepted. It may perhaps refer to the extreme animosity between François' mother, Catherine de' Medici, and Mary's, who was Marie de Guise. Apart from this, though, the reading is clear enough, since Mary, after the premature death of her husband, did indeed have a miserable life, in part because of events prefigured elsewhere, in VIII, 23:

> Letters are found in the Queen's coffers,
> No signature, no name of the author.
> By ruse [the police? spies?] the offers will
>   have been hidden,
> So no-one will know who'll the lover be.

After Francois' death, and by now installed on the throne of Scotland, Mary married the ambitious, but fly, imperious and syphilitic Lord Darnley. In 1567, however, a house in Edinburgh in which he was recovering from smallpox exploded, and he was found strangled, together with a servant, in its garden.

Mary's friend and confidant, Lord Bothwell, was suspected of murder, particularly after a casket full of love letters and sonnets – on the face of it from Mary herself to Bothwell – was discovered. Bothwell was tried and acquitted. He and Mary married – and within months she was imprisoned and forced to abdicate in favour of her infant son James VI. She escaped and fled to England, where she became enmeshed in Catholic conspiracies. She was subsequently tried and beheaded, by order of her cousin Queen Elizabeth, at Fotheringey Castle in February 1587.

THE OTTOMAN EMPIRE

The quatrain below (XII, 36) is usually taken to refer to the invasion in 1570 of the Venetian-held island of Cyprus by the forces of the Ottoman Sultan, with his power-base in what had been the great Roman outpost of Constantinople, or Byzantium.

> A savage attack on Cyprus is prepared –
> Tears in my eye as your ruin approaches –
> Byzantine fleet, Muslims, such great damage;
> Two opposing, the great waste by the rock.

The Sultan's (Muslim) fleet blockaded the island's main towns and landed thousands of troops. There was indeed 'great damage' and 'great waste', for tens of thousands of Venetians and native Cypriots were put to the sword. The island continued to be ruled by Turkey for another three hundred years and it became the launching-pad for subsequent naval attacks on the Greek islands, the Cyclades.

The climax of this first wave of expansion and conquest arrived in 1571 within the famous battle of Lepanto, which seems to be prefigured in another quatrain (III, 64):

> The lord of Persia will fill great merchant
>   ships,
> [Then] a fleet of triremes against the
>   Muslims;

> *From Parthia and Media they will come to*
> *plunder the Cyclades;*
> *A long rest shall come to the great Ionian*
> *port.*

The battle, fought in the Gulf of Corinth, did indeed pit two fleets of triremes (oared galleys) against one another: Ottoman against Christian. The Ottoman fleet, in a defeat that was more destructive of morale than of effective power, was destroyed and the Ionian ports of the islands and Asia Minor were able to secure a period of relative peace.

ST BARTHOLOMEW'S DAY MASSACRE AND RELIGIOUS UPHEAVAL

We have already seen how Nostradamus predicted important events in the immediate future history of France (the dying-out of the Valois line, the death of Henri II, the murder of the Duc de Guise, the assassination of Henri III etc.). He also seems to have predicted the St. Bartholomew's Day massacre of 1572 and the religious upheavals that followed. According to quatrain IV,47:

The Protestant Duc of Vendome, Henri of Navarre, saw his claim to the French throne come to fruition after much difficulty

The wild black one, when he has tried
His bloody hand by fire, sword and bent
  bows,
Then all the people will be so afraid
To see the greatest ones hanged by the neck
  and feet.

It is possible that the first phrase of this quatrain – in French 'Le noir farouche' – conceals an anagram involving the words 'roi' and 'France'. i.e. the king of France – in which case it can be taken to refer to the actions of Charles IX after the attempted assassination, engineered by his mother, of Admiral Coligny, the leader of the French Protestants, the Huguenots.

Charles' sister Margot was due to marry the Protestant king Henri of Navarre. As guests gathered for the wedding in Paris, Charles ordered his troops to close the city gates and slaughter every Protestant they could find. No-one knows exactly how many were killed, perhaps as many as 100,000. Admiral Coligny was finally murdered and then strung up by one foot; other Huguenot aristocrats were hanged by the neck (as above). Though Henri of Navarre escaped death by immediately converting to Catholicism and lived to fight another day, a period of profound religious unrest followed, as predicated in quatrain III, 98:

Two royal brothers shall fight it out so fiercely
That the war between them shall be mortal,
That each of them shall occupy strong places;
Their great quarrel concerning the kingdom
  and [its] life.

After the murderous madness of the St. Bartholomew's Day Massacre reached the provinces, the Huguenots found an unlikely champion in the king's brother, the Duc d'Alençon, a liberal Catholic. Thus "two royal brothers" were set against each other and the Duc's faction even went so far as to march an army to the gates of Paris to force the King to issue an act of reconciliation in 1576.

There then followed a period of stand-off, hostile peace, which allowed Henri of Navarre to leave Paris and return to his kingdom, where he reconverted to Protestantism. He later became king of France himself, as predicted in a further quatrain (X, 18):

The house of Lorraine shall cede place to
  Vendôme,
The high pulled low, and the low raised up;
The son of Hamon will be elected by Rome,
And the two great ones will be placed in
  default.

This is one of Nostradamus' most famous verses – and one of the most precise. In 1589, after Henri III had been assassinated, leaving no heir, the French throne was left vacant, open to any French nobleman who could successfully claim descent from the Emperor Charlemagne. Henri of Navarre, who was also Duc of Vendôme (as above), had what many considered the best claim. However, his renewed Protestantism – he was 'a son of Hamon', i.e. a heretic – put him beyond the pale and set him against the Catholic Holy League of the de Guise family (of the house of Lorraine, as in line 1), which had a claim of its own. They went to war for the kingdom, a war in which Henri soon had the upper hand, although the issue was not resolved until Henri reconverted to Catholicism and was approved by the Pope over his two principal rivals, the Duc de Guise and the Duc de Mayenne, the "great ones" of the last line. He was crowned King Henri IV of France in 1589.

PREDICTIONS OF PAST EVENTS

The 17th Century

The Moon at full by night upon the high
*   mountain,*
The new wise man alone with his brain has
*   seen it:*
Invited by his disciples to become immortal;
Eyes to the south, his hands at his breast, his
*   body on fire.*

This verse (IV, 31), with its mysterious language and its suggestion of visions given only to one man, is believed by many to refer to the execution by fire in 1600 of Giordano Bruno, the Dominican monk turned Kabbalist and Hermetic philosopher.

Bruno spent many years in northern Europe, hoping among other things to gather the aid of its princes against the growing Spanish-Austrian influence in Italy and the consequent hardening of intolerance in the Catholic Church. (He visited both London and the court of Henri IV in Paris.) In 1592, however, he was seduced back to Italy, to Venice – where there seems to have been a burgeoning underground Protestant movement – by the entreaties of his disciples. He was soon betrayed to the agents of the Inquisition, which imprisoned and tortured him, tearing out his tongue, before burning him at the stake.

The clampdown of the Inquisition on the pursuit of 'natural' science (i.e. philosophy and scientific investigation unsanctioned by the Church) is also prefigured in two other quatrains (IV, 18 and VIII, 71):

Some of the most learned in the celestial
*   sciences*
Shall be found fault with by ignorant
*   princes;*
Punished by edict, hunted down like
*   criminals,*
And put to death where they are found.

and

The number of Astronomers shall grow very
*   great,*
Pursued, banished and books censured;
The year 1607 by sacred glomes,
No man shall be guaranteed in the sacred.

The use of the word 'princes' in the first verse strongly suggests the so-called princes of the Church, and 'celestial sciences' can be taken to include everything from astronomy and astrology to the 'world soul' promulgated in Bruno's pantheistic philosophy, all of them targeted by the Inquisition.

The year 1607, however, for all its specificity,

The devious Cardinal Richelieu was prepared to use spies to further his political ambitions

has not yet been found by any commentator to have particular significance, except in as much as it marks the year of John Dee's final decline. Galileo, for example, was not tried by the Inquisition and sentenced to life imprisonment until twenty-seven years later. Perhaps the mysterious word *glomes* provides some kind of solution to the riddle – though no-one has yet found a persuasive translation for it.

FRANCE

Great future events in France in the seventeenth century continued, it seems, to preoccupy Nostradamus in his eyrie in Salon. In a quatrain in the third of his 'centuries' (III, 11), for example, he seems to be foretelling the final end of Henri of Navarre:

The weapons battle in the sky for a long season,
The tree fell in the middle of the city:
The sacred branch is cut, the sword near Tyson
Then the monarch of Hadrie succumbed [was killed].

In 1610, Henri IV – identified with 'Hadrie' in a number of the verses, according to some Nostradamian adepts – was preparing for war against the Hapsburg dynasty, which ruled over both the Holy Roman Empire and Spain, when there appeared in the sky over France, by report, a ghostly army, believed to presage the death of a king. On May 14th, in the centre of Paris, near the rue Tison (though the meaning of Nostradamus' 'Tyson' or 'tyson' has been

much disputed), his 'sacred' majesty was stabbed to death by a pro-Spanish French Catholic, probably put up to it by the Hapsburgs. Henri's widow quickly made peace with them.

Another major French seventeenth-century political figure seems to make an appearance in VIII, 68:

> *The old Cardinal by the young man deceived*
> *Will see himself disarmed of his office,*
> *Arles does not show a double is perceived,*
> *And the Liquiduct* [or the Aqueduct] *and*
> *   the Prince embalmed.*

Erica Cheetham, in *The Prophecies of Nostradamus*, argues that the Cardinal in this verse is Cardinal Richelieu, who in 1642 was supplanted in Louis XIII's favour by a young aristocrat called Henri de Cinq Mars. Richelieu was forced to retire. While staying at Arles, however (as in the third line), he received from his spies a copy ('double') of a peace treaty de Cinq Mars had secretly signed with the King of Spain. Richelieu travelled secretly by barge to Paris, becoming in the process 'Liquiduct' or 'Aqueduct' (literally 'led by water'), and there denounced de Cinq Mars to the King. De Cinq Mars was beheaded, and both Richelieu and Louis XIII died within the year. Their bodies were, as the verse predicted, embalmed.

ENGLAND

England though – not France – was a particular preoccupation of Nostradamus' in those predictions of his which seem to match events in the seventeenth century. For example, in III, 82 and III, 79, we read:

> *From the English kingdom, the unworthy one*
> *   driven away,*

Charles I – 'the unworthy one' alluded to in the quatrains?

*The councillor through anger consigned to
the fire,
His followers shall stoop so low
That the bastard will be half received.*

and

*The great squawker, audacious, without
shame
Will be elected governor of the army,
The stoutness of his competitor,
The bridge being broken, the city fainting
from fear.*

The first verse is generally taken to refer to King Charles I, who obstinately continued to proclaim his 'divine right to rule' in the face of an increasingly democratically-minded parliament. One of his councillors, Archbishop Laud, was indeed 'consigned to the fire' and eventually Charles was forced to take refuge among the Scots, who promptly 'stooped so low' as to hand him over to his Parliamentary enemies. The result was that Oliver Cromwell, the 'bastard', later replaced the King as Lord Protector of the Commonwealth, a kind of 'half' king, only half accepted by the English citizenry.

He had already been elected by Parliament head of the army, as in the second verse, and during the Civil War between King and Parliament his forces had twice laid siege to the Royalist city of Pontefract, which translates precisely from its Latin source as 'broken bridge' (another apparent Nostradamian word-play). Cromwell was a tough, even brutal commander (in another verse he is referred to as a 'Butcher'), and Pontefract had good reason to 'faint from fear' – as indeed did the King himself, as we can see from quatrain IX, 49:

*Ghent and Brussels will march against
Antwerp;
The Senate of London will put their king to
death;*

*Salt and wine will do it no good,
That they may have the kingdom into ruin.*

A 'king' put to death by a 'Senate': this, from a sixteenth-century perspective at any rate, was a sensational, absolutely unheard-of event and yet Nostradamus is quite clear about it. Indeed the number of this particular quatrain (IX, 49) may carry an extra significance, since it was in the year 1649 that Charles I was beheaded by order of the London Parliament.

His execution also more or less coincided (as in line 1) with a renewed attempt by Philip IV of Spain to bring to heel the Protestant Netherlands (Antwerp) from his bases in (Catholic) Brussels and Ghent. This war, as well as the Civil War in England, interrupted supplies in England of both luxury imports like wine and basic commodities such as salt. The economy ('the kingdom') did indeed suffer greatly.

Cromwell (referred to in the 'Butcher' quatrain as 'born in obscurity' and 'ruling the empire by force') died in 1658, and was succeeded by his weak son Richard, who resigned as Lord Protector the following year amid calls for the return of the monarchy. In 1660, Charles I's son, Charles Stuart, set foot in England once more and was crowned Charles II, the so-called "Merry Monarch". The events that followed, however, during the first decade of his reign, were anything but merry, for:

*The great plague of the maritime city
Shall not cease till the death be avenged
Of the just blood by price condemned without
crime;
From the great dame unfeigned outrage.*

This (II, 53) seems to be an almost *en clair* account of the so-called Great Plague of London ('the maritime city'), which swept through the English capital in 1665, killing many thousands of its citizens. Nostradamus evidently sees the plague as divine retribution for the execution of Charles I, as some contemporaries did also. Worse, though, than the plague was yet to come, as recorded in II, 51:

> *The blood of the just will be required of*
> *London*
> *Burned by fire in three times twenty and six;*
> *The ancient dame shall fall from her high*
> *place,*
> *Of the same sect many will be killed.*

The plague was followed the next year (1666, as made more or less entirely specific in the second line's 'three times twenty and six') by the so-called Great Fire of London, seemingly regarded by Nostradamus as a second vengeful act of God. The 'ancient dame' of this quatrain and the 'great dame' of the 'Plague' one preceding it are generally considered to be one and the same: Old St. Paul's Cathedral in the centre of the city, to which plague victims had flocked. It was razed to the ground 'from its 'high place' by London's Great Fire, as were more than eighty of the city's churches 'of the same sect'.

King Charles II died in 1685 and his younger brother James took the throne. James II, however, was a high-handed Catholic convert and much resented by the largely Protestant aristocracy. The upshot seems to have been prefigured by Nostradamus in verse IV, 89:

> *Thirty Londoners will secretly conspire,*
> *Against their King over a bridge a plot is*
> *made;*
> *He and his followers will not choose death,*
> *A fair-haired king elected, native of Frisia*
> [Holland].

In 1688, a group of English lords secretly approached James' Protestant sister Mary and

The old St Paul's cathedral, casualty of the Great Fire of London, and possibly the subject of quatrain II, 51

her husband, the Dutch William of Orange, offering them jointly the English throne. William cannily invited them to Holland to sign a declaration of support – hence 'across a bridge': i.e. after a sea voyage between the two countries. Later that year, with their signatures in hand, William landed with a Dutch army and entered London without opposition – James' army had melted away, and James himself and his court ('not choosing death') had escaped to France, where he became known as 'The Old Pretender'.

William was duly elected king by Parliament as foretold, the only king in English or British history ever to be so chosen; though he was not fair-haired, he was indeed ' of Orange', a colour that may be covered by the German-derived French word *blonde* in the original text.

Finally, as far as this century is concerned, Nostradamus saw the beginnings of the rise of the British empire. He wrote in X, 100:

The great empire will be in England,
The all-powerful [the great panjandrum]
  for three hundred years;
Vast armies will pass through land and sea,
The Portuguese will not be happy.

This verse is, once again, more or less completely unambiguous – and it must have come as a considerable shock to the people of Nostradamus' time when England was little more than a gadfly nuisance to the great continental royal houses. Yet it came true: from the period of the English Civil War until India gained its independence in the 1940s, the British empire steadily grew until it embraced much of the world. Portugal, which in Nostradamus' era was a great exploratory sea-power, and had been awarded by the Catholic Church suzerainty over half of the earth, was to see its star wane as Britain's waxed – much, one must imagine, to its chagrin.

William of Orange arrives in England to take the throne

The 18th *Century*

Head of Aries, Jupiter and Saturn,
Oh, eternal God, what changes!
After a long century his evil times return,
France and Italy, what turmoil!

To trouble Europe and the universe,
To put to great flight two eclipses
And to enforce life and death on the Poles.

With this quatrain (I, 51), Nostradamus apparently greets from long distance the eighteenth century, for the first alignment of Jupiter and Saturn in the House of Aries to occur after his time arrived was in December 1702. The hundred years following that date ended (in late-1802) with the consolidation of Napoleon's dictatorship in France and his successful invasion of Italy. After that, of course, came the 'turmoil' of the Napoleonic wars…

The early period between these two dates need not concern us long, since for the most part it involves events that we today remember poorly, if at all: events like the War of the Spanish Succession (IV, 2 and IV, 5), the reign of French King Louis XV (III, 14 and 15), and the signing of a peace treaty between Persia and the Ottoman Empire (III, 77) – for which Nostradamus gives the astonishingly exact date of October 1727 (*"L'an mil sept cens vingt et sept en Octobre"*, or "seventeen hundred and twenty seven in October").

Now and again, though, a new territory and a major new character looms across the Nostradamian horizon, as in VIII, 15:

> *Towards the North* [in the place of the Eagle], *great efforts by the masculine woman*

CATHERINE THE GREAT

This verse is a clear reference to the Russian Czarina, Catherine the Great, crowned Empress in her own right after the abdication (and murder) in 1762 of her husband Peter III. She was a formidably strong-willed ('masculine') woman and the commander-in-chief of a powerful army which expanded Russia's borders and brooked no opposition internally – something which certainly 'troubled' Europe, if not the universe. At the same time, she was a disciple and friend of the French Encyclopaedists, particularly Voltaire, and she originally intended to follow their principles in drastically reforming the Russian state.

As time went on, though, particularly after the beginning of the French Revolution, Catherine turned her back on such liberal notions and became increasingly imperious and reactionary. She presided over the 'life and death' of the Poles (as in line 4) via the so-called 'partitions' of Poland, which allowed the three great states which were her nearest neighbours – Russia, Prussia and the Austrian Empire – simply to absorb increasingly large swathes of its territory. And when the Poles finally rose up in revolt, Catherine presided over a final carve-up, which removed Poland from the map entirely for a hundred and twenty-five years.

Catherine the Great and her allies carved up Poland between them

Two further elements in the Catherine quatrain are worth mentioning in passing, since they may demonstrate something of Nostradamus' wit and associative wordplay: the word '*Aquilon*' in the first line, and the word '*l'univers*', which Catherine, 'the masculine woman', is said to 'make great efforts to trouble'. *Aquilon* is from the Latin word for 'northern', and it it is not usually found with a capital

letter. It also suggests the Latin word for eagle, '*aquila*,': the symbol of Imperial Russia (with its capital letter) was the double-headed eagle. Similarly, the word '*l'univers*' can be rearranged as *luni vers*, which now suggests in garbled medieval Latin or early French 'towards the moon'. David Ovason, in his *The Secrets of Nostradamus*, suggests that this phrase should be applied to 'the eclipses' in line 3, which can then be read as eclipses of the moon or crescent moons, the symbol of the Ottoman Empire – Ottoman armies were indeed twice 'put to great flight' by Catherine.

THE MONTGOLFIER BROTHERS

Occasionally, too, in those of Nostradamus' prophecies which seem to relate to the eighteenth century, an entirely familiar name shifts suddenly into sharp focus, as in V, 57:

> *One shall go forth from Mont Gaulfier and*
> *Aventine*
> *Who through a hole shall give warning to*
> *the army…*

The main thing that shouts out from the first line of this quatrain is the name Mont Gaulfier or Montgolfier, the name of the two brothers who invented and launched the first hot air balloon in 1783. Their invention was later, as the second line says, used by the army for reconnaissance and scouting missions, when a hole was cut in the bottom of the gondola for viewing purposes. The second pair of lines of this quatrain, however, are infinitely more mysterious:

> *Between two rocks the prize shall be taken*
> *Of SEXT. Mansol shall lose his renown.*

A suggestion has been made that this particular quatrain is actually a conflation of two separate prophecies, a fact signalled by the use of the word 'Aventine', one of the hills of Rome, in the first line (where it doesn't make much sense). The last two lines, however, do seems to concern Rome, since 'SEXT.' is an abbreviation of the Latin word for 'Sixth'.

This darkling figure can be identified with the first Pope to carry a 'Sixth' after his name since Nostradamus' time, Pope Pius VI and, as Erica Cheetham points out, the word 'Mansol' –

The Montgolfier brothers' invention features in quatrain V, 57

which she believes to be an ellipsis of the Latin words *'manens solus'*, 'remaining solitary' or 'chaste' – may also be another identifier.

POPE PIUS VI

Pius, who had opposed the French Revolution, was captured by Napoleon when he invaded Rome in 1797 and Napoleon forced him to hand over 'the prize' of church land, the 'rocks' on which the power of his Church rested. Certainly Pius thereafter lost both 'renown' and power. He was imprisoned at Valence, where he died in 1799, as also foretold by Nostradamus in II, 97:

> *Roman Pontiff, beware of coming near*
> *The city watered by two rivers;*
> *You will spit your blood there,*
> *You and yours when the rose blooms.*

Valence, the Pope's prison, is close to Lyon, where the Rhone and Saône rivers meet. In August 1799 Pius suffered an attack of vomiting so violent that it caused internal bleeding: he spat blood. Some of the thirty priests imprisoned with him – 'you and yours' – may well have suffered from the same illness, though there is no record that they in fact did. As for

Pope Pius himself, he died on August 29th, just as the late roses were coming into bloom.

THE FRENCH REVOLUTION

He died, of course, after the two most important developments in eighteenth-century Europe: the French Revolution and the rise of Napoleon Bonaparte – and Nostradamus, in his *Prophéties*, seems to have paid careful and grave attention to both. In VI, 23, for example, he appears to be laying out the background to the French Revolution:

> *Defences of the spirit of the kingdom*
>   *undermined,*
> *The people will be stirred up against their*
>   *King,*
> *Peace, new made, sacred laws degenerate*
> *Rapis was never in such great disorder.*

The *Rapis* of the last line is clearly both an anagram of Paris and a play on words involving 'rapine' or plunder: the quatrain as a whole is a remarkably accurate account of the chain of events – in Paris and country-wide – that led to the Revolution. Under the weight of taxation and through the folly of the tax-free nobility, the financial structure of the country virtually collapsed.

The King, under popular pressure, tried to stem the tide of enmity against him by calling for a new election of the Estates-General (a 'new peace'), which was composed of representatives of the nobility, the clergy and commoners. The nobility and clergy, however, made common cause with each other against the commoners, invoking the 'sacred laws' of the past – and the starving poor of Paris soon erupted. The Bastille was stormed. The commoners of the Estates-General formed their own legislative

The storming of the Bastille, a pivotal moment in the French Revolution, and central to quatrain VI, 23

Louis XVI's attempts at escape were futile

National Assembly. The King, by now a constitutional monarch – and more or less resigned to his lot – remained popular, particularly in the countryside. However, his Queen, Marie Antoinette, was known to be actively involved with right-wing elements within the National Assembly and she was also suspected of being in secret correspondence with her brother, the Austrian (and Holy Roman) Emperor, Leopold, who was threatening war against the new France. Under close watch in the Tuileries Palace – as a protection against the mob – Louis gave his word that the family would not try to escape – and then, in 1791, it did, before being recaptured 'in the field' (as all foretold in V, 5) near the village of Varennes:

> *Under the feigned pretext of removing*
>   *servitude,*
> *People and city will usurp power:*
> *He will do worse because of the deceit of a*
>   *young whore,*
> *Free in the field delivering a false promise.*

In 1792, Louis and the royal family again tried to escape. They evaded the guards by using a secret door in the Queen's apartments, and then boarded a coach headed for the eastern border and Austria. Their first destination was the small town of Varennes. Unfortunately for them they got lost and instead took a roundabout route to Reines, along which they were once more apprehended. It was the beginning of the end for them all – as Nostradamus seems to have predicted with breathtaking accuracy in IX, 20:

> *By night will come through the forest of*
>   *Reines [or the Queen's door]*
> *Two partners by a roundabout way: Herne*
>   *the white stone,*
> *The black monk in grey within Varennes,*
> *Elected cap. causes tempest, fire, blood, slice.*

Herne is almost certainly an anagram for the

body, the National Assembly, which rapidly took over tax-collection, drafted a new constitution, issued paper money and disestablished the French Catholic church, as foretold in I, 53:

> *Alas, how a great people will be tormented*
> *And the Holy Law in total ruin;*
> *By other laws all Christianity [ruined]*
> *When the new mines of gold and silver are*
>   *found.*

The situation in the capital soon deteriorated, with Republican demagogues using the raw power of the Paris mob to terrorize the old French word for 'the Queen', who in this case almost always wore white ('the white stone'). Louis, during the escape, wore grey and may also have had a monk's cloak. Having said that, it is the last line which firmly identifies him: he was France's first constitutional king, and thus 'elected'; he was known as Louis Capet (or *cap.*); and his attempted escape had disastrous consequences, among them the fatal 'slice' of the guillotine, which he met in January 1793.

A further verse (I, 57) seems to describe the scene as his severed head, which had once been anointed at his coronation, was held up to the mob:

> *By great discord the trumpet will tremble*
> *Agreement broken, lifting the head to heaven*
> *A bloody mouth shall swim in blood*
> *His face turned to the sun anointed with*
> *milk and honey…*

… exactly as occurs in the French ceremony of coronation.

In the end they all died (IX, 77):

> *The stolen kingdom will invite the king,*
> *The captive queen condemned to death by*
> *lottery*
> *Life will be denied to the Queen's son,*
> *And the concubine to the strength of a*
> *consort.*

Louis, the 'invited' one, was re-invited, this time to death. Queen Marie Antoinette was condemned to the guillotine by a jury 'chosen by lot' and was killed nine months after her husband. The Dauphin, the heir to the throne, was secretly murdered in prison (as has been recently confirmed by DNA testing of a newly discovered relic) and Louis' father's influential mistress, Madame Du Barry, was executed on December 7th, 1793.

THE REIGN OF TERROR

What followed the death of Louis XVI was yet more brutality, the so-called Reign of Terror. Maximilien Robespierre, one of the leaders of

Revolutionary committees frequently met during the brutal Reign of Terror to decide their next move

the Jacobin Party, who had more or less forced the decision to execute the King on the National Convention, seized control of the twelve-man Committee on Public Safety after the death of his colleague Marat. There was a series of show trials of political opponents, and the rate of execution accelerated.

This turn of events, with Robespierre becoming a virtual dictator, seems to have been forseen by Nostradamus (IV, 11 and VI, 57). Note that the word 'red' is used by Nostradamus on a number of occasions to refer to the radical Republicans of the French Revolution – though it may also perhaps refer to the colour of a cardinal's robes and hence to matters in Rome:

> He who shall be covered in a great cloak [or, who will have enshrouded great Capet]
> Shall be induced to commit some cases,
> The twelve red ones will come to soil the cloth
> Under murder, murder will be committed

and

> He who was well in front in the kingdom,
> Having red head near the hierarchy;
> Harsh and cruel, and will make himself so feared,
> He will succeed to the Sacred Monarchy.

There are further Nostradamian verses which seem to refer to the closing of the churches, the abolition of convents and monasteries, and the execution of priests and monks; to the rise of the pagan Cult of Reason and to the ultimate fate of Robespierre himself, finally overthrown by a reaction to his excesses in the National Convention – and executed.

It is time to turn now to a man whose extraordinary career Nostradamus carefully prefigured and who began to emerge as a national hero in the same year as that of the death of Robespierre: Napoleon Bonaparte.

NAPOLEON BONAPARTE

> An Emperor will be born near Italy
> Who will cost the Empire dear;
> They will say, What people he keeps company with!
> He is less a prince than a butcher.

Thus, in quatrain I, 60, Nostradamus announces the arrival of Napoleon, born at Ajaccio in Corsica in 1769, just a year after the island had been ceded by the Genoese to France. He was indeed, in the end, to 'cost the Empire dear' and he was indeed, furthermore, looked down on by many French as a *parvenu*, a provincial nobody. As a Corsican, he was something of a second-class French citizen and the people he kept company with – his wife Josephine, a Creole from Martinique, and his comparatively uneducated brothers whom he turned into kings – raised many an aristocratic eyebrow. Though his father was a relatively well-to-do lawyer and he himself a cut above a butcher, he was certainly no prince. Instead, after studying at the Brienne Military School in Paris, he rode the coat-tails of the Revolution to power.

MILITARY CAREER BEGINS

His first accolade came in 1793 at the siege of Toulon, which had turned its face against the new revolutionary government. At the age of twenty-four he was appointed brigadier-general after the port-city had been taken with the help of his artillery.

The Reign of Terror didn't reach as far as the army, and he remained secure. Then, when the Terror was put to an end by the execution of Robespierre and many of his fellow Jacobins, bread riots broke out in Paris and he was called

As soldier and Emperor, Napoleon Bonaparte engendered both fear and admiration

in by the suddenly conservative government to quell them. For this he was then rewarded with the unofficial sobriquet of 'Saviour of the Republic'.

A number of Nostradamus' quatrains seem to predict Napoleon's career as a soldier. One (VIII, 1) is particularly striking:

> *Pau, Nay, Loron, more fire than blood he'll be,*
> *Swimming in praise, the great one fleeing to the confluence.*
> *He will refuse the magpies entry,*
> *Mighty-bridged Durance will keep them confined.*

The names of the three insignificant French towns mentioned in line 1 only make sense as an anagram of 'Napaulon Roy', 'King Napaulon', a spelling which, it has been claimed, was sometimes used during Napoleon's lifetime. He was to be a military phenomenon of huge energy ('fire'), says Nostradamus, rather than a murderous tyrant ('blood'). The second half of line 2, though – after a nod to his gathering fame across Europe – seems to take us back to Napoleon's imprisonment of Pius VI at 'the confluence of two rivers' as does the use of the word 'magpies' in line 3 – 'magpies' are also known as 'pies'. 'Pies' is also the French word for the two Piuses whom Napoleon imprisoned in his ongoing war with the Church: Pius VI and, subsequently, Pius VII. Pius VI, as we have seen, was held at Valence; his successor at Grenoble. Both these cities are in south-east France, watered by the Durance river.

Other quatrains seem to carry Napoleon's story forward into Italy and elsewhere, but often degenerate in their second halves into seemingly unrelated matters. I shall quote only what seem to me the relevant lines. Thus I, 93 on the invasion of northern Italy and the growing distrust of the British:

> *The Italian land near the mountains shall tremble,*
> *The Lion [Britain] and the Cock [France] shall not see eye to eye…*

and III, 37:

> *Before the assault, an oration made,*
> *Milan taken by the eagle…*

This second verse seems to refer to a celebrated speech made by Napoleon before what he thought would be a great battle for Milan in 1796. (In fact he took the city unopposed.) He told his 'starving and half-naked' soldiers that they could not rely on the French government 'which owes you much but can do nothing for you' – only on him personally. "I will lead you into the most fertile plains in the world", he said. "There you will find honour, glory and riches". By 1798, they had them, for Napoleon's army had taken most of Italy, as predicted in V, 99:

> *Milan, Ferrara, Turin and Aquileia,*
> *Capua and Brindisi vexed by the French nation…*

There followed after the conquest of Italy what in the end proved an unsuccessful campaign in Egypt, put to an end by the British Admiral Nelson's victory at the Battle of the Nile. Nevertheless, in 1799, Napoleon was made supreme ruler of France (on the Roman model) as First Consul. Quatrain VII, 13 seemingly describes his rise to power:

> *Of the city marine and tributary*
> *The shaved head will take the satrapy;*
> *Chasing off the sordid who then oppose him,*
> *For fourteen years he will hold the tyranny.*

The 'city marine and tributary' in this quatrain is almost certainly Toulon which provided him with his first important government position ('satrapy') as brigadier-general. He was known to his troops as 'le petit tondu', the little crop-head – hence 'shaved head'. The 'sordid who then oppose him' could either be the British fleet anchored off Toulon in support of the city, or more likely the Republican government he in effect ultimately replaced. The 'tyranny' held 'for fourteen years' is similarly – even eerily – accurate. He was the ultimate authority in France from November 1799 till April 1814, a little over fourteen years, first in the short robe of First Consul, then (from 1804) in the long coronation robe of Emperor, as foretold in VIII, 57 and IV, 54:

> *From a simple soldier he will attain an*
> *   empire,*
> *From a short robe he will attain a long one…*

and

> *Of a name which no French King ever had.*
> *There was never a thunderbolt so much*
> *   feared,*
> *Italy shall tremble, Spain and the English,*
> *He shall be much taken with women*
> *   strangers.*

NAPOLEON AS EMPEROR

Napoleon was crowned Emperor in Paris by the same Pope Pius VII whom he later imprisoned. His official seal was an eagle gripping crossed thunderbolts – and 'Italy, Spain and the English' certainly had cause to fear him. He invaded both Italy and Spain and thought seriously about invading England, which had declared war on France in 1803, in the year of his coronation. He began to prepare an invasion fleet in Channel ports. However, ultimately, he turned eastward instead to take on the Austrian Empire. It was a great mistake, as foretold in VIII, 53:

> *Within Boulogne he will want to wash*
> *   himself of his faults,*
> *He will not be able at the temple of the sun,*
> [Instead] *He shall fly doing things too*
> *   great…*

The eastern campaign was ultimately a disaster and the British, not having been invaded, began seriously to fight back, particularly in and around Spain. First came the famous 1805 Battle of Trafalgar (off Spain) in which twenty ships under the command of Admiral Villeneuve were either destroyed or captured and 14,000 Frenchmen killed or made prisoners of war. The quatrain (I, 77), which seems to predict the battle and to refer both to the death of the British commander Admiral Nelson and the later suicide of Admiral Villeneuve, I have chosen to jumble, following Sampietro's method:

> 1. *Between two seas will rise a promonory,*
> 4. *Through Calpre the fleet near Rocheval,*
> 3. *The proud Neptune will fold black sails,*
> 2. *Who then will die by the bite of a horse*
> *   [pin].*

The promontory 'between two seas', the Mediterranean and Atlantic, is almost certainly the Rock of Gibraltar – an old name for which is Calpe, which, it can be seen, is very similar to the 'Calpre' of the text. Admiral Villeneuve had been ordered by Napoleon to ship an army from Cadiz via Gibraltar to northern Italy, but he ran into the British fleet about midway between the Rock and Cape Roche ('Rocheval'). The British took minor losses, but one of them was Lord Nelson himself, in mourning for whom his flagship raised 'black sails' as it returned to port. Admiral Villeneuve, taken captive at Trafalgar, was allowed to return to France the following year. On his journey homeward he committed suicide by pushing a long pin ('cheville' rather than the 'cheval' of the text) into his chest.

The British land campaign in Spain was also a major contributor to Napoleon's ultimate undoing. Originally invited to the Iberian peninsula to help Spain in a war against Portugal, Napoleon took advantage of a palace coup in Spain to install his brother Joseph on the Spanish throne (as he had – with other brothers – on the thrones of Naples and Holland). The Spanish quickly rose in revolt, and were joined, not only by their old enemy Portugal, but by a British army under the command of Arthur Wellesley, later Duke of Wellington.

By winning victory after victory over five years, Wellesley gradually pushed the French back to the Pyrenees – and eventually into French towns like Pau, as recorded in IV, 70:

Very near the great Pyrenee mountains,
A man will raise a great army against the
*   eagle;*
Open veins, exterminated forces,
As far as Pau the chief will come to chase
*   them.*

The other disaster Napoleon had to face in the final years of his hegemony, of course, was the invasion of Russia, the climax of which is foretold in IV, 82:

A great troop gathered shall come from the
*   country of the Slavs,*
The old Destroyer shall ruin a great city;
He shall see his Romania extremely desolate,
And shall not know then how to extinguish
*   the great flame.*

The 'old Destroyer' in line 2 can be interpreted as fire: the Russians abandoned their 'great city', Moscow, which earlier in its history had been declared 'the third Rome' (after Rome and Constantinople) – hence 'his' (Napoleon's) desolate 'Romania' – and then torched it as the French army arrived, thus denying Napoleon both booty and winter base. The French were

Even the heroic actions of Napoleon's Old Guard could not ensure victory at the Battle of Waterloo

unable 'to extinguish the great flame'. Many soldiers died in the attempt, and the 'great troop' was forced to retreat from 'the country of the Slavs' in winter, enduring terrible hardships and constant guerilla attacks along the way, as prefigured in II, 91:

At sunrise, a great fire will be seen,
Noise and brightness in the direction of
*   Aquilon [the North];*
Within the round, death and cries will be
*   heard;*
From sword, fire, famine, death to those who
*   waited.*

Only thirty thousand men returned from Russia – note the use of the word *'Aquilon'* again to designate the country – out of an army that had once been 600,000 strong. It was the beginning of the end for Napoleon, since all Europe was now united against him.

DEMISE

Napoleon was forced to abdicate in favour of Louis XVI's brother (Louis XVIII – the dead Dauphin having become Louis XVII after the execution of his father), and was sent into permanent exile, with a small bodyguard, on the Mediterranean island of Elba. On February 26th, 1815, though, he and his guard escaped. The new King despatched an army against him, but the soldiers defected to Napoleon's cause. He entered Paris in triumph at their head, and was carried shoulder-high to the King's palace, where people thronged the corridors for hours. He was re-crowned Emperor on March 20th. Quatrain II, 66 seems to sum up the sequence of events with remarkable economy:

> *Through great dangers the captive escaped,*
> *In a little time great* [again]*, his fortune*
>   *changed;*
> *In the palace the people are caught,*
> *The city besieged by a good augury.*

The 'good augury' in the city, however, was not to last, for the allies set against Napoleon rejected his peace overtures. They declared him an "enemy of humanity", and immediately began to regather their troops. So, too, did Napoleon.

With a new army, he crossed into Belgium on June 15th to face two separated forces, one British, under the Duke of Wellington, and the other Prussian, commanded by Field Marshal Blücher. He first took on the Prussians and forced them to retreat, after inflicting major losses. He ordered General Grouchy to pursue the remnants. Then, two days later, he took on the British on a stretch of open farmland known as Waterloo. Things did not at first go well for the British, as stated in I, 23:

> In the third month at sunrise
> Wild Boar, Leopard to the fields of Mars to
>   combat;
> The Leopard, weary, lifts his eyes to the sky,
> Sees an Eagle playing about the Sun.

It was indeed 'the third month' after Napoleon's return to Paris. The 'Wild Boar' was the emblem of the Prussian army and though the Lion was the British army's emblem, the Lion had been often dismissed by Napoleon, according to Damon Wilson, as 'the Leopard of England'.

It seemed for a while as if the French must finally break through the British lines. The Eagle of Napoleon's personal seal was definitely in the ascendant as the sun beat down. Then, though, at 4pm the Prussians arrived, and immediately began to attack the French right wing. General Grouchy had neither intervened to cut off their approach nor rejoined the main French force, as ordered. The result was a disaster, as in IV, 75:

> One ready to fight will defect;
> Chief adversary will win victory;
> The rear guard will put up a defence;
> Those falling away will die in the white
>   country.

Grouchy failed in his duty, Wellington carried the day, and without a heroic rearguard action by the veterans of Napoleon's Old Guard – who were all killed, it is said, to a man – many more French soldiers would have lost their lives. Those who survived the retreat did indeed die in a 'white country' – for white was the colour of the Bourbon flag of the now restored Louis XVIII. All was, in fact, as Nostradamus had predicted.

After the fateful battle, Napoleon returned to Paris, only to be abandoned once and for all by the generals and politicians. He made his way to the port of Rochefort, where he finally surrendered to the captain of a British man-of-war. He was again sent into exile, this time to the small Atlantic island of St. Helena and it was here that the final act of his extraordinary career was played out (I, 32):

> The great empire will soon be translated
> To a small place which soon will begin to
>   grow:
> A very miserable place of small account,
> In the middle of which he will lay down his
>   sceptre.

Napoleon died on St. Helena, perhaps poisoned, six years later, on May 5th 1821. He was just fifty-two years old.

The 19th Century

Surveying the range of Nostradamian quatrains assigned by interpreters to the nineteenth century, one is forced to the conclusion that the Sage of Salon was blinkered, preoccupied more or less entirely with his native France. I shall not examine them in any great detail here – except where they seem to show astonishing prescience – since political events in France in the nineteenth century are both complex and relatively unknown to the Anglophone audience.

Having said that, however, two extraordinary quatrains do seem to give an extremely precise account of events in France immediately following the Battle of Waterloo (IX, 86 and I, 20):

> From Bourge-la-Reine they will come straight
>   to Chartres
> And near the Pont d'Anthoni they will pause.
> Seven for peace crafty as martens
> Will make entry with their armies into closed
>   Paris.

and

> Tours, Orleans, Blois, Angers, Reims and
>   Nantes,
> Cities vexed by sudden change
> By strange languages tents shall be pitched…

What remained of Napoleon's *Grande Armée* vacated Paris before the allies arrived there, making its way precisely as Nostradamus described: travelling via Bourge-la-Reine to Chartres in the Loire valley, after bivouacking for a night beneath the Anthony Bridge. The seven nations 'for peace' which had allied themselves against Napoleon (Britain, Prussia, Russia, Austria, Sweden, Spain and Portugal) then entered the capital as occupiers. By that time, as in the second quatrain, they had already occupied the cities of northern France, which had gone through, within a period of little more than a year, the 'sudden change' of Napoleon's fall and rise and ultimate defeat. 'Strange languages' were by this time everywhere…

NAPOLEON'S LEGACY

The eerie accuracy, particularly of the first quatrain, is repeated in a verse about the assassination of Louis XVIII's son and heir, the Duc de Berry in 1820 (III, 96):

> The Chief of Fossan will have his throat cut
> By the keeper of the Hunt and the
>   Greyhound,
> The act committed by those of the Tarpeian
>   rock;
> Saturn being in Leo, February 13th.

On February 13th, 1820, the Duc de Berry, whose maternal grandfather was King of Fossano ('Fossan') in Sardinia, was stabbed to death at the opera, in an act at least interpretable as treason – the crime committed by those executed in Rome by being thrown from the Tarpeian rock. The assassin was an anti-monarchist called Louvel who worked, remarkably enough, at the royal stables...

From this point on, however, the quatrains assigned to nineteenth-century France are often extremely obscure and require a good deal of tortuous interpretation. Nostradamus, it is true, does seem to predict the future fate of the Duc de Berry's son (unborn at the time of his murder); the death of the last of the Bourbon line, Louis Bourbon Condé and the machinations behind the scenes of Louis Philippe, Duc d'Orleans. It is only, however, with the 1830 crowning of the Duc as the so-called 'Citizen King' that Nostradamus seems once more to speak, in V, 69, more or less clearly:

> No more will the great one be in a false sleep
> Unease shall take the place of repose;
> He will raise the phalanx of gold, azure and
>   vermilion.
> Subjugating Africa and gnawing it down to
>   the bone.

Louis Philippe is not, of course, clearly identified in this quatrain, although the first two lines do strongly suggest him. Now out in the open (no longer 'in a false – pretended – sleep'), he later had cause to regret becoming the figurehead of France during what turned out to be a very volatile and unsettled period ('unease in place of repose'). The third and fourth lines, however, clearly indicate that Nostradamus had him in mind. Louis Philippe was the first king of France to adopt the tricolour of the Revolution – with its bars ('phalanx') of red, white and blue – as the national flag; and in the first year of his reign, a French army captured Algiers and gradually took over the whole of Algeria – which it 'gnawed to the bone' as a colony for over a century.

In a bid for popularity ten years after his accession, Louis Philippe, who had already faced two attempted coups from Bonapartists, decided to have Napoleon's remains reburied in Paris – and once more Nostradamus seems to speak of events with some clarity (V, 7):

> The bones of the Triumvir will be found
> When they search for a deep and enigmatic
>   treasure,
> Those around will not be restful,
> This concavity of marble and metallic lead.

Napoleon, in taking on the office of First Consul, had become the leading figure in what was still, at least nominally, a council of three – hence he had been a 'Triumvir' (a member of a triumvirate). By collecting his bones from St. Helena and reburying them in great pomp in *Les Invalides* in Paris (in a 'metallic lead' coffin in a 'marble' tomb), Louis Philippe, there is no doubt, was seeking to inherit the 'deep and enigmatic treasure' of Napoleon's seemingly endless popularity with the French.

He was not in the end successful. Ten years later in 1848, "the year of revolutions" in Europe, he was forced to abdicate in favour of Napoleon's nephew, Louis Napoleon Bonaparte, who became, first president of the Second Republic in 1849, and two years later, in a *coup d'état*, Emperor Napoleon III.

THE FRANCO-PRUSSIAN WAR

The next event to come more or less sharply into focus in the *Prophéties*, after the rise to power of Napoleon's nephew, is the Franco-Prussian War of 1870 and 1871 (1, 92):

> Under a man the peace will be proclaimed
>   everywhere,
> But not long after pillage and rebellion,
> Because of a refusal, land and sea will be
>   assaulted,
> Dead and captured, a third of a million.

Napoleon III's decision to declare war on the Prussians was to ultimately prove disastrous

In the late-1860s, after fifteen or so years of his reign, Napoleon III had proclaimed: "The Empire is at peace." However, he hadn't reckoned with the ruthless Prussian chancellor, Otto von Bismarck, who first took on the tottering Austrian empire, and then, after victory in a seven-week war, turned his attention to France. By this time the Prussians had set about installing a member of their own ruling family, the Hohenzollerns, on the throne of Spain. Napoleon III objected, demanding that their nominee be withdrawn. Bismarck now formally refused. On July 19th, 1870 – much to the Chancellor's delight – Napoleon III declared war.

A Prussian force quickly invaded France with much 'pillage'; Napoleon's army was disastrously defeated in the Battle of Sedan, provoking the 'rebellion' of the Republican Commune in Paris and just under a third of a million were indeed killed and wounded in the seven-month conflict.

There are a number of Nostradamian quatrains seemingly dedicated to this war – among them VIII, 43, IV, 100 and X, 51:

Through the fall of two bastard regimes
A nephew of the blood will occupy the throne,
Within lectore there will be blows of missiles;
The nephew through fear will fold up his
  standard.

The strange word *'lectore'* in VIII, 43, is taken by some Nostradamian commentators to be a virtual anagram of Le Torcey, a suburb of Sedan in which some of the fiercest fighting took place during the decisive French-Prussian battle near the Belgian border. Napoleon III, arriving late, soon saw that the position was hopeless and surrendered (folding up 'his standard' 'through fear'). Eighty-three thousand Frenchmen were taken prisoner, including Napoleon III himself.

Fire shall fall from the skies on the Royal
  building,
When the light of Mars is eclipsed,
Seven months the great War shall last, people
  dead through evil,
Rouen and Evreux shall not fail the King.

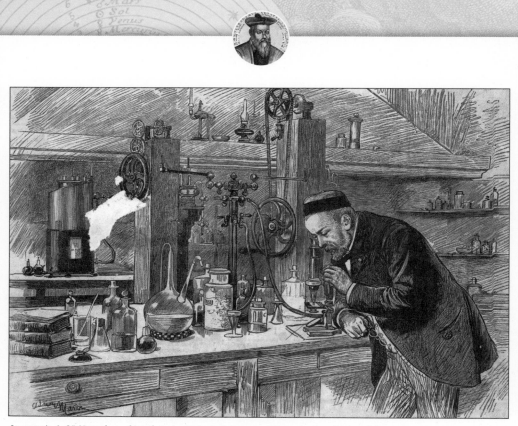

In quatrain 1, 25 Nostradamus hints that scientist Louis Pasteur was rediscovering long-lost knowledge

After the battle, the Prussians advanced on Paris to besiege it. The Tuileries Palace was destroyed by Prussian artillery and 'the light of Mars' – Napoleon's blood-line – ended at the same time as the French monarchy. Normandy [Rouen and Evreux], however, remained loyal to both even after the Emperor's capture and Paris' fall. The War in all lasted for almost exactly seven months, as predicted by Nostradamus, but not before thousands of Parisians had died in resistance, through starvation and through the 'evil' of the Communard uprising.

> *Some of the lowest places in the country of*
>   *Lorraine*
> *Will be united with lower Germanies,*
> *By reason of the siege of Picardy, Normandy*
>   *and Maisne,*
> *And in counties will be reunited.*

France lost parts of Lorraine – and Alsace – to what soon became a unified Germany, and did not receive them back until 1919. The rest of France – Picardy, Normandy and Maisne included – was occupied by the Prussians until 1873, and only became whole again after full reparations had been paid in gold, and the Prussian army had withdrawn.

LOUIS PASTEUR

Only one last quatrain relating to events in nineteenth-century France is worth serious examination – but it is one of the most extraordinary. In it (I, 25), another historical name leaps to the eye, this time that of Louis Pasteur:

> *The lost found again, hidden for such a long*
>   *cycle,*
> *Pasteur will be honoured as a demi-God;*

But before the moon ends her great cycle,
By other winds [ancient ones] *will be*
dishonoured.

Pasteur, the first propounder and demonstrator of the germ theory of disease, remains to this day, there is no doubt, 'honoured as a demi-God'. He was, after all, the founder of modern microbiology and the man perhaps most responsible for the fact that Western populations, at any rate, live as long as we do.

Modern standards of hygiene might be said to have directly evolved from his demonstration that the souring of milk can be prevented by it being heated, then placed in a sealed receptacle, in a process we still call 'pasteurization'. He showed that bacteria are living organisms producing acids (as in the souring of milk), that they are responsible for a wide variety of human and animal diseases and that many of these diseases can be prevented by the process that Joseph Lister had discovered – or rediscovered, since it seems to have been known to those whom Isaac Newton called 'the Ancients' – for smallpox: vaccination.

The usual reading of lines 3 and 4 of this extraordinary verse is that Pasteur's theories would be rejected and ridiculed by his conservative contemporaries, as indeed they were, but that he would gain general acceptance – as he eventually did with the setting up of the Pasteur Institute, after the end of a 320-year lunar cycle, in 1889. Line 1, however, remains an extremely provocative mystery. It clearly suggests that Pasteur would be rediscovering knowledge that had long been lost: i.e. that the germ theory of disease had at some time in the past been well-known; if the 'cycle' referred to in line 1 is the same lunar cycle as that in line 3, then it was known in the middle of the sixteenth century, Nostradamus' own time. It was then perhaps 'lost' through the persecutions of astronomers and alchemists that he himself

had predicted would take place in the early seventeenth century.

In a sense, this quatrain brings us back to the central mystery of Nostradamus' life and to his strange practices as a doctor, which very much flew in the face of the orthodox medical opinion of his time. It suggests that he himself might have known that many diseases, including the plague, were caused by bacilli, and that the first defence against them lay in proper hygiene.

We have already seen how Greek (and perhaps Arab) philosophers as far back as the fifth century BC seem to have had a basic grasp of atomic theory and of the fundamental laws of astronomy. Is it possible that doctors – perhaps Egyptian doctor-priests, who seem to have practised a sophisticated form of medicine – also knew about the dangers of miniscule unseen organisms, and that this knowledge was passed down through the ages as part of the Hermetic or alchemical tradition?

The answer, of course, is that we simply do not know. But the possibility remains that line 4, on the basis of this, could be read in a rather different way: i.e. that Pasteur could ultimately lose his reputation, *because he had only succeeded in penetrating part of the knowledge known to 'the ancient ones'* – the traditional reading for the French words *'autres vents'* in the last line.

Even if this phrase is translated literally as 'other winds', it may be that Nostradamus is referring, ironically, to the prevailing medical orthodoxy of his time: i.e. that diseases were caused by ill humours in the air, or 'winds'. In this case he is saying that Pasteur will ultimately lose his reputation because the germ theory is inadequate to the understanding and combating of a wholly different class of organisms only to be discovered (or rediscovered) after his time. What these may be – HIV? Ebola? a whole new category of air-borne, fast-mutating viruses? – we may not yet, to our future cost, know.

The 20th Century

Of the quatrains of Nostradamus usually assigned to the twentieth century, there are very few which are either clear or convincing and many commentators on the *Prophéties* have been forced into searching for scraps and a sort of associative flailing, to not much good effect.

There may, of course, be a reason for Nostradamus' failure to speak with much clarity about the 1900s. It is worth remembering that up till the end of the preceding century, the world which he had set out to envision was still a relatively familiar place, a place of wars that involved large masses of soldiers and sailors, for example, and weapons that had been developed along lines already laid down in his own time. (The gun-making company Beretta, it should be remembered – the same family-owned company which supplied Ian Fleming's James Bond with one of his favourite weapons and today makes side-arms for the American forces – was founded in northern Italy almost five hundred years ago.)

In the twentieth century, by contrast, Nostradamus was confronted, not only with completely new and different kinds of warfare, but also with many extraordinary inventions and discoveries for which there were not only no words, but no conceptions and no precedents at all. What he saw at the top of his spiral staircase in Salon may well have baffled him just as much as the words he wrote in response baffle us today.

THE RUSSIAN MONARCHY

Perhaps as a result of this, he appears to be at his most accurate when seemingly predicting events involving individuals – though he does in a number of the verses give glimpses of large-scale events and inventions, as we shall later see. Two of the 'personal' quatrains (VI, 72 and VIII, 80), for example, seem to involve the fate of the family of the last Tsar of Russia, Nicholas II:

> By a feigned fury of divine inspiration
> The wife of the great one shall be violated;
> Judges willing to condemn such a doctrine,
> A victim sacrificed to the ignorant people.

and

> The blood of innocents, of widow and virgin,
> So much evil committed by a great Red
> Saints' images [icons] *soaked in burning
>   candle-wax*,
> From fear none will be seen to stir.

The first of the two quatrains is a more or less accurate account of the relationship between the preacher and faith-healer Grigori Rasputin and the Tsarina Alexandra, Nicholas' wife – as well as of its consequences. The occasion of the Tsarina's growing obsession with the so-called *starets*, or 'holy man', was the illness of her son (and heir to the throne) Crown Prince Alexei, who was a haemophiliac: i.e. subject to a condition in which his blood would not clot, making even small cuts and bruises (local internal haemorrhages) potentially fatal. In 1907, Rasputin was called to the bedside of the then three-year-old after a fall had caused bruising and along with it a high fever. He prayed over Alexei for half an hour until his temperature suddenly dropped. After this, he became an indispensable confidant and advisor to the royal family.

The trouble was, of course, that the *starets* in his private life was a tempestuous and uncontrollable character, an uneducated Siberian peasant with a gargantuan appetitite for carousal and seduction. He was also said to be a member of an Orthodox Christian sect known as the *Khlysty*, whose rites culminated in orgies

(hence the 'judges who condemned' both him as an *arriviste* peasant and 'this doctrine'). Although the Tsarina herself was not 'violated' by him (except in her trust) – as was the rumour at the time – many ladies of the court flocked to Rasputin's apartment and almost certainly his bed, hoping to travel higher on the coat-tails of his gathering influence.

The final insult to the entrenched (male) Russian aristocracy came when this tough, bearded man with staring eyes became the Tsar's advisor on political appointments. With the country heading rapidly towards chaos – and with the uxorious Tsar more and more preoccupied with his domestic life – it was a recipe for disaster.

The outraged honour of the aristocracy finally found an unlikely instrument of revenge

Preacher and faith-healer Grigori Rasputin surrounded by followers from the Russian court

in the homosexual fop Prince Felix Yusupov. Two days before New Year's Eve in 1916, Yusupov invited Rasputin to a party at one of his palaces, where a small group of co-conspirators first laced his drinks with cyanide in massive doses, then shot him and beat him with a crowbar. Rasputin, however, refused to die until he was shoved, bound, beneath the ice of the River Neva and drowned.

In *The Mammoth Book of Prophecies*, Damon Wilson adds a fascinating footnote to this story:

> *In 1916, Rasputin wrote a strange document headed "The Spirit of Grigori Rasputin-Novhyk of the Village of Pokrovskoye", which was found among his papers after his murder. It begins by stating that he had foreseen that he would not live past 1 January, and that he had a message for the Tsar and the "Russian Mother" (the Tsarina). If "common assassins" killed him, especially peasants, the Tsar had nothing to fear and Russia would remain a monarchy for centuries to come. If, on the other hand, he was murdered by nobles, the Tsar and his immediate family would all die within two years, and all Russian aristocrats would have died or been driven out of the country within twenty-five years (by 1942).*

It is unlikely that Rasputin – whose own prophecy turned out to be true enough – is the 'victim sacrificed to the ignorant people' of the last line of the first quatrain quoted. This fits the Tsar (and his family) much more readily, as does the second quatrain, set against the background of the Bolsheviks' wholesale destruction of the churches. The 'great Red' involved in both the massacre of the Tsar's family and the burning of icons was Lenin; and it was under his orders that on the morning of July 17th 1918 the 'blood of the innocent' was shed.

By this time the Tsar, his family, their doctor and a number of servants were being held under close house arrest in Yekaterinburg and,

as the White Army approached the city, they were all ordered down to the cellar where they were met by a hastily assembled firing squad.

The Tsar died first, leaving his wife the 'widow' of the first line of the quatrain. Then she too – along with their 'virgin' young children – was gunned down. Their deaths were the prelude to all the deaths that followed in the concentration camps, prisons and cellars of what was later to become the KGB. It was indeed a time when, as Nostradamus writes, 'from fear [of the Great Terror] none will be seen to stir'.

WARS AND POLITICAL TURBULENCE

Why, though, did Nostradamus do so little, as far as we can see, to predict the event which helped to precipitate Tsar Nicholas' abdication and death: The First World War?

It is true that here and there among the quatrains there are references to 'the British' making 'great incursions' in terrain made perilous by 'rains and frosts' (II, 1); to what seem to be artillery shells falling on Rheims and causing vast destruction (III, 18); and to 'the greatest army' (the German, with 14 million men under arms) being put to flight and ultimately being 'driven out of France'.

However, he gives us no coherent picture of either the Eastern or the Western Front. In fact there is really only one quatrain concerning the War which seems truly prophetic (IX, 55, which again I have slightly jumbled):

> 1. *The horrible war is prepared in the west,*
> 4. *Blood, fire, Mercury, Mars, Jupiter in France*
> 3. *So horrible that young, old, beast* [will all succumb].
> 2. *The following year will come the plague.*

The 'horrible' devastation of the 'Great' War, in

which some twenty million people died, was indeed followed, a year after its end, by a 'plague', a worldwide epidemic of influenza, which claimed as many deaths as the War had – perhaps more.

After the War and the Great Influenza Epidemic, there came, of course, the founding of the League of Nations, headquartered in Geneva, and a period of relative peace, prefigured with remarkable accuracy by Nostradamus, along – perhaps – with the growth of sea and air travel (I, 63):

> With the scourges past, the world becomes smaller,
> Peace for a long time, lands inhabited,
> Everyone safe shall go by air, land, sea and wave,
> Then once more the wars begin again.

The wars began again in part because the League of Nations, which was set up to stop them, was little more than a talking shop. It could do nothing to heal the damage done by the demands for reparation forced on defeated Germany by Britain and France. Nor had it any way of imposing its collective will when new war clouds ultimately gathered, as Nostradamus seems to have well understood in two different quatrains which practically leap out of the pages of the *Prophéties* (I, 47 and V, 85):

> The sermons of Lake Geneva will become bothersome,
> Some days will be extended into weeks,
> Then into months, a year, then everything will fail,
> The magistrates will condemn their own empty laws.

and

> Through Switzerland and its neighbours,
> They shall fall to war because of the clouds,

> Lobsters, locusts and gnats,
> The faults of Geneva shall appear quite naked.

The 'clouds [of] lobsters, locusts and gnats' suggest immediately a sixteenth-century vision of the tanks, aeroplanes and artillery-ammunition that Germany began to produce in vast numbers during the process of secret rearmament in the 1930s; among 'the faults of Geneva' was the fact that it could do little or nothing about it – in 1933, Germany simply withdrew from the League to avoid both criticism and inspection, as, in the same year, did Japan when it was criticized for its invasion of Manchuria. As for Mussolini, when he was pilloried for the assault on Abyssinia in 1936, he blithely turned a deaf ear.

By the time of the coming of the Second World War, when Switzerland's neighbours (Germany, Italy and France) 'fell to war' (as in the second quatrain), the League was essentially a dead letter; after the War it dissolved – to the breast-beating of 'magistrates' who condemned, as Nostradamus wrote, 'their own empty laws' – in favour of the United Nations.

Once again Nostradamus seems better on the whole at what I have called 'personal predictions' than at the turbulence, wars and mass movements of the twentieth century. He seems, for example in X 22, to have predicted the fate of Britain's King Edward VIII, later sent into exile as the Duke of Windsor:

> For lack of will to consent to a divorce,
> He who will afterwards be recognized as unworthy,
> The King of the Islands shall be expelled by force,
> Another put in his place who has no sign of kingship.

To most Nostradamian commentators, at least, this is a virtually *en clair* account of the constitutional crisis brought about in 1936 by Edward's

Edward VIII and his brother George contemplate their respective futures at the funeral of their father, George V

ent ly refer to General – later Generalissimo – Francisco Franco, and to his role in the Spanish Civil War of 1936–9 and its aftermath. The second of them even invokes him by name:

> One of the greatest will fly to Spain
> Who for a long time after will cause blood to
>   flow,
> Passing troops through the high mountains,
> Laying waste to everything, but afterwards
>   reigning in peace.

and

> From castel Franco shall come out the
>   assembly,
> The ambassador, not satisfied, will create a
>   split,
> Those of Ribiere will be in the melée
> And withold the entry they have into the
>   great gulf.

plainly stated desire to marry Wallis Simpson, an American who had recently divorced her second husband. Because of it, he was forced by public opinion (and by the then Prime Minister, Stanley Baldwin) to abdicate in favour of his shy and stammering brother, later George VI – who had shown, indeed, 'no sign of kingship' up till then.

Edward was subsequently appointed governor of Bermuda, where there was much gossip about his involvement in an unsavoury murder. He flirted with Hitler's emissaries, and later became little more than a vapid, childless playboy. He was indeed 'afterwards recognized as unworthy' – in contrast to his brother George, who became a truly popular King.

GENERAL FRANCO

Much is also made by Nostradamians of a pair of quatrains (III, 54 and IX, 16) which appar-

In 1936, at the time of the attempted fascist military coup which led to the Spanish Civil War, Franco was in command of the Spanish army in Morocco – and he immediately set his face against the leftist civil government in Madrid. Since the Loyalists, as they became known, controlled the navy – and hence the Straits of Gibraltar which separated Morocco from mainland Spain – he negotiated with the Nazi government of Germany to provide him with air transport. He literally 'flew' (rather than 'fled') to Spain.

He and his men then marched on and took Madrid, where he was hailed by the Nationalists as their new leader and saviour; from then on he conducted a campaign of all-out war on the Loyalists ('laying waste to everything') which left deep and long-lasting wounds ('for a long time after will cause blood to flow') in the body politic. Franco certainly 'passed troops over high mountains' – Spain is, on average, the highest country in Europe, and he did thereafter 'reign in peace' – though it was a peace enforced by a one-man dictatorship.

The second quatrain is remarkable in that it both uses the word 'Franco' and connects it/him directly to events in Spain – *castel* is usually taken to mean the Spanish city of Castile (or else a reference to the Spanish word for 'castle'). The 'assembly' that 'shall come out' may well be the Spanish fascists who supported and in some cases fought for the Nazi cause – in which case 'those of *Ribiere*' referred to were certainly 'involved in the melée', since José Ribiere (in fact Rivera) was the founder of the Spanish fascist party, the Falange.

The second and fourth lines of the quatrain are altogether more mysterious, though Francis X. King in his *Nostradamus*, cited by Damon Wilson, suggests that both are to do with Hitler's request (through his ambassador to Spain) for Franco's assistance. Wilson writes:

> Hitler asked Franco [to] help him take Gibraltar from the British, thus breaking their stranglehold on entry into the Mediterranean "gulf". Franco saw that this would violate his neutrality and flatly refused [thus causing a certain frostiness and a 'split' with the German ambassador]. At the time it was a political gamble to annoy a powerful neighbour like Hitler [especially one who had been so helpful during the Civil War], but in maintaining his neutrality, Franco guaranteed his political survival when the Allies won [World War II].

WORLD WAR II

Quatrains that refer to the causes and conduct of the War itself are relatively few and often broad-brush in their outline. They can be dealt with here under the headlines of their usually accepted themes, a method adopted by Damon Wilson.

MODERN WARFARE

With the quatrains that are generally taken to refer to this Second 'Great' War of the century, we again encounter the anomaly that Nostradamus addresses, not the war itself, but (by and large) the personalities – particularly that of Hitler – engaged in fighting it.

It is not that the seer does not apparently describe the sort of weapons involved, but that references to them are scattered and usually buried in quatrains that either contain no other identifiers or else veer off in other, often impenetrable directions. Hence, we find in different verses (laid out in the order of the 'centuries') references to:

Iron fish (II, 5);

In the heavens shall be seen a long fire with running sparks (II, 46);

The dart of heaven (II, 70);

The noise of the unwanted bird (II, 75);

By fire from heaven the city shall be almost burnt (II, 81);

Fire the colour of gold from heaven to earth shall be seen…
Great murder of mankind, great loss of infants (II, 92);

Armies shall fight in the air a long season (III, 11);

There shall be heard in the air the noise of weapons (IV, 43);

He will use thunderbolts, so many in such an array,
Few and instant, then deep into the West (IV, 99);

References to modern weaponry can be found in the quatrains but are difficult to interpret

The contraption of flying fire
Shall trouble so much… (VI, 34);

Flying boats and galleys (VII, 26);

An earthquake by mortars (IX, 31).

Only very rarely, in fact, does Nostradamus devote a whole quatrain to what seem to be the weapons and techniques of modern warfare, and when he does there are no certain references to which war is meant. Thus in IV, 48:

The fertile and spacious plain round Bordeaux

Shall produce so many hornets and so many grasshoppers,
That the light of the sun shall be darkened,
They shall fly so low, a great plague shall come from them.

Some Nostradamus scholars believe that this is a direct reference to the Allied invasion of France on D-Day in June, 1944, with its vast curtain of air-cover seen here through the prism of an uncomprehending sixteenth-century mind, forced to resort to metaphor to describe what it has seen: others see it as a limited-palette picture of air-bombardment in general. One is reminded by it, perhaps because of this – and despite the reference to Bordeaux – of helicopters and gunships over the paddy-fields of Vietnam. They also suggest that a further quatrain (I, 29) accurately describes the landing-craft used during the D-Day invasion in the same, almost child-like language:

> *When the fish that is both terrestrial and*
> *   aquatic*
> *By a strong wave is thrown upon the shore,*
> *With its strange, smooth and horrifying*
> *   shape,*
> *By sea very soon to the walls enemies will*
> *   come.*

Others believe that this particular quatrain clearly refers to submarines, or else to sea-launched intercontinental ballistic missiles, just as another quatrain (I, 64) seems to invoke other aspects of modern warfare without assigning them to any particular time:

> *They shall think to have seen the sun at*
> *   night,*
> *When the half-human hog is seen;*
> *Noise, singing, a battle fought in the sky*
> *   shall be seen,*
> *And brute beasts heard to speak.*

This can be interpreted – and perhaps should be – as a primitive picture of things that must have left Nostradamus almost literally speechless: searchlights or bombs falling at night ('the sun at night'), tanks or perhaps men in anti-contamination suits ('the half-human hog'); the whizz of shells and the sound of guns in aerial combat ('noise, singing, a battle fought in the sky') and radio communication between personnel carriers ('brute beasts heard to speak').

As usual, though, Nostradamus seems generally leery, when he comes to address World War II, of anything that doesn't immediately concern human beings, individuals – people who, though surrounded by almost unimaginable weapons and inventions, are still recognizably of the same species as himself.

ADOLF HITLER

In a number of quatrains, for example, he seems to predict the birth and rise to power of Hitler, who is said to have recognized himself, much to his delight, particularly in II, 24 (again in a slightly rearranged version):

> *1. Beasts wild with hunger will cross rivers,*
> *2. Most of the field will be against Hister*
> *4. When the child of Germany shall see the*
> *   Rhine;*
> *3. In a cage of iron the great one will be*
> *   drawn.*

Hitler himself believed that the 'beasts wild with hunger' of the first line of the quatrain referred to his unstoppable armies battling for Lebensraum ('living room') to accommodate the desire for new land of the German people and that the 'Hister' of the second line was a direct reference to himself, a combination of his own (assumed) name and of 'Ister', a Latin word for the river Danube, on the banks of which he was born (at Braunau am Inn).

'Most of the field' of nations were indeed set against him when he 'saw' and crossed the river Rhine for the invasion of France, and though Hitler himself probably saw 'the great one drawn into a cage of iron' as his enemies conquered by German steel, the last line clearly applies, in its new place, to Hitler: 'drawn' into 'the cage of iron' of the bunker he retreated to during the final days of the Russian siege of Berlin.

There are other invocations of Hitler, it seems, in three further quatrains (III, 35; III, 58; and IX, 90):

> *Out of the deepest part of Western Europe*
> *Of poor people a child will be born*

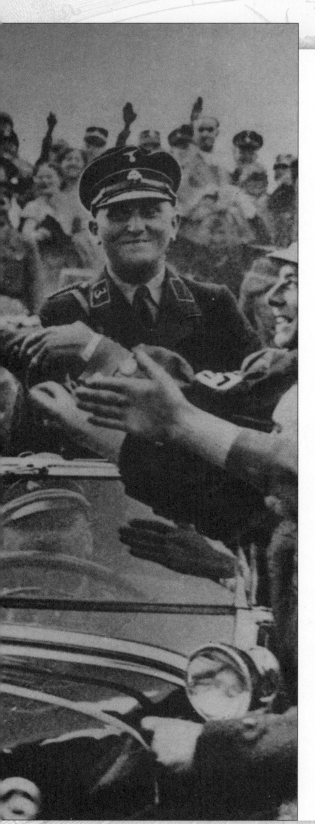

> *Who will seduce many people with his*
> *tongue,*
> *His fame will increase in the Eastern*
> *kingdom.*

and

> *Near the Rhine from the Noric mountains*
> *Will emerge a great man of the people come*
> *too late,*
> *Who will defend Poland and Hungary;*
> *It will not be known what became of him.*

and

> *A great Captain of great Germany*
> *Shall come to yield himself by simulating*
> *help,*
> *A King of Kings, the help to Hungary,*
> *Whose revolt will cause great bloodshed.*

The first of these quatrains is relatively straight-forward: Hitler was indeed born in the depths of Western Europe, in Austria; his father was a badly-paid border official; he rose to power through the strength of his oratory; and 'the Eastern kingdom' – either Russia or the whole territory east of Germany – came to know him only too well.

The other two quatrains are slightly more opaque, though the third, with its reference to 'a… Captain of great Germany' seems extraordinarily prescient, since during Nostradamus' own time there was no such thing as a 'great Germany', only independent – and often warring – kingdoms and principalities. (He speaks elsewhere, and equally presciently, of a 'great' Britain, rather than the separated countries of England, Scotland and Wales.)

Hitler 'emerges', says Nostradamus in the second verse, 'near the Rhine', a phrase which is shorthand for Germany, since the Rhine is

Adolf Hitler did indeed 'seduce many people with his tongue'

the latter's national river. He comes from 'the Noric mountains', which evokes Noricum, a Latin word for Austria. In the end, 'it will not [indeed] be known what became of him', since his body was burned after his suicide in the Berlin bunker, and what remained of his skull (which might have positively identified him) was spirited away to the Soviet Union to entertain Stalin.

The references to Hungary (and to Poland) in the last two of this set of quatrains are on the face of it even more mysterious. However, once again, they more or less fit the facts of history. Although Hungary was a German ally, it late in the War, after the disaster of the Russian campaign, sued for peace to the Allies; Hitler, proclaiming ('simulating') that Hungary needed 'help', promptly occupied it and installed a puppet government. He was later forced to 'defend' both Hungary and Poland, of course, against Soviet armies.

The 'revolt' Nostradamus describes in line 4 of the third stanza could either then mean Hitler's brutal purge of Hungarians after his occupation of the country, or the later anti-Communist 'revolt' of 1956, ruthlessly put down by Russian tanks. What is meant by 'come too late' when applied to Hitler is again not entirely clear. But perhaps Nostradamus meant that the mystagoguery and medievalism that Hitler used to give dignity both to the Nazi movement and German militarism was much better suited to an earlier age.

THE POLITICAL BACKGROUND AND THE HOLOCAUST

(II, 39)

> *A year before the Italian conflict,*
> *Germans, French, Spanish for the strong;*
> *The school house of republicanism will fall*
> *Where, except for a few, they will suffocate to*
> *death.*

Italy joined forces with Germany in 1940, so the second line refers to the situation in Europe the year before, when Germany invaded Czechoslovakia – and when Nazi-style fascism, already entrenched in Spain, had also been taken up by gathering numbers of right-wing French politicians (later to hold office in the French Vichy government). 'The school house of republicanism' in the third line is often interpreted as referring to France, but I prefer to see it as post-First-World-War Germany, which became a turbulent republic with a difficult and painful birth (and education) after the abdication of the Kaiser. Many German Jews were involved in revolutionary movements at the time, and under the Third Reich, amid the ashes of the German Republic, they died in vast numbers, 'except for a few' – 'suffocated to death' in the camps.

THE MOLOTOV-RIBBENTROP PACT OF 1939

(II, 38)

> *There shall be a great number condemned*
> *When the monarchs are reconciled,*
> *But one of them will come to such a bad*
> * obstacle*
> *That their reconciliation will not last long.*

The non-aggression treaty signed between Russia and Germany in 1939 temporarily put off the war between them that was, in the end, inevitable, given their violently antithetical ideologies. It gave Hitler time to enlarge and equip his armies for the coming task, and Stalin a chance to repair the damage done by his execution of the majority of his own officer corps. They quickly jointly invaded Poland and carved it up between themselves in the infamous so-called 'partition'.

Hitler's ambitions in the West, however, were thwarted by the resistance in the air (the 'bad obstacle') of the British. So, deciding simply to contain the British with a sustained bombing campaign, he turned his attentions back eastward. 'The reconciliation' between the two monarchs did not indeed 'last long'. Hitler invaded the Soviet Union in June 1941 – and so 'condemned' a very 'great number' to death – both German and Russian.

THE BATTLE OF THE ATLANTIC

(IV, 15)

> *From the place from which one will think to*
> *   make famine come,*
> *From there will come plenty;*
> *The eye of the sea like a greedy dog,*
> *One shall give oil and wheat to the other.*

Because Britain couldn't produce enough food to feed its own people, Hitler believed that he could ultimately starve it into surrender by interrupting its supply lines to and from the United States. His U-boats were therefore charged with destroying every British convoy they could find. If goods entering Britain could be kept to an absolute minimum, and if the United States could at the same time be frightened away from committing itself to war in Europe, he argued then all that stood between him and his dreams of empire were Russia and an oil-less, toothless, enslaved Great Britain which could be conquered and occupied whenever he chose. 'The eye of the sea' in line 3 is a striking image of the U-boat's periscope peering out from underwater 'like a greedy dog', looking for prey.

Hitler's double strategy, however, in the end failed. American troops and *matériel*, as well as wheat and oil – the use of the word 'oil' is particularly striking – were soon streaming across the Atlantic via the convoys, to permanently alter the European balance of power. Hitler's factories churned out tanks rather than more

submarines; the British soon had access to the U-boats' secret radio-codes via their computer-driven 'Enigma' programme and radar and more accurate depth-charges did the rest. Although about a quarter of all Allied merchant seamen on the Atlantic run were either killed or drowned, the death rate among U-boat crews was around three times higher.

The Battle of the Atlantic was a crucial victory for the Allies, for it made Britain a bastion – in Winston Churchill's phrase, 'Fortress Britain' – from which new assaults could be launched, new warfronts opened, as Nostradamus himself seems to have recognized in another quatrain (III, 71):

> *Those in the Islands who have long been*
> *   besieged*
> *Will use vigour and force against their*
> *   enemies;*
> *Those outside, overcome, will die of hunger,*
> *They will face a greater famine than ever*
> *   before experienced.*

The second half of this verse has often been taken to refer to scarcities and oppression faced in countries occupied by the Axis powers, particularly the countries of the Soviet Union. Having said that, the words 'a greater famine than ever experienced' suggest something much darker: the deliberate policy of starvation to death in the German concentration camps.

PEARL HARBOR

(X, 100)

> *Naval battle, night shall be overcome;*
> *Fire shall bring ruin to the ships in the West;*
> *A new stratagem, the great ship coloured;*
> *Anger to the vanquished and victory in a*
> *   fog.*

On December 7th 1941, just after dawn ('night'

The horror of nuclear warfare, prophesied by Nostradamus, became frighteningly real for the citizens of Hiroshima and Nagasaki

having been 'overcome'), the Japanese launched a massive air-attack on the American Pacific fleet from camouflaged ('coloured') air-craft-carriers off the coast of Hawaii. Fire did indeed 'bring ruin to the ships in the West' – eighteen were sunk, two hundred aircraft were destroyed, and 3,000 servicemen and women were killed.

In the United States the prevailing public mood changed overnight – pacifism was quite suddenly seen as unpatriotic ('anger to the van-quished'); even the odd phrase 'victory in a fog' is an accurate picture of part of what transpired. It could be said that the Japanese failed in the 'fog' of war to find and destroy the principal US carriers, which were out at the time on manoeu-vre and their survival unharmed was the ulti-mate reason for the eventual US 'victory' in the Pacific.

HIROSHIMA AND NAGASAKI

(II, 6)

Near the gates and within two cities

There will be two scourges, the like of which
  have never been seen before;
Famine within plague, people thrust out by
  iron,
Cries for help to the great God immortal.

'Two cities'; 'two scourges' never before seen – the clear candidate for this remarkable quatrain is the dropping of atomic bombs on Hiroshima and Nagasaki in 1945 – a candidacy that is underwritten if the French word *'portes'* or 'doors' in the first line is altered by a letter and indicates that Nostradamus perhaps intended *'ports'* or 'harbours'. (Both Hiroshima and Nagasaki are port-cities.) 'Famine within plague' suggests the effects of radiation sickness and 'people thrust out by iron' – a phrase that is extremely unclear in the original French – may in fact be 'people outwardly [as if] thrust through by the sword', bleeding, their skin torn off by an unseen agency. When considering the fourth line, there were certainly prayers for help from the dying victims – just as there are continuing prayers in the maintenance of their memory today.

EVENTS AFTER WORLD WAR II

Only a handful of Nostradamus' quatrains seem to refer directly to events after the Second World War, but they can be construed as dealing with some key moments in post-War history. One celebrated verse (III, 97), for example, refers, according to investigators, to:

THE FOUNDATION OF THE STATE OF ISRAEL

A new law will occupy a new country
Towards Syria, Judaea and Palestine;
The great Barbarian Empire will crumble
Before the Sun makes an end of its cycle.

Palestine, after World War I, became a British protectorate, though it had been promised to Britain's Arab allies in return for their wartime help. Then a classic piece of diplomatic double-talk it was also guaranteed in principle to Jews who wanted to return, after some seventeen hundred years, to their lost historic home of Judaea. After the Second World War, exhausted and demoralized by the thirty years of civil unrest and terrorism that was the result of this havering, the British announced they intended to withdraw their occupying forces in 1948, and handed over the so-called 'problem' of Palestine to the newly-formed United Nations.

The UN in its wisdom – and partly out of a collective guilt for their lack of response to the Holocaust – decreed that half of Palestine should now be set aside for the foundation of a new state of Israel. Palestinian Arabs – and the surrounding Arab countries of Syria, Jordan, Egypt, Lebanon and Iraq – were outraged. Their unity-in-opposition ('the Barbarian Empire'), however, crumbled in the face of the ruthlessness and superior military skill of the Israeli armed forces.

THE 1956 RUSSIAN INVASION OF HUNGARY

(II, 90)

By life and death the kingdom of Hungary
will be changed,
The law will become harsher than service;
Their great city will be full of howlings,
laments and cry,
With Castor and Pollux enemies in the lists.

After brutal occupation by their one-time German allies – a matter, indeed of 'life and death' – Hungarians welcomed the Soviet army when it entered Budapest towards the end of the War. A Communist régime was soon installed and from then on Hungary was ruled by the Soviets with an iron hand – 'the law will become harsher than service'. In 1956, though, students in Budapest demonstrated against being forced to learn Russian – and anti-Soviet demonstrations soon spread across the whole country. The Communists were in the end hounded from office and a multiparty democracy was declared. The Politburo in Moscow soon responded – especially after the new Hungarian government, egged on by the West, declared the country neutral – by sending in its tanks.

The Hungarians – desperately appealing to the West for help (with 'howls, laments and cry') which never came – put up what resistance they could. However, they were themselves divided: Hungarian communists ended up joining the invading forces and fighting 'free' Hungarians for their stake in the future.

Though the two sides were truly 'Castor and Pollux' – Greek heroes, born twin brothers – they became 'enemies in the lists' in the battle for control of their country. It was to be another three decades and more before Hungarians had a further taste of real freedom, though Russians who visited Hungary were, from then on, astonished by the country's prosperity and high standard of living, as compared to their own.

THE FALL OF THE BERLIN WALL
(V, 81)

> *The royal bird over the city of the sun*
> *Seven months before will give nightly*
>   *warning,*
> *The Eastern wall will fall and the lightning*
>   *shine,*

The enemies on cue at the gates for seven
days.

'The city of the sun' is identified by some Nostradamians as Berlin, the capital of North Germany, whose astrological sign is Leo – the principal sun sign; and Damon Wilson goes on to suggest as the main candidate for its 'royal bird' 'the statue of a winged Angel of Victory that stands… in the middle of [the city]… on top of the [Brandenburg] Gate', through which the Wall ran, dividing east and west Berlin.

The statue of the winged Angel of Victory atop the Brandenburg Gate, scene of much rejoicing when the Berlin Wall fell

For more or less the 'seven months' of the second line, he adds, before the Wall fell, there were demonstrations and mass meetings – as well as such events as the opening by Hungary of its border with Austria – all across the Soviet satellite states of eastern Europe. The phrase 'The enemies on cue at the gates for seven days' of line 4 may perhaps be a reference to the scenes of rejoicing as east and west Berliners came together across the razed Wall regularly and freely – for the first time in twenty-eight years.

THE DEATH OF POPE JOHN PAUL I (1978)

(X, 12 and III, 65)

Elected Pope, as elected mocked
Called at once impulsive and timid,
By too much good sweetness destined to die,
Night brings his death, fearful and upright.

and

When the sepulchre of the great Roman is
found,
A day after a Pope will be elected,
He will scarcely be approved by the Senate,
Empoisoned his blood in the sacred chalice.

Albino Luciani, who took the name Pope John Paul I, was elected at the first vote of the Conclave of Cardinals after the death of Paul VI (named after the 'great Roman' of the first line of the second quatrain, Paul of Tarsus, who was a Roman citizen). He was a man of shining goodness, but he became Pope at a time of deep corruption both in Italy and within the Vatican; when he announced that he personally was going to restore complete transparency in all financial and administrative matters and weed out those who had been responsible for a series of financial scandals involving the P2 Masonic lodge and the Mafia, he immediately made many, many enemies – not least within the Italian Senate. He was widely mocked – as in the first quatrain – as a simpleton. In the end, he reigned as pontiff for just one month.

A few days before he was due to deliver his report on financial irregularities in the Vatican Bank, he was found one night ill and 'fearful' in bed; his attendants held him 'upright'; then he died. At the request of the Vatican, no autopsy was, it seems, ever conducted. There were rumours at the time that the stomach medicine at his bedside had been tampered with, and that his blood had therefore truly been 'empoisoned' in 'the sacred chalice'.

DETENTE BETWEEN THE SUPERPOWERS

One day the two great masters will be friends,
Their great power will see itself increased
The new land shall be at the height of its
estate
To the man of blood the number is reported.

This verse (II, 89) is generally reckoned to refer to the growing friendship, particularly after the fall of the Berlin Wall, between 'the great masters', Ronald Reagan and Mikhail Gorbachev, the latter of whom is likely to be 'the man of blood' – i.e. the man with a spreading port-wine birthmark on his forehead – of line 4.

At the time, of course, 'the new land', the United States, was truly at 'the height of its estate', threatening a new escalation of the Cold War through its mooted 'Star Wars' programme. However after an agreement was reached by the two men at Reykjavik, when their 'great power' – or popularity – was indeed vastly increased, nuclear missiles on both sides were made subject to inspection. Their numbers were counted and supernumerary missiles were destroyed on home soil – all of which was reported back to 'the man of blood' in the Kremlin.

Agreement between Reagan and Gorbachev stemmed the tide of nuclear expansion

There is another tantalizing reference, it seems, to the demise of Communism in two lines of quatrain IV, 32:

> *The old stands fast, then is ousted from the middle;*
> *The rule of 'All things in common among friends' is set aside*

Indeed, in several of the quatrains, scattered through the *'Centuries'*, there are a number of extremely suggestive lines, said by Nostradamians to refer variously to the Iran-Iraq War ('Towards Persia very near a million': V, 25); to Fidel Castro's visit to America ('Into the new land the King advances far/While the subjects come to bid him welcome': VIII, 74) and to the assassination of President John Kennedy and the fate of his two brothers ('A great King taken within the hands of a young man…/When three brothers will be wounded [Edward Kennedy at Chappaquidick] and murdered [Robert Kennedy in Los Angeles]').

SPACE TRAVEL

These scraps are will-of-the-wisps when compared to perhaps the most declarative of all Nostradamus' verses generally seen as belonging to the late twentieth century (IX, 65):

Buzz Aldrin walking in the 'strange land' featured in quatrain IX, 65

He will come to arrive within a corner of the
moon
Where he will be taken and put in a strange
land;
The unripe fruit will cause a great scandal,
Great shame, to one great praise.

The first two lines of this quatrain are unequivocal: a man will eventually be landed on the moon – an event unimaginable, one would have thought, to a sixteenth-century mind. But even the details recorded by Nostradamus in his eyrie seem to be correct. For as Damon Wilson points out, the rocket which ultimately resulted in Neil Armstrong's historic moon-walk – in what was, after all, a very 'strange land' indeed – was fired on a predetermined trajectory in much the same way that the circus performer called a "human cannonball" is shot into a distant net. Since they had minimal control over the space-flight, it would therefore be accurate to say that the astronauts were "taken" to the moon [and "put" upon it].

He goes on to add that, though the moon strictly speaking cannot be said to have corners, the landing-craft of the Apollo 11 mission landed in the so-called Sea of Tranquillity, 'in the upper left-hand corner' of the 'face' that the moon – which does not rotate on its axis as the earth does – presents to us as we on earth look up at her.

As to 'the unripe fruit' which 'will cause a great scandal', he suggests (with Francis X. King) that this is a reference to the Challenger shuttle disaster of 1986, which killed six NASA crewmen, as well as the first civilian to be taken on a space mission, teacher Christa McAuliffe. This was the result of a design-fault (the shuttle was, because of it, 'unripe'), and NASA's budget, amid much anger (and 'shame') from the public, was quickly cut back. The American enthusiasm for space, which reached a pitch after Neil Armstrong's moon-walk ('to one great praise'), ebbed away.

With the space-race and its aftermath, of course, we are now in recognizably modern terrain. It is time, then, to look at Nostradamus' predictions that span the arrival of the third millennium AD and may prefigure our collective future.

The 21st Century

THE BEGINNING OF THE FUTURE

I now have to embark on the extremely per-ilous business of trying to fit some of the remaining eighty-five per cent of Nostradamus' quatrains into future time. I shall begin by look-ing once more at the strange letter of dedica-tion to Henri II which has exercised Nostradamians' minds over the years and which Nostradamus wrote for the publication of his last three 'centuries' in 1568.

It will be remembered that Luciano Sampi-etro, in his *Nostradamus: The Final Prophecies*, managed to dig out of this very odd document – to his own satisfaction, at any rate – a rough end-date for the prophecies of 2025-27, with the beginning of some sort of end-game in 1994. This was the year, also targeted by other Nostradamian commentators, in which NATO intervened against Serbia, particularly over the issue of Muslim Kosovo, and an independent Palestinian state, under Yasser Arafat, was (the-oretically) born. Sampietro goes on to quote part of section 113 of the dedication (most likely numbered – like all the other sections – by Nostradamus himself):

> And it will be near [the end of] the seventh
> millennium that the sanctuary of Jesus Christ
> will be increasingly oppressed by the infidels
> who will come from l'Aquillon, and the world
> will come near to a great conflagration…

The key word in this section is, of course, *l'Aquillon*, which has two l's, rather than the one of '*l'Aquilon*', which is used elsewhere by Nos-tradamus to mean 'the North' or 'the country of the Eagle'. Sampietro proposes that the word used here is instead the sixteenth-century ver-sion of the modern word 'aiguillon', a 'sting' or 'spur, or of "aiguille", a 'boring-needle', a 'cusp' or a 'needle-like point', particularly of rock. This word, he suggests, has a double connec-

Could the strange word 'l'Aquillon' indicate the increasing influence of the Muslim faith?

tion to the world of Islam, first through the needle-like spire set over a hemispheric roof that is typical of important Islamic buildings, particularly mosques; and secondly through the cusp or horn of the crescent or sickle-moon, the emblem of the Turkish empire and of the Muslim faith.

This theory would certainly fit with the use (in this professedly Christian context) of the description of 'the infidels who come from l'Aquillon' who will increasingly oppress 'the sanctuary of Jesus Christ' – a phrase which might be used here of the city of Jerusalem and/or the whole of Christendom (i.e. the countries of the West). Sampietro then goes on to quote another part of the section 113:

> And at that time and in those countries, the infernal power will confront the Church of Jesus Christ with the force of the adversaries of his law and it will be the second Antichrist, who will persecute that Church and its true Vicar by way of the power of its temporal Kings, who for their ignorance will be seduced by tongues that will cut better than a sword in the hands of the madman.

Writing before the destruction of New York's World Trade Center on 9/11 and the invasion of first Afghanistan and then Iraq he suggests by inference that the 'temporal Kings' are the royal families and political dynasties who control the oil of the Middle East. He contends that they will be deceived by the honeyed, but ultimately hugely destructive, words of 'the second Antichrist'.

Not every commentator agrees with this theory. As Damon Wilson points out in his *The Mammoth Book of Prophecies*:

> The Antichrist/beast was predicted by the early Church to appear shortly before the end of the world. [But his] *role as the great villain (second only to Satan) was largely the creation of*

theologians from the late Byzantine period and early Middle Ages, who felt the need for a balancing "enemy" for Jesus… [The Antichrist] is only passingly referred to in the New Testament… where he is simply a false prophet and a denier of Jesus' divinity… [and] by Nostradamus's day, the label "antichrist" was used for a wicked [anti-Christian] person as well as Christ's predicted adversary…

Which of these two was intended by Nostradamus in the present context of the dedication to Henri II is impossible to say. What he does seem to be saying, however, is that some virulently anti-Christian person or movement will seduce the 'temporal kings' into supporting him or it, to their eventual great detriment. This immediately brings to mind, not only the conscience-money given by Saudi-Arabia to fundamentalist madrassas and to organisations like al-Qa'eda, but also a very curious quatrain from the *Prophéties* (I. 87):

> World-shaking fire of the centre of the earth
> Will bring an earthquake to the tower of the
>   new city;
> Two great rocks will make war on each other
>   for a long time,
> Then Arethusa will redden a new river.

'The centre of the earth' or in other words 'The World Centre'; 'Two great rocks'… It is all too tempting to believe that 'the new city' of line 2 *must* be New York, and that 'the tower' in the same line has to refer once more to what were the city's tallest buildings.

If a comma – not present, it has to be said, in the original – is placed after 'two great rocks' in line 3 (and thus continuing: 'They will make war…'), then the phrase would become an exact description of the Twin Towers. Even if a comma is not inserted there, Nostradamus can be interpreted as saying that two 'rocks' – or equally obdurate enemies – will thereafter launch an extended war against each other, as indeed they have.

As for the last line, though the French 'Arethuse' is the name of a mythical Greek nymph transformed into a stream, Erica Cheetham suggests that the name is being used here as a hybrid-cum-anagram of 'Ares', the name of the Greek god of war, and the acronym 'USA'!

This interpretation of I, 87 is, of course, hugely seductive – though as with many other quatrains there is no absolute proof of any kind. Nevertheless, Nostradamus did seem to see the power of the United States being turned eastward, when the time came. In quatrain I, 50, he records:

> From the aquatic triplicity shall be born
> One who shall make Thursday his holiday;
> His fame, praise, reign and power will grow
> By land and sea, to become a tempest to the
>   countries of the East.

'The aquatic triplicity' may be interpreted as the three seas which engird the United States: the Atlantic and Pacific Oceans, and the Gulf of Mexico. The United States does indeed celebrate its national holiday, Thanksgiving, on a Thursday, the third Thursday of every November, and there is no doubt that since the Second World War its power 'by land and sea' has grown enormously. It has also, no doubt, with the invasions of Afghanistan and Iraq, 'become a tempest to the countries of the east'…

What we have here, then, in the dedication to King Henri II and a number of quatrains, is the suggestion of a potential future scenario, with its origins in the recent past. If Luciano Sampietro and others are right, the crucial year in this scenario is 1994, when despite – and in part because of – international intervention, Christians and Muslims were set at gathering odds with each other in central Europe for the first time in the modern era, in a war that has continued to fester, with the repeated destruction of churches and mosques.

ISLAMIC UNREST

Islamic jihadists, largely from the Middle East, came to join in the fighting, just as they have in that other continuing war between (Orthodox Christian) Russia and (Wahabbist Muslim) Chechnya. There may be references to both these conflicts in the first three lines of II, 32, where I have treated the phrase 'de baliene' (or 'de Balennes') as a barely disguised code for 'Albania':

> Milk, blood, frogs shall rain in Dalmatia.
> Conflict passed on, pestilence to nearby
>   Albania;
> The shouting will be great throughout
>   Slavdom…

Roughly contemporarily with this – the first modern meeting in Europe of ethnic/religious war and international intervention – the foundation of the Palestinian state in 1994 set the scene for other similar hostilities in the Middle East: this time the bitter enmity – a war in everything else but name – between Israel and the Palestinians under Yasser Arafat. Strong for the Palestinian cause – though divided among themselves – were virtually all the Arab (and predominantly Muslim) countries of the area, while Israel had one major ally, the United States, which was – like many other Western (Christian) countries – prepared to turn a blind eye to the land-grabbing and vengeful ferocity of the Israeli government.

Every event after 1994 – the takeover of the West Bank, the Intifada, the increasing intransigence of Jewish sects, of right-wing elements in successive Israeli governments and of terrorist organizations fostered by Arafat – may again have been predicted by Nostradamus in I, 55:

Under the hostile climate of Babylon
There will be a great effusion of blood
So that land and sea, air, sky will be unjust;
Sects, hunger, régimes, plagues, confusion.

It was, however, the intervention of al-Qa'eda in
the 1990s that, in effect, turned these two separate areas of conflict into battlefields in a single
global conflict. By intervening, with other
jihadists, in the Balkans, in Chechnya, in
Muslim Africa and against the American presence (and the existence of the state of Israel) in
the Middle East, al-Qa'eda gave notice of a war
between a theocratic and all-enveloping version
of Islam and any 'infidels' or 'heretics' who per-
secuted it or stood in its way.

There followed, of course, the events of 9/11
– and the rumour that quickly swept though the
souks of Asia that the attack had been organized by America itself, and that Jews who would
normally have been at work that day in the
World Trade Center had been forewarned. It
was one more clear sign – it was soon taken for
granted – that there was an anti-Islamist con-
spiracy between Christians and Jews.

This view was unfortunately reinforced by the
comments of US President George Bush in the
run-up to the invasion of Afghanistan and the
toppling of the Taliban régime. The military
action there was described by the president as 'a
crusade', turning Osama bin Laden in the
process into the modern equivalent of Saladin,
the heroic 12th-century warrior who fought the
Crusaders, took the city of Jerusalem and
reduced the Western-ruled Kingdom of
Jerusalem to a thin coastal strip.

THE EMERGENCE OF AL-QA'EDA AND OSAMA BIN LADEN

The emergence of Osama bin Laden as a pan-
Islamic hero and as a catalyst for anti-Western
feeling across the Islamic world is perhaps foretold in quatrain I, 84:

Moon obscured in deepest shadows,
Her [past?] brother turned the colour of iron;
The great one long hidden in the shadows
Shall cool a sword in the bleeding wound.

The 'moon obscured in deepest shadows' is

Although vilified by many in the West, Osama bin Laden has won hero status elsewhere in the world

clearly both the crescent moon of Islam (a moon mostly obscured by the shadow of the earth) and 'the great one' of the third line, who having hitherto lived in obscurity emerges onto the glare of the world stage, thereby dragging the Moon's brother (the Sun? Christianity?) into a state of war ('the colour of iron'). The identification of this figure with Islam is confirmed by line 4, since it was believed at one time by Damascus swordsmiths that, to achieve the finest quality of steel, newly forged blades should be annealed by being thrust into the bodies of living victims. Osama bin Laden, of course, can also be seen as thrusting his sword into the already 'bleeding wound' of bad relations and mutual suspicion between East and West.

Another quatrain (I, 56) again seems to warn of the coming of a great leader from the world of Islam ('the moon') to challenge Western Christianity ('heaven', 'the Sun'):

> Sooner or later you will see great change
> Extreme horrors and acts of vengeance,
> So that if the moon is led by its Angel,
> Heaven approaches its inclinations.

That there will be a major conflict between 'Sun' and 'Moon' Nostradamus seems to have no doubt – and he appears, on the basis of two verses (I, 92 and IV, 43), to believe that the 'Sun', the West, in the beginning at any rate, will have the worst of it:

> The Gods will make it appear to mankind
> That they will be the prime movers of a great
>   conflict;
> The sky once serene will show sword and
>   lance,
> On the left hand will be greater affliction.

and

> Weapons will be heard fighting in the sky
> In the same year the divines will become

> enemies;
> They will unjustly debate the holy laws;
> Through thunder and war true believers will
>   die.

It seems that Nostradamus in these two quatrains is saying that both sides in the conflict will pronounce it a holy war, a mission of God – a *jihad* on the one side, a Crusade on the other and that the sky of the first quatrain, once serene (over Afghanistan and Iraq, perhaps) will be filled (again, perhaps) with missiles and the vapour-trails of combat aircraft. 'The left hand' – the West, traditionally, in maps – will suffer 'greater affliction' in the form of increased loss of prestige, and the sort of attack that may well have been prefigured in quatrain X, 95:

> An all-powerful king will come to Spain,
> Subjugating the south by land and sea;
> He will do evil lowering the crescent,
> And lowering the wings of those of Friday
>   [the Muslim holy day].

Another quatrain (V, 55) expands on this theme:

> Out of a fertile Arabian country
> Will be born a strong master of
>   Mohammedan law,
> Who will vex Spain and conquer Granada…

THE END OF THE FUTURE

The two quatrains that end the previous section obviously involve a Muslim incursion – perhaps under the auspices of that 'strong master of Muhammedan law', Osama bin Laden – into Spain, over which Islam once had sovereignty. That it – and particularly the jewelled city of Granada – was lost to the Crescent some five hundred years ago remains the source of bitter regret and pain.

It may be that the train-bombs exploded in Madrid in 2004 – followed by the suicides of some of the co-conspirators – were just a beginning, as suggested by quatrain IX, 51:

Against the reds sects will gather themselves
By fire, water, iron, rope, peace will be
    destroyed.
Those who will conspire to the point of death,
Except one, who shall above all ruin the
    world.

What else, though, can be said, on the basis of Nostradamus' *Prophéties*, about what seems to be one of their most reiterated themes: i.e. the emergence in the East of a hugely dangerous but charismatic figure ('one who shall' – perhaps, as above – 'ruin the world')? The *Prophéties* in general are full of the distant echoes of a war caused by extended friction between West and East, Christianity and Islam. The war, on the face of it, seems to come in two phases: first a war of planetary devastation followed by an uneasy peace; and then a second war, led in the West by a new leader who manages at last to bring both victory and a golden age of peace.

The beginning of the conflict appears to be complicated in some way by the behaviour of the French (as in verse I, 18, 'Because of French disagreement and negligence/The passage will be opened to Mohammed…'). This may well refer to the French opposition to the second Gulf War. However, Turkey will ultimately ally itself to the Western cause (as in verse V, 47, 'The great Arab will march well ahead/Betrayed he will be by the Byzantines [Turks])' – though whether this means that Turkey will betray 'the great Arab' by not joining in a broad-front anti-Western (and anti-Christian) movement, or will literally hand him over to his enemies, is not clear.

The Haram mosque in Mecca, a place of annual pilgrimage for Muslims

As for the rest of the conduct of what, according to Nostradamus, will be a massive conflict, it seems best to gather the quatrains that seem relevant together here by theme. I shall also include, where germane, short passages from the dedication to Henri II in the 1568 edition of the *Prophéties*. Thus:

TERRORIST ACTION AGAINST THE U.S.A., BRITAIN, SPAIN AND FRANCE

(X, 49; II, 100; VI, 80; II, 29; V, 54)

> *Garden of the world near the new city,*
> *In the road of the hollow mountains,*
> *It will be seized and plunged into the Tank.*
> *Drinking perforce water poisoned with*
> *   sulphur.*

'The new city', one must assume as before, is New York, though the terrorist attack will come not in New York, says Nostradamus, but nearby, in New Jersey, known today as the 'Garden State' ('garden of the world'); it will affect a major city or cities, perhaps New York itself – a fact suggested by the phrase 'in the road of the hollow mountains', i.e. a canyon between skyscrapers.

Nostradamus indicates that the attack will involve the secret poisoning of reservoirs which will contaminate the drinking supply used by an unsuspecting public ('perforce').

> *Inside the islands, so horrible a tumult,*
> *Only a war-like quarrel will be heard;*
> *So great will be the predators' insult*
> *That there will be an alliance with the grand*
> *   league.*

'The islands', as before, refer to Britain, and here Nostradamus is much more vague about the nature of the attack. All he talks about is a 'predators' insult' which will unleash a huge

reaction, a 'horrible tumult'. The suggestion is made that all opposition to the war against terrorism, personified by the suicide bombers of al-Qa'eda ('those who will conspire to the point of death'), will rapidly melt away in response to the outrage, and Britain will join with new enthusiasm 'the grand league' – in all probability the United Nations – that will ultimately be set against it.

> *From Fez the kingdom will come to those of*
> *   Europe;*
> *Fire to their city and the sword will cut;*
> *The great one of Asia, by land and sea with*
> *   a great army,*
> *So that blues, pars, cross, he shall drive to*
> *   death.*

The authors of the Madrid train-bombs ('fire to their city') were largely Moroccan Arabs, and a number of them seem to have fled back to Morocco in the bombing's aftermath. Fez, of course, is one of the principal cities of Morocco, where a group of jihadists connected to al-Qa'eda and Osama bin Laden ('the great one of Asia') had already struck.

This quatrain suggests that Morocco is an important base for fundamentalist Islamic terrorists, and that they will ultimately spread their campaign elsewhere, particularly, it seems, to France (where a ban on religious dress in schools was imposed in 2004). The word 'blues' in other contexts in the *Prophéties* seems to indicate the French – and there is at least the possibility that the odd word '*pars*' stands for Paris. 'Cross' in the last line, of course, stands for Christians in general, another principal target for jihadists.

> *The Oriental will come out of his seat,*
> *Will pass over the Apennine Mountains and*
> *   see France,*
> *Shall penetrate across the sky, the waters and*
> *   snow*
> *And shall strike everyone with his rod.*

This quatrain once more indicates an attack against France, this time coming from Italy (passing over 'the Apennine mountains'). Line 3 may mean that a terrorist or terrorists will arrive in France by air from northern Italy (penetrating 'across the sky, the waters and the snow'), or that some sort of guided missile or laser weapon will be involved, one that 'shall strike everyone with his rod'.

> *From the Black Sea and great Tartary,*
> *A king there will be who will come to see France,*
> *He will penetrate through Alania and Albania*
> *And in Istanbul will leave his bloody pole.*

This is the most persuasive of all the quatrains seemingly referring to al-Qa'eda and bin Laden. Again we have 'a king' from the East – in the earlier verses described as 'the Oriental' and 'the kingdom' – but in this case he is specifically said to come from 'Tartary', the part of central Asia which traditionally includes Afghanistan, Osama bin Laden's hiding place.

Also of extreme pertinence are the two places the 'king' is described as penetrating (perhaps via 'the Black Sea') on his way to France in line 3: Alania and Albania. Alania is an old name for the territory of the Alani, a warlike race which once inhabited the Caucasus, the home today, of course, of the Chechen people – and the war in modern Chechnya against Russian forces is known to have drawn large numbers of al Qa'eda jihadist fighters – some of whom, at the time of writing, seem to be holed up in northern Georgia on the Black Sea.

Al Qa'eda also fought in the second place mentioned in line 3, once part of 'Albania': Albanian Kosovo. There it was pitched against Christian Serbs in the year which Nostradamus seems to have appointed as providing the root-cause of all disasters – many of them involving al Qa'eda – to follow. The specific reference in

the last line to Istanbul ('Bizances' for Byzantium, in the original) seems to me to clinch the ascription.

In 2004, Istanbul suffered the first of what may become an extended string of al Qa'eda bombings. Perhaps the French security agencies have already taken note both of this and of the other related predictions.

TROUBLE IN THE MIDDLE EAST

(III, 4; VIII, 96)

> *When of the people of the Moon they shall be near default,*
> *Not very far from one another;*
> *Cold, drought, danger towards the frontiers,*
> *Even where the oracle had his beginning*

'The people of the Moon' are once again the Islamic nations of the Middle East, It is foretold by Nostradamus that one of them, almost certainly Saudi Arabia, will have to confront severe social problems ('cold, drought') and at the same time a dangerous external threat that will reach even to the birthplace of Muhammad in Mecca. This is confirmed in section 75 of the dedication to Henri II: "And the city of Mecca itself will be attacked and assailed from all directions with great violence by armed people."

> *The Synagogue barren without fruit*
> *Shall be received among the infidels;*
> *The daughter of the persecution of Babylon,*
> *Miserable and sad shall cut her wings.*

This quatrain (VIII, 96) strongly suggests that the state of Israel ('the synagogue barren without fruit') will in the long run be overrun as a result of 'the persecution of Babylon', and will have to shrink back within reduced borders ("shall cut her wings'). Once again, this is in line with the dedication to Henri II (sections 74 and 78-79): 'That place where the habitation of

Abraham was shall be assaulted... And the Holy Sepulchre, held in great veneration for such a long time, will remain a great while open to the universal aspect of the heavens, the sun and the moon. The sacred place shall be converted into a stable for cattle small and large, and put to profane uses...'

NUCLEAR DISASTER AND INVASION

(V, 98; II, 3; II, 4; X, 60, VII, 6)

> [There shall] *be so great a plague that two parts of three in the world shall fail, so much so that no-one shall be able to know the true owners of fields and houses.*
>
> DEDICATION TO HENRI II
(SECTION 70-71)

> *At forty-eight degrees of the climacteric,*
> *At the end of Cancer shall be such a great drought,*
> *That fish in the sea, river and lake shall be cooked, fevered;*
> *Bearn and Bigorre by heavenly fire shall be in distress.*

The astrological reference is unclear, although it is hard to imagine fish being '"cooked" in sea, river and lake' without the sort of huge temperatures unleashed by the nuclear explosion or meltdown suggested by the phrase 'heavenly fire'. This unsettling possibility is underwritten by another quatrain from the *Prophéties* (II, 3):

> *By heat like the Sun upon the sea*
> *Around Negrepont the fish are half broiled;*
> *The inhabitants will come to cut them up,*
> *When Rhodes and Genoa are in want of biscuits.*

Several of Nostradamus' prophecies hint at the chilling prospect of nuclear disaster

Erica Cheetham contends that *'Negrepont'* (otherwise 'Black Bridge' or the name, Negriponte, of the first post-invasion American ambassador to Iraq) is a word used of the Mediterranean island of Ruboea – at the centre, it seems here, of a nuclear explosion or accident (perhaps involving a nuclear submarine).

The last two lines suggest that the dead fish will suddenly be the only food available to the survivors – and also that hunger is by then widespread from northern Italy to the Greek islands. It is significant, perhaps, that this verse should immediately precede a further quatrain which may relate to the same unnatural disaster:

> *From Monaco as far as Sicily.*
> *All the coast will be left desolate;*
> *There will not be suburbs, cities or towns,*
> *Which shall not be pillaged and plundered by*
> *   Barbarians.*

Once more, the desolation along the whole coastline of western Italy strongly suggests the presence of some sort of radiation – perhaps the poisoning (via the use of so-called 'dirty bombs') of either the sea or the littoral's main cities. Nostradamus, however, may have in mind here some more conventional form of attack, since clearly the 'suburbs, cities and towns' remain safe enough for the 'Barbarians' to pillage and plunder them – it is worth noting that Nostradamus would consider Barbarians to be non-Christians rather than people from the Barbary States. Whatever the cause of this disaster, though, Nostradamus often returns to it, as in:

> *Naples, Palermo and all Sicily,*
> *By barbarous hands shall be depopulated,*
> *Corsica, Salerno and the Island of Sardinia*
> *Famine, plague, hunger and endless evils.*

In a number of quatrains Nostradamus also refers to the island of Malta as being somehow at the epicentre of whatever disaster it is that befalls. It is also included in a further Nostradamian prediction of a disaster:

> *I mourn for Naples, Monaco, Pisa, Genoa,*
> *Savona, Sienna, Capua, Modena, Malta;*
> *Upon them blood and sword for a new-year*
> *   gift;*
> *Fire, earthquake, water, unhappy ending.*

Malta, it should be noticed, is the odd one out of the territories which, it seems, are to come under attack around New Year's Day of an unknown year. As Nostradamus would probably have had little, if any, knowledge of other belief systems which have different dates for the New Year (Chinese, Muslim etc.) it is presumed to be the Christian New Year. All the rest are Italian cities – even Monaco was part of Italian territory until the nineteenth century – due to undergo (since they haven't, apparently, yet) 'fire, earthquake, water, unhappy ending'.

A WORLDWIDE FAMINE

(I, 67; III, 42; V, 90; VI, 5)

> *The great famine whose coming I sense,*
> *Will return to different places and then*
> *   become worldwide,*
> *So great and lasting that from the woods*
> *Roots will be torn and infants from the*
> *   breast.*

No real clue is given here about the cause of the famine or its duration, although the message is repeated in several other quatrains, among them:

> *A child shall be born with two teeth in his*
> *   mouth,*
> *It shall rain stones in Tuscany;*
> *A few years after there shall be neither wheat*
> *   nor barley*
> *To feed those who faint for hunger.*

A number of quatrains deal with odd natural phenomena (or 'monsters') such as the 'child born with two teeth in his mouth' – which today is recognised as not being that uncommon. Rarer, perhaps, is the 'rain of stones' in Tuscany, which must be something other than hail – bombs, perhaps, or debris from an explosion. Certainly this possibility is held out in a quatrain in the fifth of Nostradamus' 'centuries' relating, not to Italy this time, but to southern Greece:

> *In the Cyclades, in Corinth and Larissa,*
> *In Sparta and all the Peloponnese*
> *Shall be so great a famine and plague by*
> *   false connisse*
> *So as to last nine months in all the southern*
> *   peninsula.*

What exactly this 'false *connisse* which will cause famine and plague' may be, is again something which varies amongst Nostradamians. Damon Wilson believes the word might derive from the Greek word for dust, konis; whilst Erica Cheetham believes that a 'false dust' refers to something man-made: i.e. some sort of chemical or biological attack. The combination of 'famine' and plague', however, seems elsewhere (in the quatrain that refers to the destruction of Hiroshima and Nagasaki, for example) to allude to the effects of radiation poisoning. So the famine and plague might be caused, once more, by nuclear fall-out.

This same possibility re-occurs in a very odd quatrain from the sixth 'century':

> *Such a great famine by a pestilent wave,*
> *Through long rain will come the length of*
> *   the arctic pole;*
> *Samarobrin a hundred leagues from the*
> *   hemisphere,*
> *Living without laws exempt from politics.*

Once more, commentators are at a loss as to what the word '*Samarobrin*' may mean, or how it can be 'a hundred leagues from the hemisphere' without being in orbit round the earth. Again we have in this quatrain the combination of 'famine' and 'pestilence' which seems to suggest the effects of radiation, perhaps carried in this case by a 'long rain' over the whole of the northern hemisphere.

Alternatively what may be being referred to here is the effect of a guided missile carrying both a nuclear warhead and, say, plague bacilli. If, as I have suggested, some form of fundamentalist Islam has by then taken over large parts of the Middle East – and Israel has suffered, at the very least, a crushing setback – then there will be no shortage of such weapons in the hands of anti-Western and anti-Christian jihadists.

Another possibility, first advanced by Damon Wilson, is that the 'famine and pestilence' may be caused by debris from a comet crashing into the earth's atmosphere from outer space – this might also explain the 'raining of stones' over Tuscany in the earlier verse quoted. Wilson cites in evidence Sir Fred Hoyle's theory that cosmic debris from comets has, at different periods in earth's history, brought with it the building blocks of matter – and potentially the makings of new, hitherto unknown viruses. Perhaps this is indeed the case here. The upshot, whatever the source of the 'famine' and 'pestilence', is the same, according to Nostradamus: the breakdown of civil society.

DROUGHTS AND FLOODS

(I, 17; III, 12)

> *For forty years the rainbow will not appear,*
> *For forty years it will be seen every day;*
> *The parched earth will grow even drier*
> *And a great flood when it shall be seen.*

It is entirely possible that Nostradamus sees in

In quatrain I, 71 Nostradamus suggests that there will be a profound change of climate, leading to drought and flood

this quatrain two successive periods of forty years, making eighty years in all, of drought followed in turn by flood. What I believe he means, in fact, is that drought and flood will occur simultaneously for a period of forty years in different parts of the world, that there will be, in other words, a profound change of climate due to global warming. This is to some extent born out by a further quatrain in the third 'century':

> *By the swelling of Heb, Po, Tag, the Tiber of*
> * Rome,*
> *And by the Lake of Geneva and Arezzo [?];*

> *The two chief cities of the Garonne,*
> *Taken, dead, drowned, human booty divided.*

The Heb here is either the river Hebrus in Thrace or the river Ebro in Portugal – probably the latter. Tag – the Tagus – is also in Portugal, while the Tiber and Po are rivers of Italy. The two chief cities of the Garonne are Toulouse and Bordeaux and the fate that Nostradamus seems to hold out for all of them is vast flooding. Lakes like those of Geneva and Arezzo in Italy, he suggests, will flood their banks because of the melting of icecaps on mountain tops, while rivers like those described will represent a

danger from two sources: a vast new burden of water flowing downstream and a general rising of sea-levels worldwide because of the melting of the ice at both poles. As a result, major cities in France like Bordeaux and Toulouse, he says, will also face inundation.

ECONOMIC COLLAPSE

(VIII, 28; IV, 50)

> *The copies of silver and gold inflated,*
> *That after the theft were thrown in the lake,*
> *On discovery that all are destroyed by debt,*
> *All bond and scrip will be cancelled.*

This, with one small correction, is a very clever translation (from extremely complex and opaque French) by Damon Wilson. He rightly points out that paper money ('copies of gold and silver') was undreamt of in Nostradamus' day, as was inflation, yet Nostradamus "seems to have seen these economic commonplaces of the future."

Rapid inflation of the kind that appears to be predicted in the quatrain would indeed be an inevitable concomitant of the sort of disasters (war, drought, nuclear accidents, invasions etc.) seen above: there would quickly be a total collapse of the money supply. Wilson allows, however, that this is a very generic prediction, and

In several quatrains the spectre of economic collapse is raised

that it could equally apply to the Third World debt crisis of the 1980s. He states:

> Throughout the 1970s, the world banks lent vast amounts of money to impoverished nations, then increased the interest payments to an impossible extent. Finally, when Mexico threatened to default, it was realized that the whole world economy could collapse as a result. (The banks relied on the regularity of the debt payments to secure their own borrowings – if the Third World nations had refused to pay en masse, the banks would have collapsed, taking every currency in the world with them.)

> Partial debt cancellation was hurriedly organized with the aid of the major governments (and their taxpayers' money) and the disaster was narrowly averted, As of this writing (2003), however, the world banks and national governments still insist on holding impoverished nations to crippling debts originally run up (and paid for, bar the vast interest) decades before.

Having said this, of course, it remains one of the aims of al Qa'eda and of its shadowy inspiration, Osama bin Laden (by all accounts a multi-millionaire) to bring the Western banking system and the economy in general to its knees. The reaction of the stock markets and of growth indexes in the United States and Europe after the events of 9/11 was not lost on him.

THE COLLAPSE OF THE ASIAN ECONOMY

This further quatrain is quoted by Wilson as one which may describe a future economic collapse in Asia (brought on by the events described above).

> Libra will be seen to reign over the West

> And have the rule of Heaven and Earth;
> No-one will see the strength of Asia die
> Until seven have held by rank the hierarchy.

'Libra' is an astrological sign which indicates wealth and prosperity, seen here as ruling over the West. (The phrase used by Nostradamus in the original French for the West, 'Les Hesperies', meaning 'the people of the evening star', which sets in the west, probably indicates, more specifically, America.) Wilson does once more acknowledge, however, that this prophecy may once more refer to the past – this time to the collapse of the Asian 'Tiger' economies (and of the Russian rouble) in 1997-8. This interpretation seems on the face of it more likely, given the last line: 'Until seven have held by rank the hierarchy'. For, in Wilson's words:

> For many years, the forum of the world's seven most industrialized capitalist nations (Canada, France, Germany, Great Britain, Italy, Japan and the USA) was called "G-7" (for "Group 7"). In 1997, Russia applied to join the group and the title was [subsequently] changed to "G-8". [Application for membership, though, did not prevent Russia's own economy from collapsing in August, 1998.] This may be the end of the "hierarchy" of seven mentioned by Nostradamus in the last line. Shortly afterwards, the previously bullish Asian-Pacific economies unexpectedly collapsed through bad investment and massive state incompetence and corruption.

This is perhaps true, but the French of the last line of the quatrain is, as so often, ambiguous. The possibility thus remains that another (future) economic collapse in Asia is intended, perhaps at a time when seven successive nations have held (one after the other) the leadership of 'the grand league' set against jihadist forces mentioned earlier.

CRISIS WITHIN THE CHRISTIAN CHURCH

(I, 15; X, 65; II, 93; VIII, 99; VI, 25)

> *Mars threatens us with warlike force;*
> *Seventy times he will cause blood to be shed,*
> *The clergy will be exalted and ruined*
> *And by those who wish to hear nothing from*
>   *them.*

'Mars' here means, of course, 'war'; and the 'us' who are threatened suggest Nostradamus' French – and hence European – readership. On the other hand, the 'seventy times' Mars will 'cause blood to be shed' seems an extremely high number unless either terrorist attacks or a series of local wars breaking out at flashpoints all over the world are intended.

The upshot, however, is clear from lines 3 and 4: the clergy of the West will at first be exalted as a moral authority to deal with the crisis (and their Christian God sought as a refuge), and then – when the clergy is unable to respond (and God seems oblivious) – the public will turn its collective back on organized religion and look more to so-called pagan religions and the 'New Age' movement as a whole.

> *O mighty Rome, thy ruin is drawing near,*
> *Not of thy walls, but of thy blood and*
>   *substance,*
> *The rough by letters shall make so horrid a*
>   *notch*
> *Sharp iron thrust in all the way to the shaft.*

This quatrain holds out the same prospect for the Roman Catholic Church in particular: i.e. the undermining of faith and a consequent huge loss of prestige ('ruin… not of thy walls, but of thy blood and substance'). Propaganda against the Church ('the rough by letters') will have such a profound effect, suggests Nostradamus, as to wound it mortally.

Of the people of the church blood will be
*   drawn,*
Like water, in such huge abundance,
And will not be staunched for a long time.
*   Alas, alas, to the clergy ruin and torment.*

One of the reasons for the ecclesiastical crisis, suggests Nostradamus, is that Christians in general ('the people of the church') will be a particular target for terrorists. Attacks will be made on congregations and major church buildings. The result, he says, will be rapidly falling church attendance and a crisis both of confidence and conscience among clerics ('ruin and torment'). The Dedication to Henri II predicts that many will actually leave the Church in sections 65 and 66: "And the chief men of the Church shall be put back from the love of God and many of them shall apostatize from the true faith".

Very near the Tiber hurries Libitina
A little before a great inundation;
The master of the ship captured and put in
*   the well,*
A castle and palace in flames.

One terrorist attack, this verse suggests, will be made on the Vatican itself, 'very near the Tiber' in Rome. 'Libitina' is the Greek goddess of funerals – and hence of death; and the 'master of the ship' (prior to its 'great inundation') in line 3 is the heir to the 'Fisherman', the first Pope, St. Peter. The inference is that Castel Sant' Angelo and the Pope's palace in the Vatican – supreme symbols of the power and splendour of the Church – will both be attacked and perhaps fire-bombed. Line 3 suggests strongly that the Pope himself will be taken hostage.

Castel Sant' Angelo – a possible target of a terrorist attack?

By the power of the three temporal Kings
The holy see will be put elsewhere,
Where the substance of the material spirit
Will be recognised and accepted as the true
  See.

Perhaps as a result of this attack (and also, perhaps, the death of the Pope in the process – see below), the Holy See, according to Nostradamus, will be moved from Rome and established elsewhere, just as it was (in Avignon in what is now France) during the so-called Babylonian Captivity (1309-78). This move, says Nostradamus, will be generally accepted as necessary.

By setback in war shall the monarchy
Of the great fisherman be brought into
  ruinous trouble
Young black red will take the hierarchy,
The traitors will undertake it on a misty day.

This quatrain is possibly a reference to the terrorist attack on the Vatican and Castel Sant' Angelo described above. (If so, then it will take place 'on a misty day') It may also refer to some internal putsch within the church hierarchy, perhaps involving young cardinals from the Third World ('young black red'). What is certain is that Nostradamus did indeed foresee a crisis in the hierarchy brought on by 'setback in war', as we shall see in the last two of the quatrains that seem to relate to the immediate future.

THE TAKEOVER OF THE PAPACY

(V, 56; X, 91)

By the death of a very old Pope,
Shall be elected a Roman of good age,
Of whom it will be said that he dishonours
  the seat,
And shall live long and be of stinging
  courage [labour?].

The 'death of a very old Pope' may well refer to the death of Karel Woytila, John Paul II. The inference here is that his successor will be a much younger man 'a Roman of a good age'. This new Pope, however, will bring disrepute to the Papacy (perhaps by echoing the militancy and fundamentalism of movements like al Qa'eda, setting Christianity and Islam on a collision course, therefore, in the George W. Bush manner). He may also be the same Pope referred to in a verse near the very end of the last 'century' of the *Prophéties*, though the date, on the face of it, is palpably wrong:

The Roman clergy in the year one thousand,
  six hundred and nine,
At the head of the year will make a choice
Of one grey and black, come out of the
  country,
Never as malign a one was there ever.

It is worth recalling here *The Prophecies of St Malachi*, a list of (at the time) future Popes which was supposed to have been seen in a vision by the Irish Saint Malachi in 1139 and given by him during his pilgrimage to Rome to Pope Innocent II.

THE MALACHI LIST

Each future Pope was described by Malachi in a short Latin phrase, and though the list is now regarded to be a forgery of the late sixteenth century, it has still by and large proved astonishingly accurate. The present Pope (2004), John Paul II, for example, is described by (the true or false) Malachi as *De Labore Solis* ('About the Labour of the Sun') – and this too seems extraordinarily prescient. John Paul II has worked ceaselessly for the Church – as per Nostradamus, 'the Sun'. He also comes from the east (Poland), towards the rising sun, and he was born on May 18th, 1920, when there was a total eclipse of the sun in the northern hemisphere.

After John Paul II, however, only two Popes remain on the Malachi list. The first is described as *Gloria Olivae* ('The Glory of the Olive'), and it is said of the second:

During the last persecution of the Holy Roman Church, there shall sit Petrus Romanus [Peter the Roman], who will feed the sheep amid great tribulations, and when these have passed, the City of the Seven Hills [Rome] shall be utterly destroyed, and the dreadful Judge will judge the people.

The 'dreadful Judge' invoked here is generally seen as God at the Last Judgment. It is entirely possible, however, that the 'City of the Seven Hills' will be destroyed by a much more mundane agency, one connected with the quatrains discussed above, and that the 'dreadful Judge' might be some other personage, dispensing a new law – perhaps even the strict Muslim law of Sharia.

It is worth recalling, too, the so-called Fatima prophecy, recorded by the last survivor of the children who claimed to have seen and spoken with Our Lady of the Rosary at Fatima (in Portugal) in May 1917. At a much later church enquiry, Lucia dos Santos claimed that Jesus had also later appeared to her and had given her a special prophecy about the future which was not to be revealed to the world until 1960. A transcript of the prophecy was taken to Rome in secret and it wasn't revealed for some reason until June 2000. Told as a story, it contained these words:

> [The] *Holy Father* [the Pope] *passed through a big city half in ruins and half trembling with halting step, afflicted with pain and sorrow, he prayed for the souls of the corpses he met on his way.*

Was this city Rome? We do not know. But, according to the prophecy, the Pope – together with "bishops, priests, religious men and women, and various lay people of different ranks and positions" – was later executed.

That Nostradamus questioned the stability and very future of the Church in its recognized form in his *Prophéties* gave validity to those who thought him to be nothing more than a charlatan who used spurious methods to achieve results. It is now time to consider the question that was asked first by contemporaries of Nostradamus and is still being asked by commentators today.

X

NOSTRADAMUS: GENUINE OR FRAUD?

Coming events cast their shadow before.
JOHANN WOLFGANG VON GOETHE

NOSTRADAMUS' prognostications appeared in English even before his death, when his almanac for the year 1559 – full of predictions of 'divers calamities, weepings and mournings' and 'civil sedition and mutination of the lowest against the highest' – was published in London. The publication came shortly after the coronation of Queen Elizabeth I and almost immediately Nostradamus was attacked as both politically seditious and a threat to the somewhat shakily re-established Anglican Church. One contemporary writer, in a book published two years later, said:

> The whole realm was so troubled and so moved with blind enigmatical and devilish prophecies of that heaven-gazer Nostradamus… that even those which in their hearts could have wished the glory of God and his Word most flourishing to be established were brought into such an extreme coolness of faith that they doubted God had forgotten his promise.

Archbishop Parker dismissed the predictions as 'a fantastical hotch-potch', and the government took legal action against the booksellers who sold them. Their influence, however, was great. As William Fulke, another contemporary, wrote of Nostradamus:

> None almost of them that gave any credit to prognostications durst be bold to open their faith and religion… Without the good luck of his prophecies it was thought that nothing could be brought to effect… Except the true preachers of God's Word had sharply rebuked the people for crediting such vain prophecies, there should have been none end of fear and expectation.

Nostradamus, in other words, was generally seen in England as an underminer of good order, uninterrupted work and true religion, at least when made accessible, through the printed word, to ordinary people. Nothing was seen to be wrong at the time *per se* with astrology or prophecy, it should be understood. The new Queen, after all, had called on the astrologer/alchemist John Dee to set the date of her coronation – and he quickly became an important figure at her court. There were astrologer-dons at Cambridge, like John

While Elizabeth I privately supported astrology and prophecy, her government did its best to prevent the dissemination of Nostradamus' work

Fletcher at Caius College and throughout Elizabeth's reign the aristocracy flocked to such alchemist/astrologer/doctors as Simon Forman. No, it was only in the hands of common people, unfamiliar with such esoteric matters, that prophecies like those of Nostradamus were harmful. What was wrong, in other words, was not prophecy but printing. For all the lordly public disapproval of the Sage of Salon, however, his *Prophéties* continued to be printed and reprinted in English in one form or another during the centuries that followed.

In the seventeenth century, for example, the *Prophéties* were used as propaganda in the wars against the Dutch and the French, and as an explanation for the so-called Glorious Revolution of 1688 which overthrew James II and brought to the throne William of Orange. Between 1672 and 1691, five different editions of the *Prophéties* were published with titles like

The Fortune of France, from the Prophetical Predictions of... Michael Nostradamus; *A Prophesie... of Michael Nostradamus that Charles II... shall have a son of his own body*; *A Strange and Wonderful Prophecy for the Year 1688*; and *A Collection of Many Wonderful Prophecies... plainly Foretelling the Late Great Revolution*.

The *Prophéties*, in fresh British editions, kept on appearing and reappearing. They were invoked to show that the American War of Independence and the French Revolution had both been foreseen in the upper room at Salon almost two and a half centuries before – it can be seen that the 1790s were a particularly active period.

As for the twentieth century, there was a further publishing boom during the First World War and after that the newspapers took over, constantly calling upon Nostradamus to predict or to explain future or past events – as they still do today. During the Second World War, both sides, the Germans and the British, also used Nostradamus for propaganda purposes, as a story told by André and Lynette Singer in their *Divine Magic: The World of the Supernatural* well illustrates:

> *The Nazis became aware of a young Swiss astrologer and Nostradamus interpreter called Ernst Krafft. Goebbels, the propaganda minister, saw the potential for spreading a Nostradamus prediction which pointed to a German victory. Krafft was employed to come up with suitable interpretations from the Prophéties. As British intelligence became aware of Goebbels' activities they resorted to similar methods. Their most painstaking achievement was a faked edition of 50 Nostradamus quatrains which pointed to Hitler's defeat and death.*

None of this – the uses made of Nostradamus' verses by propagandists and by profit-driven publishers and newspaper editors over the years – proves one way or another, of course, whether he was a true prophet or not. All it proves is that the majority of his quatrains are vague enough – and/or so run through with evasions and alchemical coding – to admit many interpretations.

As we have already seen, when we looked in detail at the quatrains, it should be remembered that not all of his quatrains are vague. The verses relating to the execution of King Charles II, to the assassination of the Duc de Berry, to the existence of Pasteur, Great Britain and greater Germany, for example, are almost astonishingly accurate – and there are many, many more of their kind.

It is also worth remembering that of all the so-called seers and spurious prophets published over the years – among them Mother Shipton, John Dee, Merlin and even Thomas à Becket – Nostradamus is the only one whose works have

Nostradamus: genuine or fraud?

survived. He, at least, is a real historical figure. We have a biography by his disciple and assistant to prove it, and his own written words, a great many of them published in his own lifetime. There is even a portrait of him at the age of fifty-nine – after he had repeatedly turned down a position at the French court as the Royal Astrologer – a portrait which agrees with Jean de Chavigny's description of him:

> [He was of a] *little less than middle height, robust, cheerful and vigorous. His brow was high and open, the nose straight, the grey eyes gentle, though in wrath they would flame... A severe but laughing face, so one saw allied with severity a great humanity. His cheeks were ruddy even into extreme age, his beard thick, his health good.*

In examining Nostradamus' status as a prophet, then, we have, first of all, to look at his claims for himself from the perspective of his own times. Was he a plain charlatan, for example, doodling out his rhymed verses (the rhyme-scheme in the quatrains is always the same: ABAB) as a con? Surely not. He believed profoundly in the truth of his prophecies, however much, as he himself said, he was forced to disguise them. Was he involved in practising a con on himself, by putting his trust in words written down in a (chemical- or smoke-induced) trance or as a result of a dream? Again, no – then why should he have had further to disguise them? He clearly thought that his predictions were based on science – and it is worth briefly once more taking a look at exactly what in his times that 'science' (or '*scientia*,' knowledge) was.

NOSTRADAMUS' USE OF ASTROLOGY AND ASTRONOMY

Nostradamus was, it is clear, first of all a predictive astronomer, what we would today an astrologer. It is instructive that at the end of his sixth 'century' of quatrains he wrote, in roughly rhyming Latin, what he called "A Legal Caution Against Inept Critics". Its four lines may be translated as:

> *Those whosoever read these verses, let them*
> *weigh them with a mature mind;*
> *Let not the profane and vulgar crowd be*
> *drawn to them;*
> *And let all Astrologers, Fools, Barbarians*
> *stay away;*
> *He who has done otherwise, let him be cursed*
> *according to rite.*

"Let all Astrologers", as well as "Fools" and "Barbarians stay away": it seems, on the face of it, a hypocritical injunction, given that Nostradamus was himself an astrologer. We know, for example, that he cast the horoscopes of the

princely sons of Catherine de' Medici and that he did a good trade with the aristocracy while staying in Paris at the house of the Archbishop of Sens. One commentator on the quatrains, David Pitt Francis, in his *Nostradamus – Prophecies of Present Times?*, argues that he wasn't 'really' an astrologer, since no more than ten

A representation of sixteenth-century astronomy, which combined scientific exploration with esoteric knowledge

Copernicus' view of the zodiac and the heavens

per cent of the quatrains contain astrological images or references – and surely there should be more if he was one. This argument won't really wash – especially since it was precisely as an astrologer that Nostradamus was offered an official position at court.

Rather more persuasive is the view of David Ovason, who maintains, in his *The Secrets of Nostradamus*, not that Nostradamus wasn't an astrologer, but that he practised astrology at a level far beyond the capacities of almost all his contemporaries – let alone the populist newspaper-stargazers of today. He also, in Ovason's words (quoted by Wilson), made use of

astrology in the *Prophéties* in a highly idiosyncratic manner:

There is no evidence that, in the quatrains, at least, Nostradamus used astrology in a conventional way at all, either as a tool for prediction, or as a standard system of symbols for elucidation. In this sense, his quatrains are not astrological predictions. On the other hand, there is a vast body of evidence to show that Nostradamus made use of astrological references to designate specific time-periods in his quatrains.

Ovason's point is that Nostradamus added astrological references to the mix of word-play, classical allusions, anagrams, medieval heraldry and the rest which he used to cover his tracks in his verses. He also used it to deliver a message, to those who could understand, about exactly when an event would take place. Ovason gives as an example III, 3:

> *Mars and Mercury and the silver joined*
> *together.*
> *Towards the south extreme dryness,*
> *To the depths of Asia word will come word of*
> *an earthquake*
> *Corinth and Ephesus then in perplexity.*

The first line is obviously a reference to an astronomical event. Mars, Mercury and the Moon (commonly described at the time as 'the silver one') will be in alignment, announces the quatrain, during the year in which the prophecy will come true. The trouble is, this happens fairly regularly, so Nostradamus buries an extra clue in the first words of the second and third lines: 'Vers' meaning 'towards' and 'Au' meaning 'to the'. The result is 'Versau', the French word for the Zodiacal sign Aquarius, which may also be indicated in the words 'the south extreme dryness'. In the complex astrology of Nostradamus' time Aquarius was both a southern sign and a symbol of heat, and therefore – paradoxically, since it is also a water sign – of dryness. The upshot of this, according to Ovason, is that we should look for a year in which Mars, Mercury and the Moon align in the House of Aquarius.

The first year after the publication of the *Prophéties* in which such an alignment actually took place was 1571 – and with this identification, everything else in the quatrain now falls into place. This was the year in which the Ottoman empire suffered a severe psychological setback at the naval battle of Lepanto.

The empire suddenly had to confront the fact that it was not insuperable, especially at sea. This was the 'earthquake' of which word 'will come to the depths of Asia' and it certainly did leave Corinth and Ephesus in 'perplexity'. It meant that the Greek port of Corinth, which had been in Ottoman hands for close to a hundred years, and Ephesus, an Ottoman port-city on the coast of Asia Minor, both suddenly became vulnerable to attacks from Christian corsairs. The Ottomans – once regarded as the biggest conceivable threat to Christian Europe – no longer ruled the waves. They had to rely in the future on their land armies.

It is all very well, of course, just to say sniffily, as Ovason does, that Nostradamus was using 'astrology in a form which is so arcane as to be beyond the understanding of most modern astrologers' (especially in the process of 'solving' the 'problem' of one of his quatrains), or to add as a footnote, as Wilson does: 'We dabble with kindergarten horoscopes while Nostradamus was an initiate of doctoral level'.

This may in fact be no less than the unvarnished truth, for astrology, which was revived and popularized in the nineteenth century in a somewhat bastardized and simplified form, was in Nostradamus' era regarded as the most intellectually demanding of all the sciences. It was also an important part of every educated man's world-view. Keith Thomas, in his *Religion and the Decline of Magic*, says of its practice in the sixteenth century:

> *Astrology was… less a separate discipline*
> *than an aspect of a generally accepted world*
> *picture. It was necessary for the understand-*
> *ing of physiology and therefore of medicine. It*
> *taught of the influence of the stars upon the*
> *plants and minerals, and therefore shaped*
> *botany and metallurgy. Psychology and*
> *ethnography also presupposed a good deal of*
> *astrological dogma. During the Renaissance,*
> *even more than in the Middle Ages, astrology*
> *pervaded all aspects of scientific thought. It*

An alchemist bearing a flask containing the elixir of life, 1582

was not a coterie doctrine, but an essential aspect of the intellectual framework in which men were educated... No-one denied [at the time] *the influence of the heavens on the weather or disputed the relevance of astrology to medicine or agriculture. Before the seventeenth century, total scepticism about astrological doctrine was highly exceptional, whether in England or elsewhere.*

As a result of this, experts in astrology were in extremely high demand: individuals who had carefully studied what Keith Thomas describes as the 'ancient body of learning initiated by the Baylonians, developed by the Greeks and Romans, and further extended by the Arab astrologers of the early Middle Ages.'

It is my contention that it is precisely these 'experts' – classified with 'Fools and Barbarians' – that Nostradamus was warning away from his *Prophéties* at the end of the sixth 'century' with a threat of being 'cursed by rite'. What he was saying, in effect, was that astrology was useless in, and of, itself. It had to be combined with other techniques drawn from alchemy and ancient methods of divination.

CLUES PROVIDED ABOUT ALCHEMY AND PROPHECY

In the fourth of Nostradamus' 'centuries', there are three quatrains immediately following one another (IV, 28, 29 and 30) which are clearly directed at initiates, people who were aware of alchemical procedures and codes:

When Venus shall be covered by the Sun,
Under the splendour there will be an occult form;
Mercury in the fire will have discovered them;
By warlike rumour it will be provoked.

and

The Sun hidden and eclipsed by Mercury
Will only be set for the second heaven;
Hermes [Mercury] *will be made a prey to Vulcan;*
The Sun will be seen pure, shining and yellow.

and

The Moon will not want the Sun more than eleven times,
All increased and lessened in degree,
And put so low, that little gold the secret,
So that after hunger and plague, the secret discovered.

These verses, which directly precede – perhaps significantly – the quatrain predicting the death of the Hermetic philosopher Giordano Bruno, are more or less meaningless to us today, apart from their overall significance as relating to alchemy ('gold', 'fire', 'Mercury' and so on). They seem to refer to the alchemist's (successful, in this case) transmutation of base metals to gold ('the Sun... pure, shining and yellow'). The last two lines of the third quatrain, however, are significant: "... that little gold the secret/So that after hunger and plague, the secret discovered'.

What Nostradamus was saying was a) that the ultimate secret of his verses could only be discovered by following the path of the alchemist, and b) that this was something from which 'mere' astrologers should stay away. Nostradamus was sending a clear message to alchemists that his predictions were accessible to them, and belonged to the world of alchemical codes and practice.

There is one further set of clues to Nostradamus' methods which it is worth taking another quick look at before moving on. The first of these clues is in the second quatrain of the first 'century', which we have examined before:

The wand [divining rod] *in hand, placed in
the middle of the branches,
I wet with water both the limb and the foot;
In fear I write* [a fear and a voice?],
trembling by the hands [sleeves?];
*Heavenly Splendour; the Divine is sitting
nearby.*

The use of the word *'branches'* in the first line –
exactly the same word as in the original French
– is taken by some to be a hidden reference to
Branchus, a Greek demigod who possessed the
gift of prophecy and the ability to pass it on to
his followers. Damon Wilson quotes a fourth-
century writer, Iamblichus of Chalcis, on the
activities of a priestess of Branchus' cult:

> *The prophetess of Branchus either sits upon a
> pillar, or holds in her hand a rod bestowed by
> some deity, or moistens her feet or hem of her
> garment with water...* [By] *these means...
> she prophesies. By those processes she adapts
> herself to the god, whom she receives from
> without.*

This is, of course, eerily close to the practice
apparently described by Nostradamus: 'I wet
both the limb and the foot [of the garment'?]
with the result that 'the Divine' – 'received from
without', in Iamblichus' words – 'is sitting nearby'.
Another much discussed quatrain (I, 42), seems
to give a further clue about what Nostradamus
was up to at the top of his spiral staircase:

> *The tenth of the Calends of April by the
> Gothic account,
> Raised again by malicious people,
> The fire put out, a diabolical assembly,
> Seeking the bones of d'Amant and Psellin.*

The first line of this extremely odd verse is
thought to refer to an event that took place six-
teen years after Nostradamus' death: the

reform of the Church calendar by Pope Gregory
XIII, which decreed the removal in that year of
a number of days: i.e. the tenth of the old
Julian Calends of April (April 11th) promptly
became the Calends (April 1st). The 'Gothic'
states of Protestant central Europe, however,
continued for a time to persist with the old
Julian calendar, and the Russian Orthodox
Church, in calculating the days of its festivals,
continues to make use of it today.

Our concern for the moment, though, is with
the last two lines: 'The fire put out [by?] a diabolical assembly/Seeking the bones of *d'Amant*
and *Psellin'*. The first of the lines suggests the
death of what might be called the old learning,
the putting out of the alchemist's 'fire' by the
'diabolical assembly' of the Inquisition,
although it is with the second line that we begin
to shift into something like focus. The word
'Psellin' can only be a guarded reference to the
Byzantine philosopher Michael Psellus, and the
odd word associated with his name – *'d'Amant'*
(literally 'of Lover) – to his most famous work
De Daemonibus ('Concerning Spirits'), a treatise
on the magic of Asia Minor.

There is a section in *De Daemonibus*, as it happens, on the history of prophecy, and within it,
truffled out by Wilson, is the following remarkable passage:

> *There is a type of predictive power in the use
> of the basin, known and practised by the As-
> syrians... Those about to prophesy take a
> basin of water, which attracts the spirits of the
> depths. The basin then seems to breathe as
> with sound... Now this water* [in] *the basin...
> excels the power imparted to it by the charms
> which have rendered it capable of being im-
> bued with the energies of the spirits of
> prophecy...* [A] *thin voice begins to utter pre-
> dictions. A spirit of this sort journeys where it
> wills, and always speaks in a low voice.*

As we saw earlier, on the evidence of the very

first of all Nostradamus' quatrains, he sat at night, by his own account, at a brass tripod, which almost certainly held a basin of water. He was, in other words, a 'scryer' of the sort described by Michael Psellus, just as John Dee's assistant Edward Kelly was; it is at least possible that the last two lines in the same quatrain – 'A slender flame coming out from the solitude/ Making me pronounce what is not in vain' – refers not only to the 'thin voice' out of the depths described by Psellus, but also to the actual presence of the 'spirit' – or perhaps 'thin-flamed' angel – which 'journeys where it wills, and always speaks in a low voice'.

One is reminded in all this of John Dee and Edward Kelly's secret angel-language, Enochian, and there is one last quatrain (II, 13) that seems to me to yoke Nostradamus and John Dee together in one enterprise even more strongly:

> The body without soul no longer being at the
>   sacrifice,
> On the day of death brought to birth,
> The divine spirit will make the soul happy,
> Seeing the word in its eternity.

It will be remembered from an earlier chapter, which discussed, among other things, the alchemical project, that the ultimate goal of professed alchemists like John Dee was precisely that offered by Buddha's example and Buddhist teachings: 'awakening' or 'enlightenment'. I wrote there:

> What this 'enlightenment' or 'awakening' consists of, we have, of course, no idea. But the analogy with Buddhism suggests that it involves a gradually achieved or else instantaneous perception of the Oneness of the universe, a fusion, if you like, in the individual of the two worlds of Heaven and Earth that are connected, in one of the most enduring symbols of the Kabbala, by the tree of the soul.

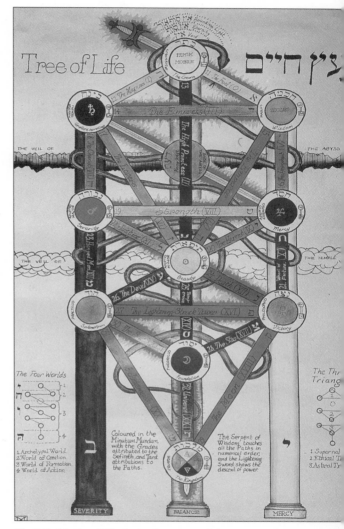

The Kabbalistic Tree of Life, showing the routes to enlightenment

> And it brings within its gift, according to [both] alchemical traditions [and Buddhist teachings], immortality: the ability to stand outside time and be connected to both the past and the future – as is suggested in the case of Nostradamus.

In the quatrain quoted above, we have further

evidence via Nostradamus' words of a connection between the alchemical project and Buddhism. The first two lines – 'The body without soul no longer being at the sacrifice/On the day of death brought to birth' – clearly refer to the soul leaving the body at the instant of death and being reborn into another body, a belief central to the Buddha's teachings.

'The spirit divine' of line 3, which 'makes the soul rejoice', is, it seems to me, an invocation of the 'Great Soul', the universal Buddhic entity with which Buddhist initiates seek to blend through constant purification over several lifetimes or via a moment of instantaneous, veil-stripping perception. The last line, equally, which offers 'the happy soul' the sight of 'the word in its eternity' is at one and the same time an invocation of the first thunderous words of the Gospel of St. John – 'In the beginning was the Word, and the Word was with God, and the Word was God' – and a description of the Buddhist Nirvana – in which, according to Damon Wilson, "the universe and eternity can be viewed as one by the purified soul".

All of the above is a (perhaps necessarily) roundabout response to the central question of whether Nostradamus was, in some sense, a fake. And the answer, of course, must be: No. On the contrary, he was involved in an enterprise which, however mysterious it may seem to us today, had its roots in the far distant past: in the Indian subcontinent, in Assyria, Greece, Egypt and Asia Minor; almost certainly in that great confluence of eastern and western thought we now call Gnostic Christianity, and in the pioneering science and technology given to us by the Muslim world.

What the connections between all these exactly were – how ideas and influences travelled from India to Greece and Egypt, for example, let alone to a lonely study in Salon in France – we do not know. We should appreciate from the above, I believe, that Nostradamus was, at the very least, extremely serious; that he was talking, at least in part, to fellow-initiates and that, however much he disguised his language, he was relating what he truly believed were accurate predictions of the future.

He was, if you like, the John Dee of France, exploring the frontiers of what was knowable about the nature of the world according to the traditions of Isaac Newton's 'ancients' – but a John Dee muzzled by the Inquisition and condemned to live for most of his life in the shadows. Only with the publication of the *Prophéties* – having burnt his books, by his own account, like another wizard, Shakespeare's Prospero in *The Tempest* – did he finally emerge from his self-imposed obscurity and give up to the world the summa of his knowledge, implicitly saying in them and through them: "He who has eyes to see, let him see".

There is of course, one last recourse for the deeply sceptical: Was Nostradamus, then, simply deluded or perhaps mad, or the victim of an inevitably benighted ignorance – doing his gullible, foolish best, in other words, in a world without the benefit of 'modern' science?

Again, the answer must be: No. Although the *Prophéties* – in modern hands, at any rate – have never proved remotely useful as a simple guide to the future, again and again they have uncovered events in the recent, and not so recent, past, sometimes with breathtaking – if retrospective – accuracy.

In the final analysis, at some point along the route we have lost the key to Nostradamus – which lies somewhere in the Rosicrucians' 'Magic, Alchemy and Kabbala'. And today we seem unlikely to find it.

INDEX

Page references in italics indicate illustrations

PICTURE CREDITS

The Art Archive
pp 35, 151, 173, 190-191, 195, 198, 203

Getty Images Ltd
pp 33, 64-65, 67, 70-71, 74, 95, 98, 104, 116, 124, 126, 129, 130-131, 133, 134, 136, 137, 138-139, 140, 141, 143, 146-147, 152, 155, 158, 160, 162-163, 166, 168, 170 (Time & Life), 171, 176-177, 179, 182-183, 186-187, 188, 196, 197

Mary Evans Photo Library
pp 12, 18-19, 20, 21, 25, 28, 30-31, 36-37, 39, 42, 44, 46, 48, 51, 53, 57, 59, 62-63, 73, 76, 78, 81, 92, 107

Science Photo Library
p 121 (Detlev Van Ravenswaay)

Topfoto
pp 10, 15, 17, 32, 83, 87, 88, 96, 101, 110, 112, 200